Psychotherapy After Kohut

A Textbook of Self Psychology

Kathleen Cavins
310-859-2424

Psychotherapy After Kohut

A Textbook of Self Psychology

To Kathleen
You're the BEST
Love
Heinz

Ronald R. Lee

J. Colby Martin

THE ANALYTIC PRESS

1991 Hillsdale, NJ London

Published by
The Analytic Press
365 Broadway
Hillsdale, NJ 07642

Set in Garamond Light type by
Sally Ann Zegarelli, Long Branch, NJ 07740

Library of Congress Cataloging-in-Publication Data

Lee, Ronald R.
Psychotherapy after Kohut : a textbook of self psychology / Ronald R. Lee, J. Colby Martin.
p. cm.
Includes bibliographical references and indexes.
ISBN 0-88163-129-9
1. Self psychology. 2. Psychotherapy. I. Martin, J. Colby.
II. Title.
[DNLM: 1. Ego. 2. Psychoanalytic Theory. 3. Psychotherapy. WM 460.5.E3 L479]
RC489.S43143 1991
616.89'14'01—dc20
DNLM/DLC
for Library of Congress 91-31485
CIP

Printed in the United States of America
10 9 8 7 6 5 4 3 2 1

Contents

Acknowledgments

We gratefully acknowledge pastoral counseling's nourishment of our early development as psychotherapists; the value of the New England Educational Institute's Cape Cod Seminars in self psychology; and students at the Illinois School of Professional Psychology, whose playful engaging of us helped shape the material that follows.

Our thanks to our families, who endured with us each step of the writing/publishing process; to the Metra Conductors of the 4:50 a.m. train from Fox Lake, who made commuting-writing possible; and to Paul Stepansky, Ph.D., Editor-in-Chief, and Eleanor Starke Kobrin, Managing Editor, The Analytic Press, for their very valuable assistance.

A special thanks to Richard Chessick, M.D., Ph.D., without whose example of therapeutic skill, scholarly dedication, philosophical wisdom and plain hard work, this project would never have been attempted. We also thank the following people for their valuable criticisms: Fred Levin, M.D., Marc Lubin, Ph.D., David Terman, M.D., and Eduardo Val, M.D.

1

Introduction

The emergence of self psychology in the 1970s and 80s has brought significant changes to the theory and practice of psychotherapy. One change, for example, has been to increase understanding of, and improve treatment success with, narcissistic patients, who were considered untreatable using the old paradigm. A description of self psychology's ideas, how they developed, and the major changes they produced forms the subject matter of the chapters that follow.

Self psychology represents a major paradigm shift that was not evident until the later stage of its development. Paradigms can be said to be "universally recognized scientific achievements that for a time provide model problems and solutions to a community of practitioners" (Kuhn, 1962, p. viii). For example, a paradigm shift occurred in physics when Einstein's wave theory of light replaced Newton's corpuscular theory. In this volume, we present psychotherapy as employing three major paradigms: (1) healing based on what we refer to as a magical covenant, (2) classical analysis, and (3) self psychology. Our major interest is in the paradigm shift from classical analysis to self psychology and the divergent opinions of self psychologists about the nature of this shift.

The publication of an increasing number of books on the subject of self psychology signified its emergence as a new paradigm. Kohut himself, the pioneer theorist of self psychology, followed his two early papers on empathy (1959) and narcissism (1966) with three major books: *The Analysis of the Self* (1971), *The Restoration of the Self* (1977), and *How Does Analysis Cure?* (1984). These were then followed in the 80s by a stream of books from Kohut's former colleagues and students, who not only used Kohut's ideas, but extended them beyond the issues of narcissism. With such a plethora of books on the subject, why another?

This book arose out of a need for a textbook for psychotherapy students. The chapters initially evolved from material prepared for a class on self psychology at the Illinois School of Professional Psychology. At the beginning, the students knew buzzwords —"idealizing transference" and "mirror transference"—but seemingly little else. Those who attempted to study self psychology soon floundered in an overabundance of articles and books shaped for polemical debate rather than the systematic unfolding of ideas.

Students did not readily grasp the significance of the new ideas represented by self psychology. In clinical practicums they seldom encountered patients with the clearly definable narcissistic transferences Kohut had described, because they were assigned either brief counseling cases or very disturbed patients with difficult archaic transferences. Even when definable narcissistic transferences occurred, they were not recognized by students or supervisors untrained in a self-psychological approach.

Many who independently tried to study Kohut became confused and discouraged after attempting *The Analysis of the Self*, perhaps the most difficult of Kohut's books. Had they first read two early papers (Kohut, 1959, 1966), the going might have been easier. And the few who knew of the empathy paper (1959) mistakenly thought of self psychology as another version of Rogerian theory. Given such misconceptions, it was evident that the major problem with teaching self psychology to clinical psychology students (or social workers, pastoral counselors, or counselors), as compared with teaching students at a psychoanalytic institute, was a lack of grounding in psychoanalytic theory. Nonpsychoanalytic students were unfamiliar with such major works by Freud as "On Narcissism" (1914), "Mourning and Melancholia" (1917), and "The Ego and the Id" (1923). Although some had read about Dora, the Rat Man, and the Wolf Man in secondary sources, few had read the primary documents, the cases written by Freud himself.

The students also were not aware that drive theory, the keystone of classical analysis, had been subjected to mounting criticism in recent decades and had actually been abandoned by many analysts. Nor were they aware of the self psychology literature by such analysts as Basch, Goldberg, Stolorow, and Wolf.

In developing the course, we initially set out to provide an overview of the major concepts of self psychology. We used White and Weiner's (1986) *The Theory and Practice of Self Psychology*, which followed a similar outline to our original course syllabus, as our basic text. The problems we encountered using the White and Weiner text were with the simple overview approach. Basic concepts, disembodied from their historical nexus and the issues and problems with which psychotherapy had wrestled for several generations of therapists, were not given the importance and meaning they deserve. The authors expounded solutions without adequately presenting the problems the solutions were meant to solve. Using the White and Weiner book meant that we were constantly explaining the issues and showing how self psychology's ideas differed from those of the classical paradigm.

To reduce the need for repeatedly explaining aspects of the classical paradigm to illuminate the importance of Kohut's ideas, we developed supplementary written material. We also found ourselves frequently explaining how the self psychology paradigm itself evolved and how it had originally been presented as an expansion of the old paradigm, the "widening scope," that Stone (1954) had described.

Eventually, it became clear to us that we were committed to a brief historical approach to the major concepts of self psychology, a narrative describing the development of concepts, rather than a general overview of concepts isolated from their context. We deliberately developed a simplified narrative that invited later refinements and modifications. Further, we wanted to avoid becoming bogged down, spending an inordinate amount of time teaching classical material as an introduction. We sought to cover enough of the introductory material to establish useful comparisons and encourage students to dig deeper into both paradigms. We were forced to be selective. We focused on the main issues of classical analysis and other precursors of self psychology, with a view to showing the emergence of self psychology theory all the more clearly.

Another problem was the tendency for clinical psychology students to think of self psychology as being solely Kohut. On the contrary, in the decade since Kohut's death, other self psychologists have so expanded the Kohutian beachhead that to view self psychology as solely Kohut is to miss the important clinical and theoretical advances of the 80s. We decided to present self psychology from a broad perspective. Narrowly conceived, self psychology consists of the ideas of Heinz Kohut, ideas that apply to the understanding and treatment of narcissistic disorders. Thought of more broadly, self psychology strives to be a more general theory, applicable to a broad range of clinical syndromes defined as disorders of the self. How broadly self psychology theory can be extended, and how useful these theoretical extensions are to clinicians, has yet to be explored fully.

The early chapters here are designed to help the reader gain a sense of continuity about self psychology. Though self psychology is hailed by many as a new paradigm, writers differ on the extent of its variation from the old. It had its forerunners. Self psychology can be said to be "radical" only if the work of many pioneers, including Ferenczi and theorists of the British school, are ignored. Like Kohut, those pioneers (and the defectors, Jung and Adler) also attempted to broaden the scope of psychoanalysis to include more than the treatment of neurotics. When their work is conceptually linked with self psychology, it can be argued that Freud, Ferenczi, the British school, and self psychology constitute the mainstream of psychotherapeutic thought. Classical analysis, thought originally to be the major highway of psychotherapy, is increasingly being viewed as a conceptual dead end, abandoned only with great difficulty by those heavily invested in it. Emerging as a new major paradigm in psychotherapy, self psychology takes us toward a more functional, "experience-near" theory and better psychotherapeutic results.

Eventually a broad outline for a manuscript emerged. It divided naturally into three parts: one covering the pre-Kohut material to show the conceptual linkage and continuity between religious healing, Freud, Ferenczi, the British pioneers, and self psychology; the second about Kohut; and the third exploring attempts at a broader theory beyond Kohut. By presenting the material this way, we hope to reinforce a broad-based professional identity.

We also recognize that once the major ideas of the self psychology paradigm are accepted, the old paradigms may be viewed differently. The new paradigm unavoidably influences what we consider important in religious and classical analytic paradigms and in the pre-Kohutian material. Thus, when we looked for themes in the old paradigms, such as idealization, it was because we already knew it was a key concept in self psychology. This is a bias that we openly acknowledge. In fact, the new paradigm enables us to see new threads of continuity.

Using each chapter as material for a two-hour class session, we found that students discussed more freely in class if the chapter contained a clinical case. Where possible, we sought to include well-known cases, already published, because these are the classics, which will be discussed and debated in the years ahead. For example, we included material on Freud's cases of Dora and Ernst Langer (the Rat Man), Kohut's case of Mr. Z, and Tolpin's case of Mrs. A. The Wolf Man (Dr. Serge Pankejeff) is covered in chapter 20. Where necessary, we included clinical material of our own to illustrate and concretize theory. As the reading recommended for each chapter reveals, we encouraged students not just to rely on our summary, but to read the cases in the primary sources.

The subject of chapter 2 is the magical covenant. From a long-range perspective, the development of modern psychotherapy is merely another stage in the ubiquitous task of psychological healing. Its beginnings are rooted in healing conducted by high-status persons, especially religious authorities. Religious healing goes back thousands of years; until 100 years ago, it was a major form of psychotherapy. Then, when Breuer and Freud published "Studies on Hysteria" (1893-1995), psychoanalysis was born. As Basch (1988a) defines it, "psychoanalysis . . . refers to a research method into human motivation, to a particular form of intensive psychotherapy, and to [Freud's] proposed general theory of mental functioning" (p. 4n).

Even though psychoanalysis added a new method and theory to the psychological approach to healing, it never completely replaced religious healing. In the United States today, for example, because of the sheer numbers of the clergy (priests, ministers, rabbis), the total amount of counseling by religious professionals is probably more than that of all other psychotherapists combined. Worldwide, this is undoubtedly so. Yet even if classical psychoanalysis has never been the only form of psychotherapy, undeniably it has been, for almost a century, the major force in understanding the psychological functioning of human beings and the conduct of healing. For this period it was the predominant paradigm, just as religious healing was for thousands of years before.

Now the influence of classical psychoanalysis is waning. Basch (1988a) concludes that "Freud fell short of his goal. He was unable to establish a theory that would serve both as a scientific basis for psychotherapy generally as well as a foundation for the investigation of human nature" (p. 3). Self psychology's emergence as a dominant paradigm now raises new issues and stimulates further research. It has the added attraction of being far more inclusive than the classical paradigm it replaces.

The critics of self psychology doubt whether this new paradigm is truly psychoanalysis (see chapter 16, this volume). Perhaps more important is the shift that self psychology has wrought in the distinction between psychoanalysis and psychotherapy (see chapter 17, this volume). Self psychologists still see a difference between them, even though they acknowledge that a similar dynamic process takes place in all forms of psychotherapy, including psychoanalysis. The distinction between these two modes of therapy lies in the aims of the treatment and the extensiveness of the working through.

Self psychology's view that psychoanalysis and psychotherapy involve a similar process is an important shift in attitude based on a change in theory. This shift is of great significance for all who practice psychotherapy, especially those whose professional roots are anchored in the broader psychotherapeutic community —general psychiatry, psychology, social work, the ministry, and counseling—yet who embrace self psychology's theoretical contribution to their work. While self psychology had its birth and early nourishment in the psychoanalytic tradition, the issue is not whether the new paradigm is psychoanalysis, but where in the new paradigm the old psychoanalysis fits. In self psychology the ideas central to psychoanalysis have been so transformed that it is now difficult to consider psychotherapy an inferior form of healing.

The last section of the book, commencing with chapter 18, looks at some trends in self psychology during the 80s and 90s after the death of Kohut. These developments have been accompanied by a proliferation of published material suggesting ways to build on the theoretical advances of Kohut. The intersubjectivists, for example, led by Atwood, Brandchaft, Lachmann, and Stolorow, claim that psychoanalysis is the "science of the subjective" (see chapters 18, 19, and 20, this volume).

Basch and Goldberg, on the other hand, emphasizing epistemological issues, are among those who resist a strictly phenomenological approach to psychotherapy and want to include the nomothetic results of observational research in infant development studies (see chapter 23, this volume) and new concepts emerging from the neurosciences (see chapter 4, this volume). Yet another position is held by Mitchell, whose relational theory subsumes the self psychology ideas of Kohut, the object relations position of Fairbairn, and the interactional approach of Sullivan in one broadly based general theory that is oppositional to drive theory. Other developments focus on affect theory in chapter 21 and trauma theory in chapter 22.

Finally, to cover the wide range of healing from religious counseling to psychoanalysis to self psychology, we use "psychotherapy" as a generic term for healing, from the Greek word to make whole. Healing in the religious paradigm focuses on the soul; in psychoanalysis, on the mind; and in self psychology, on the self.

To facilitate classroom discussion, we include recommended reading for the next chapter in each preceding chapter.

General Readings: Kohut, 1984; Chessick, 1985; Stolorow, Brandchaft and Atwood, 1987.

Readings for Chapter 2: Frank, 1963; Wise, 1966; Lee, 1979.

2

The Magical Covenant

The magical covenant, the basis of a long tradition of religious healing, was the paradigm of psychotherapy practiced extensively for thousands of years before Freud made the discoveries that led to psychoanalysis. As Stone (1951) acknowledged, "Psychoanalysis is a special and relatively new branch of psychotherapy" (p. 215). In a magical covenant, a passive supplicant expects an active, omnipotent healer to use status and power miraculously to bring about healing. Known historically as "the cure of souls," religious healing has been defined as "helping acts done by representative Christian persons, directed towards the healing, sustaining, guiding and reconciling of troubled persons" (Clebsch and Jaekle, 1964, p. 4). Such a definition may be applied to the healing by all religious faiths.

Just as magical healing was the healing paradigm prior to the therapeutic revolution initiated by Freud, self psychology may be the major new healing paradigm. Thus, it may be more appropriate to compare the paradigm shift from psychoanalysis to self psychology with that from magical healing to psychoanalysis than to compare the shift with Einstein's change in the theory of light from the views of Newton. When self psychologists claim their new theory represents a paradigm shift, do they mean that it is as radical as the one that took place under the leadership of Freud?

Magical healing was not completely eradicated with Freud, even though he sought to purge psychoanalysis of any form of suggestion. It is present in pastoral counseling today and also takes on secular forms. It resurfaces in self psychology, in the transformation of the narcissistic transferences. In what follows we examine (a) the magical covenant in religious healing, (b) secular forms of the magical covenant, (c) modern pastoral counseling, and (d) paradigm shift.

THE MAGICAL COVENANT IN RELIGIOUS HEALING

In a healing act, the religious representative (shaman, priest, minister, rabbi) utilizes his status, enacts religious rites of his faith community, refers to basic religious beliefs, and recommends a plan of action to calm and relieve those among the faithful who are distressed. This treatment, as Lévi-Strauss (1963) points out, is almost an inversion of the psychoanalytic cure.

> Both cures aim at inducing an experience, and both succeed by recreating a myth which the patient has to live or relive. But, in one case, the patient constructs an individual myth with elements drawn from his past; in the other case, the patient receives from the outside a social myth which does not correspond to a former personal state. When a transference is established, the patient puts words into the mouth of the psychoanalyst by attributing to him alleged feelings and intentions; in the incantation, on the contrary, the shaman speaks for the patient. He questions her and puts into her mouth answers that correspond to the interpretation of her condition, with which she must become imbued [p. 198].

Religious healing is sanctioned by centuries of tradition. For example, since the earliest days of the Church, if someone was sick, a priest prayed, anointed with oil, administered the sacraments (wine and bread) and prescribed herbs and medicine. Even though the 20th century has seen a decline in these religious healing rites, those still practiced give glimpses of a past when religious healing was the only resource in the community for those with troubled souls.

Example 1: Mr. J

The treatment of Mr. J, a 25-year-old single male, illustrates such religious healing. Mr. J sought help from a religious healer for his extremely "nervous" condition and his inability to sleep. His personality was characterized by extreme conscientiousness, overscrupulousness, self-doubt, phobias, and ruminating obsessions. When agitated, he would pace nervously.

When Mr. J was five years old, his parents first noticed a problem when, at a restaurant, he turned to his mother and anxiously said, "I'm going to have a heart attack." Years later, when Mr. J graduated from high school, a major crisis occurred and the symptoms enumerated earlier were overtly manifest. Following the practice of his church's tradition, he visited a religious lay woman held in high regard, an expert in diagnosing and exorcising this condition. She tested him by carefully placing drops of olive oil on water, and when these did not float, he was diagnosed as having the "evil eye." After the exorcist recited prayers to "cure" this condition and Mr. J was assured it would go away, he felt better.

Subsequently, on several occasions the "evil eye" took control of Mr. J, once after John Lennon was assassinated and again when Mr. J was complimented for being a "wonderful son" and a "nice looking boy." Every time this "evil eye" took charge of Mr. J, counseling consisting of assurances and religious rites of exorcism gave him fairly prompt relief. As he grew older, the ceremony progressively lost its potency and ability to relieve him with each incident of the "evil eye."

The power of suggestion played an important part in relieving Mr. J's subjective state. Such suggestions by a religious healer, however, derive their efficacy from the perceived omnipotence of the believer's faith community and its god. Religious healing is based on a magical covenant. The rites, rituals, and prayers, as well as the priest's presence, are mutative because of the depth of the believer's attachment to his faith community and its beliefs. These beliefs form a shared world view between the religious healer and the disturbed religious member, that enables expectations to be realized (Torrey, 1972). To the extent that the healer and the patient have divergent world views, religious healing becomes more difficult, if not impossible.

Example 2: The Shaman

Gillin (1948) describes the treatment of a 63-year-old Guatemalan Indian woman who had her eighth attack of "espanto," or "soul loss" (depression). This espanto occurred when she and her husband passed the place where he had been seduced by another woman. With the shaman's encouragement, the woman complained about her husband's infidelity and then broadened her complaints to many of life's frustrations and anxieties. The healer gave her a confident prognosis and detailed instructions about preparing for a healing feast four days later.

The ceremony went from 4:00 in the afternoon until 5:00 the next morning. It began with light refreshments and social chit chat and then moved into a large meal. The patient did not eat, but was complimented by all present on the food she had prepared. Then the healer went through many rituals, including making wax dolls of the chief of evil spirits to whom the healer appealed for the return of the patient's soul. The healer massaged the patient with whole unbroken eggs, which were believed to absorb some of the sickness from the patient's body. The medicine man and the chief took the eggs and other paraphernalia to the place where the patient had lost her soul, and they pleaded with the spirit to restore it.

On returning to the patient's home, the shaman was comforting. Then followed prayers at the house altar and rites to purify and sanctify the house. The climax came at 2:00 a.m., when the woman, naked except for a loin cloth, had her entire body sprayed with a "magical fluid" that had a high alcohol content. Then she had to sit naked and shivering in the cold for 10 minutes before drinking a pint of fluid. The healer massaged her vigorously with eggs and with one of his sandals. The woman then dressed, lay down on a bed, and was covered by blankets. She was thoroughly relaxed. After the shaman pronounced the cure finished, the patient fell into a snoring sleep. Eventually, when the woman recovered from her fever, her hypochondriacal complaints, her nagging of her husband and relatives, her withdrawal from social contacts, and her anxiety symptoms all disappeared.

Example 3: The Miracles at Lourdes

The magical covenant is evident in the healing rites still practiced in such places as Lourdes, France. There is evidence that some people who go to Lourdes for their afflictions are helped, temporarily at least (Weatherhead, 1951). To substantiate the claim of religious healing, however, the religious authorities at Lourdes have concentrated on carefully documenting "definite organic illnesses." A Dr. de Grandmaison, who studied 20 "cures," lists cases of pulmonary tuberculosis, cancer of the tongue and the breast, tuberculosis of the spine, ulcer of the leg of 12 years' duration, compound fracture of the leg for eight years, and fracture of the femur of three months' standing (Weatherhead, 1951, p. 147).

Example 4: New Testament Healing

The idea of a magical covenant forms the background to the New Testament accounts of healing in the Early Church. Weatherhead (1951) lists seven healing acts by Disciples Peter, John, Ananias, Paul, and Silas. These acts include healing lameness, blindness, palsy, paralysis, dysentery, and spirit possession. Although it is evident from these New Testament accounts that the person being healed is susceptible to the suggestions of the healer/disciple, it is the healer's imputed magical power that seems to be a major factor in inducing change. Hence, religious healers act in the "name" of, that is, the power of God or Jesus, or a status person, so as to invite an aura of personal power and to increase suggestibility.

SECULAR FORMS OF THE MAGICAL COVENANT

The magical covenant exists in secular forms. It can be seen in the placebo effect, in the Hawthorne effect, in the unrealistic expectations of patients seeking psychotherapy, and issues of therapy arrangements, such as scheduling.

Example 1: The Placebo

Studies of the placebo effect in medicine suggest that the magical covenant is never completely eradicated in a secular society; it is merely transformed. Frank (1963) defines a placebo as "a pharmacologically inert substance that the doctor administers to a patient to relieve his distress when, for one reason or another, he does not wish to use an active medication" (p. 66). He asserts:

> Since a placebo is inert, its beneficial effects must lie in its symbolic power. The most likely supposition is that it gains its potency through being a tangible symbol of the physician's role as a healer. In our society, the physician validates his power by prescribing medication, just as a shaman in a primitive tribe may validate his by spitting out a bit of bloodstained down at the proper moment [p. 66].

The placebo effect can be seen in the treatment of warts and peptic ulcers and in patients resistant to using medications. Painting a wart with a brightly colored but inert dye and telling the patient the wart will be gone when the color wears off is as effective as any other form of treatment. In a study of patients with bleeding peptic ulcers, 70% showed excellent results when the doctor gave them an injection of distilled water and assured them that it was a new medicine that would cure them. And of patients who feared drugs and distrust doctors, those given placebos had severe reactions of nausea, diarrhea, and skin eruptions (Frank, 1963, p. 68).

Frank also thinks that the placebo effect operates in mental healing.

> Using double-blind techniques, it has been found that some of the beneficial effects of tranquilizers, especially when they were first introduced into mental hospitals, were really due to the hope they inspired in both staff and patients. They increased the therapeutic zeal of the staff, and this in itself helped the patients. In this connection, the mere introduction of a research project into a ward in a veterans hospital was followed by considerable behavioral improvement in the patients, although no medications or other special treatments were involved at all. The most likely explanation seemed to be that participation in the project raised the general level of interest of the treatment staff, and the patients responded favorably to this [pp. 68-69].

Example 2: The Hawthorne Effect

That simply being part of social research can enhance functioning and productivity is so well documented in social psychology that it is named after the place where it was observed. The "Hawthorne effect" was noted at Western Electric's Hawthorne plant near Chicago when it was found that no matter what changes were introduced in the factory, they all temporarily improved productivity and morale (Roethlesberger and Dickson, 1939). Apparently the fact of being studied and contributing to "important" social research energized and mobilized employees to greater efforts. This is a subtle form of the magical covenant where the high status of the research itself functions as a placebo.

Example 3: Miss K

Miss K, a very disturbed woman in her early 40s, sought a magical covenant from a secular psychotherapist. Over the preceding 20 years, she had sought help from many counselors and psychotherapists. These relationships had never lasted beyond three or four sessions and always had a negative outcome. She reported a well-practiced "package" of suicidal thoughts, seemingly to gain the attention of the therapist. Her story was one of bitter recrimination against her parents and other relatives, whom she had ostracized, and against all the incompetent therapists she had seen and deemed unworthy of her idealization.

After half an hour of invective, she stopped and began to notice plants in therapist's office. She stood up, walked to the plants, tested for moisture, and declared they needed watering (even though they had been watered the day before). She then watered the plants, using a cup and water from an office sink. After finishing, she criticized the therapist for his neglect and then proceeded to work herself into a tirade. Miss K angrily demanded to know, because of her disappointments with other therapists, if he could cure her. When he would not guarantee such a cure, she stated that she wanted someone with whom she could form a "special relationship" (magical covenant), then left, never to return.

Example 4: Scheduling

Just as impatience over being evaluated and the need for an instant cure are the signs of Miss K's wish for an archaic magical covenant, other signs may occur when the first appointment is set up. Potential patients seeking a magical covenant often want the scheduling to suit their convenience, and they expect to receive the psychotherapist's services for virtually no fee, even though they can afford the fee. For example, one morning Dr. F, who worked in a group practice in Chicago's loop, received a telephone call from a woman who had selected his name from the phone book because his office was convenient to where she worked. She wanted to see him and bring her boyfriend at 7:30 p.m. that evening but said that she could not afford to pay more than a nominal fee.

When Dr. F indicated he had other commitments that evening, but had an opening in his schedule several days later and would see them for half fee, the woman declined. She could not wait; she had fought with her boyfriend and wanted someone to confirm, in front of the boyfriend, that she was right. When Dr. F mentioned two marriage and family centers, the woman was not interested in a referral. She then abruptly ended the conversation, obviously annoyed that Dr. F would not drop everything to meet her need.

The usefulness of the magical covenant cannot be completely discounted. Torrey (1972, pp. 102-114) provides evidence that "therapists" from a wide variety of cultures, whether witchdoctors, priests or psychiatrists, receive roughly the same kind of treatment results with their patients. It is possible, then, to make the case that over the short term, as long as the patient is highly bonded to the priest's religious community, the priest with sacraments may be as effective as the psychiatrist using medications, but without the side effects!

MODERN PASTORAL COUNSELING AND PSYCHOTHERAPY

Twentieth-century pastoral counseling and pastoral psychotherapy are new developments in religious healing. These movements involve attempts, in varying degrees, to incorporate the new scientific theories and techniques of psychotherapy, especially of Freud's psychoanalysis, while employing, as much as possible, shared religious beliefs and the natural idealization by parishioners of a pastor as a person of religious status. Stated another way, competent pastoral counselors often work within a magical alliance.

Where possible, the goal of pastoral counseling is to help people move from a magical covenant where healing is done for them, to an alliance where healing involves the patient's taking major responsibility for change. That pastoral psychotherapy is thriving indicates that this blend of the traditional and the technical, a mix of the magical and the therapeutic alliances, has made a useful contribution to the mental health of a large number of people.

One modern expression of religious healing, pastoral care, is not a specific activity of the minister, but a stance taken while the clergyman is engaged in activities associated with ministering to a religious community. This stance is expressed through the caring and commitment that a dedicated religious leader has toward his community members. This caring is focused specifically and concretely on the parishioners' need. As Wise (1966) says, "Pastoral care is the art of communicating the inner meaning of the Gospel to persons at the point of their need" (p. 8). Without such a commitment to a believer's long-term interests, religious counseling loses much of its potency.

The modern pastoral care movement, through an emphasis on training in a clinical setting, has sought to enhance the pastoral effectiveness of religious leaders. The movement is generally acknowledged as having begun in the 1920s, when Anton Boisen, the chaplain of Worcester (MA) State Hospital, established there the first clinical training program (Boisen, 1960). A handful of theological students spent three months at the hospital, full time, gaining experience in a counseling ministry under Boisen's supervision. By the 1970s, most theological students in mainline Protestant seminaries were benefiting from clinical training and receiving academic credit for it.

In the early 1960s, pastoral counseling grew out of the clinical training movement and became organized under the American Association of Pastoral Counselors with the goal of providing ordained pastors with specialized training in counseling (Wise, 1951). These pastoral counselors worked in large churches or independent pastoral counseling centers. The centers became places for local pastors to make counseling referrals. As part of their training, pastoral counselors studied theories of crisis intervention, grief, marriage and family counseling. They received supervision and undertook their own personal psychotherapy.

Eventually some pastoral counselors acquired the knowledge and skills to undertake intensive psychotherapy aimed at structural change. They took further training at the doctoral level and underwent their own extensive personal psychotherapy. After training as psychotherapists, they were, "pastoral psychotherapists" (Lee, 1981). They had retained their identities and ecclesiastical standings as pastors, garnering at the same time as technical a knowledge of the psychotherapeutic process as possible. In their role as pastoral psychotherapists, which stressed acceptance more than interpretation, such specialists often found themselves working with narcissistic and borderline personalities at a time when such disorders were considered untreatable. An emphasis on relationship in the pastoral care tradition and the need to avoid religious dogma made pastoral psychotherapists wary of an interpretive approach.

Pastoral counseling and pastoral psychotherapy, modern forms of religious counseling using a therapeutic alliance, do not ignore the magical covenant. Rather, they seek to change it. For example, in the beginning sessions of pastoral counseling, it is not uncommon for the person seeking help to request a prayer and receive it. When the person returns for further sessions, the pastoral psychotherapist attempts to involve the patient in the treatment, thereby building a working alliance out of a magical (totemic) covenant (Lee, 1979). In a working alliance, the pastoral psychotherapist is seen as less omnipotent, and the person seeking help feels more accepted as an imperfect human being. A partially transformed magical covenant sometimes stubbornly coexists with a therapeutic alliance, with reasonable results, depending on the empathy and skill of the pastoral psychotherapist.

The Pastoral Counseling and Consultation Centers of Greater Washington exemplify the kind of service that pastoral psychotherapy offers. Established in 1966 as a "not-for-profit" organization, this organization employs 45 staff clergy with specialized training. They conduct approximately 60,000 psychotherapy sessions a year to help people cope with such "problems of living" as difficult or broken marriages, feelings of failure, anxiety, depression, home or work difficulties, alcohol and substance abuse, teen problems, the search for meaning, grieving, school problems and senior citizen's feelings of neglect and isolation. These centers claim that the hallmarks of their services are "caring and quality."

The Center for Religion and Psychotherapy in Chicago (Mason, 1980), staffed by pastors with extensive training in psychotherapy, offers services similar to those conducted at the Pastoral Counseling and Consultation Centers of Greater Washington. At the Chicago center, "predominant presenting problems relate to marital and family issues and vocational concerns, though many clients come with a vague sense of uneasiness and personal discomfort as well" (p. 411). Because the center's major consultant was a member of the Institute for Psychoanalysis of Chicago, the center was introduced to the ideas of Kohut and has operated out of this theoretical framework. Of this self psychology influence, Mason has this to say:

> The psychology of the self has helped clarify data previously observed but unexplained, and called to attention other data previously overlooked. While there is awesome power in the broad theoretical sweep of the psychology of the self, it is the clinical aspects of Kohut's theories that have proven the most powerful, convincing, and exciting in our work [p. 407].

On the basis of the work of these two pastoral counseling centers and others throughout the country, there is every reason to believe that pastoral psychotherapy, modern religious healing, offers a valuable service to persons in need, especially those who are committed members of faith groups.

PARADIGM SHIFT?

To summarize, traditional religious healing has been heavily anchored in a magical covenant based on the projected power of the religious leader. This alliance was undergirded by a theological system of beliefs (metapsychology) that emphasized "God's action" and a set of rites and rituals (techniques) designed to induce God to act. Religious counseling did not produce clearly defined operational theories close to the experiential data. The techniques that evolved, however, survived the winnowing of several thousands of years. As Campbell (1975) contends, practice that has withstood the test of time has its own evolutionary form of validation.

Our contention is that natural selection has left behind three factors that make up the core of religious healing: the idealization of the religious healer; the healer's caring commitment to the patient; and a community with a shared belief system. Religious healing raises the question of whether these are components to any successful psychotherapy.

The subject of a magical covenant has not received attention from self psychology theorists. Yet this reminder of the radical shift in the healing paradigm about 100 years ago provides another context in which to place the claims of a paradigm shift from psychoanalysis to "whatever," in this case, self psychology. When self psychologists say that self psychology is a new paradigm, do they perceive it to be as radical as psychoanalysis was conceived to be in comparison with religious healing? Or is self psychology another modification, albeit major one, of the psychoanalytic paradigm, as the more conservative self psychology theorists claim?

Religious healing also reminds us that Kohut's change in attitude toward the idealizing transference was, in one sense, a rediscovery of its constructive potential, an experience familiar to religious healers. In another sense, however, as a manifestation of a therapeutic bond, Kohut's discovery of the idealizing transference was unique. Both religious healing and self psychology were able to accept that idealization could be useful. In religious healing the idealization may be used, among other things, to restore the patient's oneness with the faith community and his trust of the community's values. In self psychology, the goal is to use the idealizing transference to help form new structures in the patient through micro-internalization and leave the patient with a lessened need for archaic forms of dependency.

The magical covenant also makes clear that until Freud discovered free association and understood the importance of transference, his early attempts at healing were not markedly different from the suggestions of religious healers functioning under a magical covenant. This fact makes his discovery of psychoanalysis as a new healing paradigm, discussed in the next chapter, all the more remarkable.

Readings for Chapter 3: Breuer and Freud, 1893-1895; Freud, 1905b; Freud, 1909; Lipton, 1977; Swales, 1986.

3

Freud as Clinician

A knowledge of the major ideas of Freud is essential for understanding the contribution of self psychology to the practice of psychotherapy. Freud's clinical challenges, discoveries, and theoretical solutions heavily influenced the shape and direction of modern psychotherapy. His ideas have left problems that self psychology has sought to answer. So, any effort to understand the significance of the self psychology paradigm, needs to take into account the ongoing influence of Freud.

In this chapter, Freud's discovery of free association leads to the important case of the Rat Man (Dr. Ernst Lanzer). We also cover seven early cases: Anna O (Bertha Pappenheim), Emmy Von N (Baroness Fanny Moser), Lucy R, Katharina (Aurelia Kronich), Elizabeth Von R (Ilona Weiss), Cäcilie M (Baroness Anna von Lieben), and Dora. Freud's famous case of the Wolf Man is examined later in chapter 20. In the two chapters that follow this one, we briefly review Freud's theory of the mind and his drive/ conflict theory of psychoanalysis. With the steady decline of support for his theoretical model, Freud's major legacy may turn out to be his discovery of free association and his example as a researcher/clinician. In this chapter we view Freud's clinical work under the headings of the (a) seduction/ trauma theory, (b) technique of free association, (c) transference of creativity, (d) case of Dora, and (e) case of the Rat Man.

THE SEDUCTION/TRAUMA THEORY

As is well known, Freud first treated hysteria. He viewed the hysterical condition as one in which a person, usually a woman, suddenly finds her legs or arms paralyzed and is seized by dizzy spells or headaches, or loses vision or hearing, all without "physical cause." The symptoms of Breuer's case, the famous Anna O, give a clear description. Anna's mother says:

> Since December 7, [Anna] has refused to get out of bed. I called in neurologists because her right arm and both legs seem completely paralyzed. But the neurologists couldn't find any physical cause. She can move the fingers of her left hand a little, but not enough to eat. Her governess has to feed her, though all she will eat is oranges. She has trouble turning her head. Her neck seems paralyzed too [Freeman, 1972, p. 4].

In "The Aetiology of Hysteria," published 16 years after Breuer began treating Anna O, Freud (1896b) presented the seduction hypothesis. He stated that the neurotic symptoms of hysteria resulted from childhood sexual trauma instigated by servants, relatives, family friends, or even by incest-prone parents. How did Freud arrive at this conclusion?

First, Charcot taught Freud the importance of childhood trauma in Paris during the autumn of 1885. Second, Freud attended autopsies at the Paris morgue, where Professor Brouardel documented child sexual abuse (Masson, 1984). And, third, his own cases provided evidence. In "Aetiology of Hysteria," Freud said his theory of hysteria was based on 18 cases. More specifically, in "Heredity and the Aetiology of the Neuroses" (1896a), he said, "I have been able to carry out a complete psycho-analysis in thirteen cases of hysteria . . . . In none of these cases was an event of [sexual abuse] missing" (p. 152).

The Viennese medical community responded to Freud's linking neurosis to sexual seduction with shocked rejection! One of the most respected Viennese physicians at that time, Breuer, who had developed the "talking cure" with Anna O and who had collaborated with Freud on "Studies on Hysteria" (Breuer and Freud, 1893-1895), immediately distanced himself from Freud. Professionally isolated, Freud struggled with the issue of the importance of sexual trauma in the etiology of hysteria.

By 1897, in a letter of September 21 to Fliess (Jones, 1961, I, p. 292), Freud was expressing doubts that patient reports of sexual trauma were real. He suggested that sexual seductions might take place in fantasy only. It was not until eight years later, in "Three Essays on the Theory of Sexuality", that Freud (1905a) publicly abandoned the theory of sexual seduction as the basis of hysteria.

THE TECHNIQUE OF FREE ASSOCIATION

As he was developing his seduction theory of hysteria, Freud experimented with techniques for treating these patients. Returning to Vienna in February 1886 from his six months study under Charcot, he began his private practice using electrotherapy, baths, massage, and occasionally hypnosis.

In December 1887, he abandoned electrotherapy and placed major emphasis on hypnotism. Then, in May 1889, he began the case of Frau Emmy Von N (Baroness Fanny Moser), using techniques similar to those used in the treatment of Anna O as his point of departure and encouraging talk about events associated with the trauma while the patient was under hypnosis. He also used baths, massage, and rest. This case revealed that many beneficial effects of hypnotic suggestion are transitory because they arise from the patient's need to please the physician and fade when contact is withdrawn (Jones, 1961). Associated with this desire to please was the idealization of the physician.

The cases reported in "Studies on Hysteria" reveal steps along the road to discovering free association. In addition to Breuer's

Anna O, and the case of Frau Emmy Von N, another case, that of Katharina (Aurelia Kronich), involved a conversation at a mountaintop lodge where Freud often vacationed. This case has been referred to as "wild analysis," but because such a term conjures up images of treatment "out-of-control," Swales (1988) clarifies two points. First, Freud was not attempting treatment with Katharina. He was gathering data for his research, and Katharina's history contained a clear example of incest and symptoms of hysteria. Second, this was not the casual encounter depicted by Freud.

Swales, in an impressive piece of historical research, identifies the mountain where Freud met Katharina as Raxaple in the Austrian Alps and traces the ownership of the lodge in the early 1890s to Gertrude Kronich, the mother of Katharina, who had separated from her womanizing husband, Julius. Swales makes the convincing case that Freud, who had climbed this mountain many times, knew a great deal about the family, including Julius's inability to leave women alone. We wonder at the effect on Freud's growing interest in free association of Katharina's unburdening of herself in one informal session, compared with his wealthy clients who were trained by upbringing to censor everything they said.

Another patient, Frau Elizabeth Von R (Ilona Weiss), Freud was unable to hypnotize. Her resistance to hypnotism induced Freud to use catharsis without hypnosis. Freud's constant questioning so irritated her that she criticized him for interrupting her flow of speech. When he stopped the questioning, Freud found that her speech flowed freely, and she demonstrated a talent for hermeneutical inquiry (Swales, 1986). Hermeneutics is the theory of interpretation developed by biblical scholars to establish the meaning of a text. It involves an iterative process in which the meaning of a particular text is determined by its relation to the whole passage, and then the meaning of the whole is determined by studying particular texts. The philosopher Dilthy applied hermeneutics to history. Freud used it working with Frau Elizabeth von R as a part of what he called free association.

In the case of Frau Lucy R, whom he also could not hypnotize, Freud used hand pressure on the patient's head, a holdover from the laying-on-of-hands technique of the renowned hypnotist Bernheim and plainly related to well-established religious healing rituals. Freud then relaxed the pressure and asked the patient to tell whatever came to mind. She, like Frau Elizabeth von R, responded well to free association. Freud's success gave him a distinctive treatment and obliterated the controversies and sensationalism that accompanied the increased use of hypnotism by physicians at that time.

The fragment of the treatment of Frau Cäcilie M is reported by Freud at the end of the case of Elizabeth von R. There are now good reasons to believe that Cäcilie, even more than Elizabeth or Lucy, led Freud to his revolutionary discoveries and to developing further his theories of the mind. Frau Cäcilie was the name Freud gave to the 40-year-old Baroness Anna von Lieben, whom he began to treat intermittently around 1887. In a well-conducted piece of historical inquiry, Swales (1986) discovered much about Anna, who had mothered five children despite suffering "nervous illnesses" for nearly 30 years. Breuer, the family doctor, eventually brought in Freud after other specialists floundered.

Swales documents a pathogenic extended family with many members showing signs of severe mental illness. Anna herself suffered insomnia so severe and chronic that she hired a chess player to be available outside her door at night and also summoned her children to her bed in the middle of the night as company. At times the whole household could hear her crying, screaming, and raving while she went through yet another crisis. Swales, who thinks she was a morphine addict, concludes "that she was in a chronically borderline state, forever on the brink of lapsing into psychosis" (p. 23).

In a tentative scenario, Swales has Freud, by 1887, being used intermittently as a neuropathologist to treat Anna's facial neuralgias under the supervision of Breuer. Sometime in 1888 Anna received treatment from Charcot in Paris and when she returned to Vienna underwent regular hypnotic treatment by Freud, perhaps daily. Using the technique of suggestive influence, Freud gained some success by autumn, 1888. After an old memory returned to Anna, "for nearly three years after this she once again lived through all the traumas of her life" (Swales, 1986, p. 33). During this time Freud saw her twice a day.

At first Freud used the cathartic method with Anna von Lieben in conjunction with hypnosis. Swales, however, claims, on the basis of material from Brill (the New York analyst who studied under

Freud), that Freud's introduction of the technique of free association was primarily through this intelligent poetess with a vivid imagination. For reasons of discretion, help in the discovery of free association was attributed to Lucy R and Elizabeth von R, but in an encoded acknowledgment to von Lieben, Freud gave the name Anna to Bertha Pappenheim. Not surprisingly, Freud later referred to Anna von Lieben as his *lehrmeister* (teacher). Swales goes further and says that "in discussing Freud and his 'teacher,' there can be no question but that we are talking about the very *birth* of psychoanalysis" (p. 52).

One aspect of this case is of special interest. In a diary entry years later, Sandor Ferenczi noted that Freud had described how, early in his practice, he had lain on the floor, sometimes for hours at a time, accompanying a patient through hysterical crises. Swales thinks this is a reference to Anna von Lieben (p. 50). He also reports that the family descendants spoke of an "extraordinary kind of rapport—some extraordinary intensity of mutual 'infatuation' —between Anna von Lieben and Freud" (p. 50). There is a hint here of Freud's efforts to be a "twin" to his patient similar to the twinship transference discussed in chapter 13.

Sometime in 1893 Freud mentions having "lost" Frau von Lieben. Apparently Anna talked so much that Freud instructed her to write everything down, but even this grew out of hand. Swales thinks that because the family believed Freud's treatment was not bringing a permanent improvement, and was devouring Freud, they intervened, with Breuer's approval, and ended it.

These six cases reflect Freud's movement from techniques of massage, hot baths, and hypnotic suggestions, to the cathartic method during hypnosis, and then to free association. Unquestionably, with free association, Freud made a major discovery. It was a method for exploring the unconscious and created a common, shared belief system between patient and therapist to enhance therapeutic effect. Freud's new method eliminated the need for totemic representatives identified with a specific set of values of an ethnic subculture, religious group, or social cause to serve as therapists (Lee, 1979). Through free association, Freud gained access to the patient's unconscious world view and belief system.

In these six early cases, hysterical symptoms disappeared, at least for a while. Freud's psychoanalysis, like religious counseling, had an effect; it brought relief, but did not yet produce what Freud called a "complete restoration." Psychoanalysis needed to demonstrate permanent changes in a patient if it was to be accepted over other methods, religious or medical. For example, Freud treated Frau Emmy Von N for approximately seven weeks (six times a week) and a year later for about eight weeks; then several years later she urgently sought treatment with someone else. Freud's early analytic treatment, nevertheless, created hope.

Most of Freud's treatments in the beginning of his career were relatively short. Frau Emmy's lasted a total of 15 weeks. Lucy R's treatment took nine weeks; Elizabeth Von R's took eight months. On the other hand, the treatment of Frau Cäcilie M was intense: daily or twice-daily treatments for nearly three years. The challenge to demonstrate permanent change, however, proved more difficult than the optimistic Freud and his colleagues anticipated.

THE TRANSFERENCE OF CREATIVITY

As important as Freud's work with patients was eventually for the theory and practice of psychotherapy, the way Freud sustained himself during his creative discoveries may have been just as valuable. For a decade Wilhelm Fliess played an important function for Freud and hence for the evolution of psychoanalysis. Fliess "was precisely the intimate [Freud] needed: audience, confidant, stimulus, cheerleader, fellow speculator shocked at nothing" (Gay, 1988, p. 56). Freud recognized Fliess's role as "the only Other . . . the alter" (p. 56). Fliess, referred to as Freud's intimate friend, was a diligent and perceptive reader of Freud's manuscripts; Freud may have formed an idealizing (see chapter 12, this volume) or twinship relationship (see chapter 13, this volume) with Fliess as a means of energizing himself, an experience that Kohut (1984) later referred to as a selfobject. A selfobject is "that dimension of experience of another person that relates to this person's shoring up of . . . self" (p. 49).

Kohut calls Fliess's energizing function for Freud a "transference of creativity." This transference is reflected in Freud's need for and "overestimation of Fliess during the years when he made his most daring steps forward into new territory and [in] his realistic reassessment and subsequent dropping of Fliess after he had made his decisive discoveries" (Kohut, 1980, p. 493). Kohut sees Fliess's function with Freud as similar to the idealized Wagner's function with Nietzsche when Nietzsche began pouring out his most original work. Kohut also compared Freud's relationship with Fliess to Eugene O'Neill's "lifelong, desperate search for the selfobject that would satisfy his need for perfect 'mirroring,' for that 'gleam in the mother's eye' which his drug-addicted mother had not provided for him" (p. 493).

For Freud, this understandable need for an enlivening relationship was not confined to Fliess. Gay (1988) indicates that Freud's nephew John was an intimate friend in Freud's early childhood. According to Jones (1961), Freud idealized six figures who played an important part in his early life (p. 3). He lists Brucke, Meynert, Fleischl- Marxow, Charcot, Breuer, and Fliess. Jones also thinks that Freud's self-analysis eventually eliminated the need for such an idealizing relationship, but Jones's statement may reflect Freud's theory of development from autoerotism to independence rather than Freud's actual experience. Any growth from Freud's self-analysis may be explained as a spreading of his dependency needs, including his presumed need for affirmation from a special intimate, to a number of devoted colleagues. In chapter 14, we see that Freud's need for a circle of reliable lieutenants corresponds to what Kohut understands as a "selfobject matrix."

THE CASE OF DORA

The search for a way to effect permanent change with hysterics led Freud to publish "The Interpretation of Dreams" (1900). In this major book, Freud worked from a theory of a conscious and an unconscious mind (topographic), a theory formed in treating hysterics as they resisted making their traumatic memories conscious. Importantly, this work indicates Freud's increasing interest in unconscious wishes and fantasies as well as traumatic incidents and memories. From "The Interpretation of Dreams" it is clear that Freud had shifted away from a theory of sexual seduction as the etiology of hysteria, even though it was not until 1905 that he publicly renounced it. According to Freud, reports by patients of sexual seduction reflected wishes and fantasies rather than what actually occurred. He hoped that with free association, including association to dreams, unconscious motivating fantasies would be uncovered, leading to more permanent changes in hysterical symptoms. The search for permanent change also led him to Dora.

Dora, who is described in "Fragment of an Analysis of a Case of Hysteria" (1905b), was a vengeful 18-year-old female who saw Freud for three months. Her termination of the analysis was unexpected: "Her breaking off so unexpectedly, just when my hopes of a successful termination of the treatment were at their highest, and her thus bringing those hopes to nothing—this was an unmistakable act of vengeance on her part" (p. 109). Chessick (1985) recommends that this case be carefully read by every psychotherapist because it represents a clinical failure. Those who believe that progress in scientific knowledge is more dependent on experimental failures than on successes agree. We need to take advantage of Freud's courage as a scientist to report his failure and learn from it.

The case of Dora was written at the time Freud was preparing "The Interpretation of Dreams" (1900) for publication. Writing it to demonstrate the use of dreams in analysis, Freud spent nearly half of the case analyzing two dreams in great detail. Freud waited five years to publish that work, until he publicly changed his theoretical focus from seduction to sexual fantasy in "Three Essays on the Theory of Sexuality" (1905a). By then he may have felt that the need to illustrate the role of sexual fantasy and the process of dream interpretation outweighed the risks involved to Dora's identity. From Dora's dreams, Freud made the point that Dora's fantasy of giving fellatio to a man was linked to the symptoms of an irritation in her throat and coughing.

The case of Dora also alerted the psychotherapeutic community to the importance of interpreting a patient's negative transference reactions. Freud believed that Dora had an erotic transference and that the basis of this transference was Dora's sexual impulses toward her father. Dora then projected these impulses to her father, who was bad because of them, and to all men, who were bad because they were sexually interested in women. Freud believed that Dora's sexual feelings, and the accompanying belief that all men were bad, were awakened in the analysis. By leaving treatment, Dora was enacting her contempt of men and was avoiding facing her sexual longings. Freud admitted that he had disavowed the importance of this erotic transference until after Dora had left treatment.

Reading the case, it is clear that Dora's sexual impulses were only one part of a complex web of intimate relationships. The K family, who were among her parents' closest friends, had Dora stay with them many times, and Dora had shared with Frau K many confidences. From the time Dora was six, her father had an affair with Frau K the nurse who had taken care of him in a sanitarium when he had tuberculosis. When she was 14, Dora was passionately kissed by Herr K and reacted to it with great disgust.

Such disgust was exacerbated by Dora's thinking "that she had been handed over to Herr K as the price of his tolerating the relations between her father and his wife; and her rage at her father's making such a use of her was visible behind her affection for him" (Freud, 1905b, p. 34). Dora felt betrayed not only by her father, but also by both Herr K and Frau K. She told her father about Herr K's sexual advances, and her father asked Herr K to explain. Herr K denied the accusation and responded by speaking disparagingly of her because she read pornographic books. He said "no girl who read such books and was interested in such things could have any title to a man's respect" (p. 62). Thus, not only did Herr K lie about his sexual advances, but Frau K, who was the only one who knew about Dora's pornographic books, had betrayed Dora. It is easy to see how Dora could view relationships as deceitful, manipulative, selfish, and ending with betrayal.

Deutsch (1957) inquired about Dora 20 years after the girl broke off treatment with Freud. An informant described her as "one of the most repulsive hysterics" he had ever met (p. 167). The middle-aged Dora suffered from migraine, unbearable noises in her right ear, and dizziness when she moved her head. She was, as predicted by Freud, a very hostile and bitter person, still acting out revenge on men, especially her husband, who died tortured by her reproaches. She expressed great disgust with marital sexual life and clung to her son, the major object (selfobject) of her reproaches once her husband died.

Wolf (1980b) takes another approach to the case of Dora by empathizing with the 14-year-old. She has arranged to watch a procession from a store owned by friends of her father. The owner, alone with the girl, closes the shutters, clasps the girl to him, and gives her a kiss. Wolf asks if she was sexually aroused, as Freud claims she must have been. Wolf's friends, after being told this story, described her inner state with such adjectives as startled, frightened, embarrassed, and angry, but not erotically stimulated. Dora herself said she experienced disgust. Freud, however, "who usually was a most introspective and empathic analyst, could not or did not really empathize with Dora" (p. 41). Instead, Freud thought she was sexually stimulated and that her disgust was simply a manifestation of a reversal.

Wolf (1980b) writes:

> It is clear that Freud is not thinking of a young girl, of a person, or of a self in a particular situation, a situation which may be experienced as a frightening attack, a humiliating assault, a stimulating intimacy, or perhaps a betrayal of a trust. Freud appears to be thinking only of seeing a nubile sexual apparatus which in proximity to an arousing sexual stimulus failed to respond with sexual excitement. It is as if the girl were merely an appendage to this sexual apparatus, and, therefore, Freud is bound to diagnose the failure to respond with overt conscious sexual excitement as a kind of pathology, as hysteria. In this rare instance Freud has not been empathic with the girl but has put his theory first, the theory which says that the ubiquitous sexual instincts are at the root of most psychopathology. . . . The disgust experienced by Dora had little to do with whatever sexual arousal may or may not have occurred. Her disgust was the appropriate response of an adolescent to the betrayal of trust [p. 42].

Consistent with Wolf's position, the transference in Dora's case may not have been just a displacement from her past experiences of betrayal by her father, Herr K, and Frau K, but also was grounded in her experience of Freud. She entered the therapy hoping that Freud would function as a selfobject, that is, be invested in her, affirming her or allowing himself to be idealized by her. Instead, she became the selfobject for Freud's theory, just as she had been a selfobject for others. Bitter about being constantly used as a selfobject, Dora turned Freud into a selfobject of revenge. According to Deutsch's (1957) description of her 24 years later, Dora was a person in need of selfobjects of revenge to maintain her self cohesion.

THE RAT MAN

The Rat Man was a 29-year-old single man who saw Freud for an 11-month period commencing October 1, 1907. Mahony (1986) discovered that he was Dr. Ernst Lanzer, previously referred to in the literature as Paul Lorenz (Lipton, 1977). Dr. Lanzer's presenting symptoms "were fears that something might happen to two people of whom he was very fond—his father and a lady whom he admired. Besides this he was aware of compulsive impulses—such as an impulse, for instance, to cut his throat with a razor" (Freud, 1909, p. 158). Freud evaluated this case as follows:

> This case, judged by its length, the injuriousness of its effects, and the patient's own view of it, deserves to be classed as a moderately severe one; the treatment, which lasted for about a year, led to the complete restoration of the patient's personality, and to the removal of his inhibitions [p. 155].

More than anything, the treatment of Ernst Lanzer helped the medical community accept psychoanalysis as a potentially effective therapeutic agent. It was seen as a longer treatment, with more permanent results. Mahony (1986), however, questions this generally accepted belief. He claims that Freud saw the Rat Man for regular, six-times-a-week psychoanalytic sessions for "several months" and that for the next six months Freud saw him very intermittently. He also questions the "complete restoration of the patient's personality."

Unfortunately, we have only limited evidence of the permanent gains of Freud's treatment because the Rat Man was taken prisoner by the Russians during World War I and died four days later. In a letter to Jung at the time of the Rat Man's announced engagement to be married, however, Freud wrote, "he is facing life with courage and ability. The point that still gives him trouble (father-complex and transference) has shown up clearly in my conversations with this intelligent and grateful man" (Mahony, 1986, p. 84). Mahony sees the Jung letter as evidence that the Rat Man was "a public instance of Freud's therapeutic exaggeration" (p. 85). Mahony goes on to explain that "Freud desperately wanted the appearance of a complete case to impress his recently won international followers and to promote the cause of the psychoanalytic movement" (p. 85). This case also served as a selfobject for Freud's theoretical interest.

Treatment of Ernst Lanzer shifted Freud's theoretical attention from hysteria to obsessional neurosis. In a brilliant extension of his technique of dream interpretation, Freud's strategy of treating obsessional fantasies as elements of a dream led him to invite Lanzer to associate to them. From these associations, Freud soon realized that Ernst Lanzer's fears of being punished, and the accompanying fantasies, were the result of unacceptable wishes, particularly wishes for revenge on those to whom he was deeply bonded—his father and his girlfriend. Through a careful, painstaking investigation and collaborative effort, Freud and Ernst Lanzer gradually uncovered the revengeful wishes behind the fantasies of punishment. This uncovering process so involved Lanzer, that he became convinced that his symptoms were a manifestation of such unacceptable affects.

Chessick (1980a) believes that Freud's associative and interpretive work played a minor part in the personality changes in Lanzer:

> In my judgment, the case represents what is generally known in psychotherapy as a transference cure; that is, it is the interaction in the transference and the countertransference between the patient and the therapist, rather than any brilliant symbolic interpretations, that brought about improvement in the patient's mental health [p. 146].

Supporting Chessick's position is Salzman (1980), who believes that the obsessional's intellectual and behavioral maneuvers are designed to give the illusion of control over the obsessional's destiny and to substitute for significant personal relationships. He writes, "There is now good reason . . . to believe that the obsessional defensive mechanism is the most widely used technique whereby man achieves some illusion of safety and security in an otherwise uncertain world" (p. xii). The obsessional can make brilliant intellectual associations to dreams or symptoms with relish, without changing his personality, because "the ability to displace any symptom into something far removed from its original conformation is a main characteristic of his illness" (p. xv). Salzman's position is bolstered by those patients, analyzed for years, who gain much insight into their own dynamics and can explain the theory behind their condition, but who retain their symptoms. Clinical experience suggests that Freud's success came from other than what he thought—many following his techniques literally, have not been able to replicate his results.

Lipton (1977) also confirms Chessick's position. From a detailed analysis of the case of Ernst Lanzer (Paul Lorenz), Lipton concludes that "Freud's technique in that case was his definitive technique" (p. 255) and was different from the modern classical technique of strict neutrality. Modern technique, has not been an advance, but a "disadvantageous" development. The difference between Freud's technique in the Lanzer case and modern technique is a "real relationship." Lipton claims that Freud had a real relationship with his patients separate from any techniques. He thinks "that a central, important difference between Freud's technique and modern technique is the redefinition of technique to incorporate the personal relationship which Freud excluded from technique" (p. 271). In the Lanzer case, the real relationship is reflected in Freud's behavior, which is now criticized by adherents to modern techniques. For example, in the second hour Freud made a self revelation and introduced general talking; he did not challenge Lanzer when he got off the couch and paced in the room; he sent him a postcard signed 'cordially'; he asked for a photograph of Lanzer's lady friend; and he gave Lorenz a meal.

> The meal was no more than a courtesy which Freud extended to Lorenz personally and by no means a disguised therapeutic measure. Exigencies which impel the analyst to offer the patient some courtesy or some assistance on a personal basis occur occasionally, and every experienced analyst I have spoken to about this subject has had his own unique confirmatory experiences to report [p. 259].

Lipton's arguments about Freud's real relationship suggest that Ernst Lanzer was changed by Freud's honesty, integrity, and genuine, humane attitudes and behavior while he kept him involved in the analytic work of dream and symptom interpretation. Biegler (1977) also thinks that an important therapeutic factor in the analysis of Lanzer was Freud's personality, implying the successful result comes from a corrective emotional experience rather than interpretation. Chessick (1980a) adds:

> This case has led some therapists astray in that the exposition emphasizes symbolic and intellectual material; in my opinion, however, the key to the success of the treatment is Freud's personality as well as his interpretation of the patient's *feelings* in the transference. I cannot help but wonder if such a case—in which during the second session the dazed and bewildered patient calls the analyst 'captain' and gets up from the sofa—would these days be considered a suitable case for formal psychoanalysis [p. 150].

Further support for the idea that the real relationship was the major therapeutic agent of change in the case of Ernst Lanzer comes from reports of those who had their training analysis with Freud. Lipton (1977) states:

> The books by Wortis (1954), Doolittle ('H.D.', 1956) and Blanton (1971) and the shorter accounts by Riviere (Ruitenbeek, 1973, pp. 128-131, 353-356), Grinker (ibid. pp. 180-185), de Saussure (ibid. pp. 357-359) and Alix Strachey (Khan, 1973), all demonstrate the cordial relationships which Freud established with his patients [p. 261].

Freud the clinician emerges from the cases he conducted, especially that of Ernst Lanzer, as extremely dedicated and intuitive. Gay (1976) writes of Freud, "He was more humane than he readily allowed. His case histories and his private correspondence disclosed his pleasure in a patient's progress, his delicacy in managing a patient's feelings" (p. 44). Chessick (1980a) also says:

> Freud's overriding life purpose—to know and to understand what goes on in the human mind—which tended to make him seem single-minded, one-sided, and imperious, produced a high level of concentration on his work that patients experienced as an intense form of caring about them, and as an insistence that the patient take a similarly scientific attitude toward his own psyche. I am certain that both of these aspects of Freud's approach to

> patients were essential to his therapeutic results; he wrote little about these aspects simply because he took them for granted as the obligation or calling of any physician who is dedicated to his patient's welfare [p. 154].

The case of the Rat Man was an important step forward for Freud and psychoanalysis, even though Freud's claim at the time may have been overly optimistic. In the next chapter we turn from Freud's clinical experiences, and their theoretical implications to an exploration of Freud's theory of the mind. Using the analogy of a machine, he called the mind a "mental apparatus." We examine this model's philosophical assumptions and in the light of a modern understanding of the brain's functions, its inadequacy for the task given it.

Readings for Chapter 4: Ryle, 1949; Basch, 1975a; Levin, 1990.

4

Freud's Mental Apparatus

In seeking to explain psychotherapy, Freud developed a theory of the mind that used the concept "mental apparatus." The inadequacy of this concept ultimately resulted in the loss of scientific support for the drive theory of the classical psychoanalytic paradigm. The mental apparatus model raises many issues, which we examine under the following headings: (a) Descartes's mechanistic strategy, (b) materialistic thinking, (c) an energy model, (d) a consciousness model of perception, and (e) an image theory of thought.

DESCARTES'S MECHANISTIC STRATEGY

In theorizing about the mind, Freud built on René Descartes's idea proposed 400 years ago. Descartes expanded the boundary of science by using the analogy of the then recently invented clock to replace the animistic notion of the human body with a mechanistic one. By arguing that the health or disease of a body depended on the body's constitutional parts working harmoniously, he became the father of modern medicine. The mechanistic model enabled the body to be autopsied and studied without risking the hostility of organized religion: viewed as a machine, the body is not a living organism, which can then be examined or cut without risk of being sacrilegious or guilty of killing. To his mechanical view of the body Descartes made one exception—the brain.

Descartes deflected the issue of religious heresy by retaining the notion that six weeks after conception, as a result of divine intervention, the soul was implanted in the human brain's pineal gland. In keeping with church doctrine, this soul differentiated human beings from all other earthly creatures by instilling in them a sense of morality, the ability to reason, and the gift to know and potentially to chose good and evil—that is, to will freely. Descartes's dichotomy of brain and soul was expanded to include brain/mind and body/mind dichotomies. Descartes also equated reason with thought, thought with consciousness, and consciousness with self-awareness.

While extending Descartes's mechanical model, Freud nonetheless challenged Descartes's equating consciousness with mind by demonstrating the existence of an unconscious reasoning process. He also wanted to extend, through the idea of mental apparatus, the deanimation of the body to the brain as well. Hence the brain was a mental machine that ran on instinctually generated energy. Thought was the discharge of such energy. To Freud, the brain functioned like a steam boiler that constantly needs to discharge, through thought or action, the excess energy produced by the sexual (and later) the aggressive drives.

MATERIALISTIC THINKING

A major problem inherent in Freud's idea of a mental apparatus was the prevailing 19th-century physics' materialism, which represented reality as a thing. Freud reasoned that if the mind was not a material thing, it had to be a nonmaterial "thing," a mental rather than a physical apparatus. Such a materialistic view of reality has become outdated; under the influence of Einstein, physics itself has shifted from a materialistic to a structuralistic (the pattern or structure of the interaction) philosophical position (Basch, 1975a). Structuralism and general systems theory describe the world as the ordered relationships between events rather than as the events themselves. Moreover, what is considered an event is altered by how it is perceived in relationship to other events. By utilizing the prestige of physics, particularly mechanics, to form a machinelike analogy for the mind, Freud gave credibility to psychoanalysis as a scientific endeavor. Freud's use of the mechanistic thinking and materialistic language of the physics of his time to make psychoanalysis scientifically respectable limited his drive theory.

> Metapsychological theory, while useful, perhaps even necessary for certain purposes, has led psychoanalysis into a virtual *cul de sac* that is isolated from empirical and conceptual articulation with biological sciences. When theoretical constructs that are beyond the reach of psychological and physical methods are regarded as real, the possibilities for fruitful dialogue and conceptual articulation with the natural sciences slip away [Reiser, 1984, p. 7].

Once the materialistic philosophy of physics had changed through the study of atomic and subatomic particles, the concept of a mental apparatus lost theoretical appeal.

Using the ideas associated with structuralism, it is now possible to describe mental functioning without resorting to such constructs as "mind," which the philosopher Ryle (1949) calls "the ghost in the machine." According to Ryle, "'my mind' does not stand for another organ. It signifies my ability and proneness to do certain sorts of things" (p. 168). He goes on:

> To talk of a person's mind is not to talk of a repository which is permitted to house objects that something called "the physical world" is forbidden to house; it is to talk of the person's abilities, liabilities and inclinations to do and undergo certain sorts of things, and of the doing and undergoing of these things in the ordinary world.

If we discard the concept of mind as a machine, we are left with a neurophysiological organ of the body, the brain. This brain uses small amounts of calories to make signal processing possible. We also need a term to describe the vicissitudes of encoded patterns that are stored and compared in the brain and for the brain's ordering-abstracting activity. The brain's message processing may itself be a signal leading to more message processing that is unconnected to muscular or glandular reactions. Message processing is thinking. Recent developments in identifying the localization of brain functions indicate that thinking is associated with increased regional cerebral metabolic rate and increased regional cerebral bloodflow. The totality of past experience, abstracted, and ordered becomes the "self" in self psychology.

A way to understand the concept of the self is related to the functions and communications between the two cerebral hemispheres. Levin (1991) uses the term "bicameral" to refer to specialized and related anatomical asymmetries of the two cerebral hemispheres. He concludes that one of the outcomes of successful psychoanalysis (and by implication, of any successful in-depth psychotherapy) is that there are greater connections, both functionally and anatomically, between the two hemispheres. These increased connections help overcome repression and disavowal (p. 41).

Freud's model, on the other hand, conceived of the brain, a living organism, as a closed system in which the brain sought a stimulus-free "nirvana." "Conceived in this fashion, the brain, left to its own devices, would follow the laws of thermodynamics and move from a state of high organization and unstable differentiation to an amorphous, stable steady state" (Basch, 1975a, p. 492).

Far from seeking the lowest level of equilibrium, the brain is continually in need of optimal stimulation. As sensory deprivation studies have shown (Spitz, 1945; Bexton, Heron and Scott, 1954), instead of welcoming a state of rest, the brain engages in a veritable frenzy of activity in its search for stimuli. If none are available, it artificially provides them through fantasies and hallucinations. In contrast to Freud's view, the brain is now conceived of as a living system that proceeds from a less differentiated to a more complex state and resists disintegration. Unlike Freud's closed system, open systems do not respond passively to intersystemic and intrasystemic changes, but use these as signals that determine the nature of their response. Open systems influence their environment by selective interaction and actively participate in shaping their own future through behavior.

AN ENERGY MODEL

Freud's notion of psychic energy, even if understood as a metaphor, is now considered scientifically untenable. The brain does not function as an energy-transmitting organ. The passage of nerve impulses is signal propagation, not an energy transmission, according to neurophysiologists (Basch, 1975a). The brain has signaling functions that control the systems that build up and expend energy. The necessity for an energy theory of the mind disappears once the concept that the brain seeks nirvana is discarded. Only a brain that seeks inactivity needs to be "driven" into action. Since the function of the brain—indeed its very structure—depends on the reception and ordering of stimuli, there is no more need to postulate driving forces for the brain than there is for any other organ of the body. An alternative to this drive-energy theory of mentation is now provided by communication theory.

Several theorists (Rubinstein, 1973; Kent, 1981; Basch, 1985; Levin, 1990), for example, are firmly committed to an information-processing model. Basch (1975b) has pointed out that Freud (1895) hinted at such an information-processing model but ultimately chose the energy discharge model of drive theory. Given the science of his time, especially the influence of physics, Freud can hardly be criticized for pursuing his model. Yet it is now clear that such a model has long been obsolete and unsatisfactory.

Communication theory depends on information. Information consists of a coded signal that reduces the uncertainty about acting when one is confronted by alternatives. It limits rather than expands options and increases the readiness to act: "The amount of information in . . . statements is a measure of how much they reduce the number of possible outcomes" (Miller, 1963, p. 124). Every living cell processes signals and creates order, but the brain carries this function to specialized heights. It has the obligatory function of continuously abstracting, that is, of registering and connecting sensory signals into figure–ground patterns that become strategies for decision making and acting. The central nervous system selects, collects, and connects these impulses into message patterns. In this sense, reality is the product of the brain's creative activity reflecting external conditions in such a manner as to formulate effective action.

Recent research and theorizing, relying on an information--processing model, understands the brain as a complex computer with the capacity to program and reprogram itself. In this view, the cerebellum functions much as the central processor of a computer, receiving input from and sending output to every other part of the nervous system. Levin (1991) contends that, as such, it has "'the computing power' to contribute to the integration and coordination functions that we assume human learning involves" (p. 66).

Levin also assigns to the cerebellum the role of coordination of several major functions of the central nervous system.

> On this basis it seems possible that the cerebellum could be involved in part of the overall orchestration of a number of nervous system activities that range widely. These include the major affective elements within the brain (prominently the limbic system and thalamus), the motor system (of which it is the principal regulator), and the brain's systems of integrating sensory modalities of every kind (which keep the cerebellum in continuous touch with both the external and internal milieu) [p. 65].

Levin also believes that the cerebellum plays a critical role in our emotional lives and preeminently contains a representative of the body/self; it also monitors the body parts and their relationship to each other, as well as posture, acceleration, and the like. The view of the brain as a computer of exquisite complexity and with the ability to program and reprogram itself is a far cry from Freud's energy-disposal mental apparatus, which functioned in a crude, mechanical manner. Perhaps decades from now neuroscientists will look back at the "computer model" and find it equally deficient.

A CONSCIOUSNESS MODEL OF PERCEPTION

In the brain of mammals and especially humans, direct stimulation to act is replaced by stimulation that has been delayed by and compared with the beliefs and generalizations that form perception. Thus, neocortical brain activity that is not blocked by percepts stimulates the limbic system of the brain. The importance of percepts shifts the emphasis from information processing to the processes whereby percepts are formed and changed. The process of perception refers to the ordering of signals into neural connections that form a permanent record of experience, making recognition and adaptation possible. Perception is another name for the brain's abstracting and generalizing activity.

Contrary to Freud's formulation that perception equals consciousness, we now know that perception is a not-conscious process. The sensory experiences that we are aware of and mistakenly call "seeing," "hearing," and so on come after the fact of perception; that is, our percepts formed from past experiences play a major role in what we see and hear now. Consciousness seems to be one subpart of the perceptual feedback cycle. It consists of signals and information that cannot be made to fit established perceptual patterns and hence are recycled by the brain until they are either incorporated into the established order or form the basis for new patterns of abstraction. In other words, consciousness is not the equivalent of thought; it is but one aspect of problem-solving thought. Consciousness assures that signals arousing attention, but not matching existing patterns, will be temporally retained and not be disregarded until their significance, if any, for the organism becomes comprehensible.

Levin (1990), pointing out how highly idiosyncratic the process of abstracting sensory input is on an individual basis, writes:

> This suggests that the abstracting phase of long-term memory (LTM) is more individually variable than the sensory phase of memory. That is, as we process information and go from the

> sensory to the LTM storage stage, we make progressively more arbitrary choices about how to store particular knowledge. It is possible that the *meaning* [italics added] of all experience is more idiosyncratic than we might ever imagine. From this perspective it seems logical that the "filing" code of LTM is probably highly personal [pp. 51-52, n.6].

The highly personal meanings of long-term memory interest the practitioners of psychoanalysis and intensive psychotherapy.

AN IMAGE THEORY OF THOUGHT

Freud's (1911) theory of thought was based on the wish-fulfilling hallucinations that take place as a part of the primary processes operating according to the pleasure principle.

> Whatever was thought of (wished for) was simply presented in a hallucinatory manner . . . . It was only the non-occurrence of the expected satisfaction, the disappointment experienced, that led to the abandonment of this attempt at satisfaction by means of hallucination [p. 219].

This abandonment of hallucinating pleasure coincides with the development of the reality principle: "The psychical apparatus had to decide to form a conception of the real circumstances in the external world and to endeavor to make a real alteration in them" (p. 219). Freud believed, for example, that through the visual image of the breast associated with feeding, the baby learns to differentiate between an hallucination and external reality. Thus, to Freud, thought was a complex association of sensory images, an idea with which cognitive psychologists disagree.

In answer to Freud, cognitive psychologists point to the first 16 months of life. Piaget's (1969) findings, for example, indicate that nonreflective action, not recall through symbolic representation, is fundamental to learning. The first phase of development, termed the sensorimotor phase, is imageless. As Church (1961) indicates, there are "frames of reference," "cognitive maps," or "schema of mobilization," but not symbolic images. The idea that sensory stimuli set off specific behavioral reactions, such as sucking, presents no problem to physiologists (Basch, 1975a). It is precisely because infants are incapable of representation of past experience, and therefore cannot hallucinate, that their early attempts at pattern closure, when stimulated by need alone, become frustrating and lead to adaptive action and learning. Were an infant able to hallucinate, he would die, for hallucinations totally gratify. Travelers who were about to die of thirst in the desert and then were rescued have testified to giving up trying to solve problems of surviving once they began to hallucinate.

Disagreement with Freud today is not over the general idea that the mind (self) forms images; it does, but after about 16 months of age. Even then, however, such images should not be equated with thinking, as Freud does, because they represent only one aspect of thinking. Furthermore, even after 16 months, when we say we "compare images," we really do not. What is actually compared is the neurological activity of the new stimulus to the past neurological patterns established in the brain. Sometimes the end result of the brain's activity becomes conscious and assumes an image. It is a mistake to call this end product thinking.

Another form of thought is sign behavior. In Pavlov's famous experiment, the bell set off complex gastrointestinal preparations for digestion because the ringing sound had become a sign for food. Gastrointestinal reactions had become reflex behavior. Such reflex behavior does not come from the primitive, subcortical brain. Although not voluntary, reflex behavior involves perceptual input and evaluation. Once a pattern of sign behavior has been thoroughly mastered, it proceeds automatically when stimulated and turns into reflex behavior essential to survival. The experienced pianist or automobile driver is able to process and respond to many more signals quickly and efficiently than is the novice, for whom the activity has not yet become reflex. Absence of conscious reflection is not an indicator of lack of complexity or of inferior thinking. Quite the contrary, consciousness of action indicates a lack of mastery.

Physiologically, the old brain, not the neocortex, initiates and coordinates the actual activity that supports attraction or avoidance behavior (Simeons, 1962). The diencephalon, cerebellum, and brainstem (the subcortical brain), precipitate and mesh the activities of glands and muscles. As experiments with animals and the experience of humans with massive strokes show (Simeons, 1962), the vital activities of the body can go on without the participation of the cortex; although the reverse, that the cortex can continue without the vital functions, is not true. To Simeons, the associational cortex is a complex set of feedback loops whose activity prevents the older brain from overreacting to stimuli. The more primitive animals must respond more directly to stimuli from the outside. The lower the animal is on the evolutionary scale, the more likely that every signal it receives is a sign initiating behavior of some sort.

More recent research indicates that the neocortex is not only capable of inhibiting the older brain from overreacting to stimuli but also that it remains almost infinitely "reprogramable" throughout the life cycle. The most useful view of the brain is "an ecosystem, not as 'hardwired' like that of lower animals" (Levin, 1991, p. 44). The connections between mammalian nerve cells are established with a great deal more flexibility (Hagen, cited in Levin, 1991). This is a situation where "the synaptic deck is capable of being continuously reshuffled . . . in which many mechanisms create a flexible and dynamically changing pattern of connectivity . . . . Together these studies illustrate that *the human brain is a self-organizing and plastic organ that continues to change and adapt throughout life*, not a static machine with unchangeable 'hardware'" (p. 44).

As animals became more independent of their environment, not all stimuli required a response. Not every potential danger is a real danger, nor does every inviting stimulus necessarily represent an achievable goal. The associational cortex developed as an organ to delay response, that is, to delay stimulation of the old brain, until signals could be further evaluated. The primitive brain is the final common pathway for motivation of behavior, and once it is triggered, the reaction precipitated runs its course and will resist interference.

Freud (1895) spoke of sheltering the cortex from overstimulation, but, in fact, it is the cortex that acts as a protective mechanism for the old brain. The diencephalon provides the key to activity. It triggers inherited self-preservative or reproductive patterns of behavior. These dispositional patterns are encoded in the old brain's blueprints. In mammals, inherited patterns of behaving allow for considerable latitude in the manner of achieving goals. For example, mammals have a wide choice of foodstuffs and are not nearly as limited in what they may and must eat as are amphibians, reptiles, and insects. Should a dietary deficiency arise, mammals will become more alert to any nutrients containing the needed ingredient and are free to search far and wide.

A major inherited disposition is the infant's capacity to learn from the environment (mother) in the first critical months of life. The infant's autonomic nervous system processes information about the environment and facilitates communication with the mother. The mimetic musculature of the infant's face is also highly developed (Tomkins, 1962-63). There are eight or nine distinct sets of muscle reactions that an infant can reveal facially. These reflect the subcortically based affects of surprise/startle, interest/excitement, enjoyment/joy, distress/anguish, anger/rage, fear/terror, contempt/disgust, and shame/humiliation. Through these mimetic responses, the infant gains significant control over the mother-child symbiosis. Far from passively being shaped by the mother, the infant forms a system with her, using her capabilities in the interest of his needs. By his mimetic musculature, he indicates whether he is optimally stimulated; if he is not, he sends signals that encourage the mother to search for and correct whatever is wrong. It is not the specific affect but the stimulus gradients that are responsible for the infant's behavior. Affective behavior is synonymous not with emotion, feeling, or mood, but with the nervous system's nonreflective, involuntary responses to stimulation.

A clinical example of affect can be seen in a patient's uncontrollable crying and sadness during a session after his therapist notified him of an impending vacation (Basch, 1975a). The patient had lost his father when an infant. The infant was, of course, incapable of experiencing emotions at the time of his father's death. His crying now represented distress he had experienced as an infant when his mother became depressed and was unable to invest in him. Hence as an infant he had experienced repeated frustration and mounting but unrelieved tension. The sobbing was an automatic reaction to prolonged helplessness, with its immobilizing disorganization. Sobbing is a distress signal. The patient's anguished crying was a reliving of his early autonomic reaction to the indescribable experience of being helpless in the face of unrelieved tension. (In the past this behavior has been seen as "blocked emotion," rather than an autonomic reaction that needs relief.)

Freud's image theory, modified, has applicability after the age of 18 months. Soon after 18 months, the infant begins imaginative play, imitation in the absence of a model, daytime fantasy, and nighttime dreams. All of these activities require symbolic capacity. They thus mark the beginning of a symbolic life in which the infant can re-present what has been experienced previously. A sign evokes the action appropriate to the object signified, but a symbol arouses the concept of the object (Langer, 1951). This symbolic capacity represents an evolutionary advance with momentous consequences. The child can now do more than match stimuli in the here and now with established neural patterns; he can recall them and experience a mental life independent of the immediate situation. Experience can now be divided into past, present, future, and into subjects and objects.

Our manner of objectifying reality is based on our abstractions from, symbolization of, and reflection about our sensory experiences. The world of so-called material objects is a part of the symbolic world; it belongs to the world of ideas as much as our dreams do. This is not to deny that there is a reality apart from our reflections to which we react through perceptions, but this reality is one we never know directly.

Conceptualization of experience as a generality precedes conceptualization of individual objects. Indeed, the eventual existence of particulars is made possible only by the conceptualization of universals. This generalizing capacity, which Church (1961) calls physiognomic perception, is based on the ability to extract and symbolize the essential form from the totality rather than building up a hierarchical classification atomistically. This formation of universal symbols antedates the use of speech; indeed, the development of language is based on the presence of symbolic concepts. Rational verbal speech is a prime example of discursive symbolization. And with the advent of symbolic capacity the associational cortex is no longer limited to triggering sign-induced behavior. Now, instead of serving the old brain and its instinctual patterns of self-preservation and reproduction, the associational cortex, through symbolic function, to a great extent controls the dispositional power of the subcortical patterns.

In summary, Freud's attempt to build a mental apparatus theory as the basis for psychoanalysis foundered under the accumulative weight of empirically based knowledge of how the brain functions. Freud's brilliant guesses stimulated research. Yet his conception of the way the mind functions and his notion of a machinelike mind have come under increasing criticism as a basis for a theory of psychotherapy. As Basch (1988a) summarizes, "Freud's valiant attempt at creating a mental machine survives to this day; but in spite of the tinkering that it has undergone in the last one hundred years, it still does not run and never will" (p. 13).

Not only has Freud's theory of the mind been discarded by many psychoanalysts, so has drive theory, for the two go together. In the next chapter we examine drive theory and the metapsychology associated with it.

Readings for Chapter 5: Bibring, 1941; Freud, 1923b; Hartmann, 1950; Klein, 1973.

5

Drive and Conflict Theory

To enhance the explanatory power of a mechanical model of the mind, Freud found it necessary to propose some form of mind energy. Just as a machine runs only with a power source driving it, such as steam or electricity, a mental machine needs mental energy. Freud originally thought this energy was sexual, but then used the more general concept of libido, a "quantity of excitation" he referred to as "Q" (Freud, 1895).

Freud's concept of libido, which he probably arrived at from philosophy prior to his early cases (Holt, 1976), helped explain puzzling clinical phenomena. From his experience with hysteria patients, Freud could view difficulties in recalling traumatic events as repression of memories and thoughts, that is, without the concept of the libido. Freud, however, took an important step by conceiving of thought, sexual feelings, and action as manifestations of and opportunities for the discharge of libido. This conceptual arrangement parallels Kant's idea of phenomena (thoughts, feelings and action) and noumena (libido).

According to Freud's concept of libido, repression of thought (memories are stored thoughts) is an example of repressed libido. Libido blocked from discharge through thought seeks discharge in some other way such as sex, overt actions, symptoms, or obsessional rituals. The mechanistic model and libidinal theory offered a way to link together and explain a multitude of functions and behaviors. With time, however, what Freud began as an elegant, simple model became excessively complex. In what follows we explore (a) the evolution of drive theory, (b) Freud's metapsychology, and (c) conflict theory. Drive theory and conflict theory form an important interface for the classical and self psychology paradigms.

DRIVE THEORY

Bibring (1941) summarizes how Freud's drive theory developed from its relatively simple beginning into a complex explanatory analogy. Dualistic from the start, it underwent four major revisions. In the first stage, Freud categorized two groups: the sexual (libidinal) and the ego instincts. He first concentrated his theorizing on the sexual instincts, leaving the ego instincts relatively unknown. This theoretical emphasis on libidinal (sexual) repression and discharge sufficed, provided Freud confined his explanations to the clinical behavior of hysteria and obsessional neuroses.

In the second stage, Freud sought to explain clinical behavior associated with narcissism, which, as Freud used the term, subsumed what we now understand as the spectrum of narcissistic, borderline, and schizophrenic disorders. He did so by developing further the concept of ego instincts. The ego, he said, may become the aim of the discharge of libido, even though the ego also retains a nonlibidinal component called interest. To Freud, the ego becomes the target of libido when all other aims are blocked. A heavily libidinal attachment to the ego helps explain the symptoms associated with the "narcissistic" disorders. This stage in Freud's thinking represents a significant step toward making drive theory more inclusive.

The third stage in drive theory attempted to explain what Freud called sadistic behavior. He said there was an aggressive drive essential to the ego instincts. In the last sections of "Instincts and Their Vicissitudes," Freud (1915) discusses how love and hate reveal that the ego can discharge both libidinal and aggressive instincts. This change in drive theory to include an aggressive instinct was used to explain not only why love can turn so quickly into hate in personal relationships, but also why nations can so quickly turn from mutually beneficial activities to the bloodiness of a world war.

The fourth stage in drive theory came with the development of the structures of the mental apparatus: the vital stratum (id), an organized part (ego), and the unconscious part of the ego (superego). This change meant that the aggressive drive was no longer seen as primarily associated with the ego instincts, but as existing independently, like sexual instincts, in the id (Freud, 1923). The ego instincts now ceased to be independent entities and derived partly from the libidinal and partly from the aggressive instincts.

In his final revision, a fifth stage was added to drive theory. Freud then labeled the libidinal and aggressive instincts, postulated as primary instincts, as the instincts of life and death. Thus, the process of expanding drive theory into a more general explanatory theory had resulted in increasing abstraction until eventually there were two basic principles resting on biological assumptions. These two basic drives—a life instinct of libidinal (sexual) energy and a death instinct of aggressive drive—were perceived as the motivation behind all human behavior.

Another important part of drive theory was Freud's idea that desexualized libido was a source of neutral energy available to the ego. The ego as a subunit of the mental apparatus needs energy to drive it. But if the energy that drives the ego is pure libido, its defenses and organizing functions are immobilized, overwhelmed by raw drive. The answer to this quandary is that while the id supplies energy to the ego, this drive is neutralized by the ego before it becomes available for the functions of the ego.

Hartmann (1950) greatly elaborated and refined this construct of neutralization. He defined neutralization as energy that discharges in a far less peremptory manner. Neutralization involves the aggressive as well as the libidinal drives and takes place constantly as a function of the ego. The idea of neutralized instincts enables us to conceive of autonomous ego functions. Ego interests, that is, goals set by the ego independently of the need for targets of discharge for the libidinal and aggressive drives, are an example of autonomous ego functions.

Rapaport (1959), hypothesizing ways the ego could neutralize the drives, suggests neutralization occurs from actions of the ego that introduce delay and detour. He talks about raising the discharge thresholds of drive energies and building new dams to impede direct discharge. Threshold levels are inborn but can be altered through learning; they form the nucleus of the conflict free sphere of the ego. Furthermore, building structures to increase discharge thresholds utilizes drive energy. According to Hartmann, however, structures are built from drives that first have been neutralized (Applegarth, 1971).

FREUD'S METAPSYCHOLOGY

Freud's instinct theory has been heavily criticized. Swanson (1977) claims that a major reason for the unresolvability of the "psychic energy" controversy is the difficulty in agreeing on a commonly accepted definition. In reviewing Freud's use of the term, Swanson found five explicit frames of reference: interactional, subjective, classificatory, abstract theory, and neurophysiological.

The first of these, interactional, refers to the interaction of mind and body. The nonmaterial mind is activated by a nonmaterial "fluid" that flows along nonmaterial pathways. This language, and even the idea of psychic energy discharging through the motor apparatus, is understandable as a metaphor; but when psychic energy is said to convert into physical energy, the metaphor no longer applies. This frame of reference is untenable because it postulates energy discharge from the mind into the body, a process with no support in contemporary biology, and employs an unacceptable shift from analogy to the language of causation.

The second frame of reference uses such terms as "psychic energy" as descriptions of subjective experiences. Swanson argues that as the language describing subjective experiences is already rich, he sees no value in adding a new set of technical terms. Even so, it is clear that Freud was not just renaming subjective experiences but trying to explain them. Swanson (1977) continues critically:

> People do often feel as though they were seized with impulses, suffused with excitement, paralyzed by fear, or otherwise overcome with emotion. Furthermore, these feelings all must have physiological correlates. But to hypothesize feelings as psychic substances is to play games with words, not build a theory [p. 615].

The third frame of reference examines drive theory as classificatory. Psychic energy is defined as an abstract concept having no referent that actually exists; it is merely convenient for organizing clinical data. If this is so, writes Swanson, "there is no issue of verification, refutation, or testability of statements, nor, of course, of violating energy conservation, for this framework admits of no theoretical-explanatory claims" (p. 615). Unfortunately this frame also renders the theory useless.

The fourth frame of reference is abstract theory. Such theories are intended to explain clinical data and predict behavioral tendencies, but drive-discharge concepts cannot be verified by any subsequent appeal to observation of behavior. Therefore psychic constructs become irrelevant to the theoretical/investigatory process.

The fifth frame of reference, the neurophysiological, creates a hypothetical model of a living organism. Freud conceived of psychic energy as being physical in nature, but he left the particular form unspecified. The problem with this model lies in connecting this physical energy with subjective experience. Freud kept trying but never really succeeded. Freud's clinical ideas are more useful when they are "experience near" and not based on abstract analogies.

Klein (1973) made a similar case. According to him, Freud had two theories of psychoanalysis: a clinical theory and a metapsychological one. The 20th century responded with interest to Freud's clinical theories and not to his metapsychological explanations. Unfortunately, when analysts began to formulate their ideas systematically, they abandoned clinical theory for Freud's metapsychology and adopted the parlance and mannerisms of natural scientists by talking about energies, forces, cathexes, systems, layers, mechanisms, and physical analogies, rather than meanings.

Clinical theory is close to the factual, observational core of analysis (Rapaport, 1959). Many clinicians still believe that Freud derived his idea of *Trieb* (the German word Freud used for "drive") directly from clinical experience (Holt, 1976). Evidence supports the idea that Freud brought his preconceived metaphysics to the clinical situation:

> In its starkest and clearest form—essentially as stated in the "Project" (Freud, 1895b)—the metapsychology of motivation is an explicit, coherent, but untenably mechanistic theory, which has the virtue of being testable and the misfortune of being mostly wrong. It is demonstrably the result of Freud's effort to remain true to Helmholtz and Brucke, his scientific ideal father imagos; about all that is original to him in his theory is his synthesis of his teacher's ideas [Holt, 1976, pp. 162-163].

Freud thought that concepts of purposefulness and meaning were unacceptable as terms of scientific explanation (Klein, 1973). Behaviorism had the same assumption. Believing that regularities described with concepts of purpose will ultimately be explained through the use of purely physiological models, Freud wanted to purge explanations of teleological implications. Freud thought it was important to ask "how" rather than "why." In emphasizing the word "how," Freud tried to convert and reduce psychology to the universe of space, force, and energy (Gill, 1976). He considered such constructs as meaning, purpose, and intention to be unscientific.

Freud's philosophy developed in the tradition of the Brucke-Meynert scientific value system, which held as axiomatic that no phenomenon could be considered "explained" except in physical-chemical terms. Thus, when, toward the end of his career, Freud had doubts about the adequacy of the mind-machine/drive model as a general theory to explain an expanding array of complex clinical syndromes, he did not abandon neurophysiological modeling as such (Klein, 1975). Nor did he abandon the notion of a better metatheory to explain a clinical theory.

"Freud . . . did not in fact abandon a single one of the major errors of assumption that his medical and neurological training had built into his thinking" (Gill, 1976, p. 76). When there is a conflict between procedural evidence (assumptions) and validating evidence (observations), procedural evidence always takes precedence (Rychlak, 1968). The assumptions are not perceived as being wrong; there is something wrong with our observations. For Freud the positivist and determinist, the mechanisms of matter were all-important for understanding, and he was unable to give up his scientific assumptions.

Klein's (1973) position, in contrast to Freud's, is that metapsychology is mostly irrelevant to the clinical enterprise, because one cannot explain clinical data with metaphysical constructs. He believes that "the essential *clinical* propositions concerning motivation have nothing to do with reducing a hypothetical tension; they are inferences of *directional* radiants in behavior and the *object-relations* involved in these directions" (p. 108). There is need for only one psychoanalytic theory, a clinical theory that is tied to the treatment situation. In the analytic enterprise there are not mechanisms, but challenges, crises, relationships, wishes, frustrations, values good and bad, varieties of pleasure and pain. The core of the analytic process consists of the meanings that emerge.

The idea of separate approaches to the "why" of meaning and the "how" of mechanics gains support from Polanyi (1965a, 1965b, 1966), according to whom a comprehensive entity can have different "orders of reality" depending on the "focus" or the "clue" domain. Focus depends on what is foreground and what is background in looking. Any act of knowing proceeds from incidental awareness of the clues to focal awareness of the leading element of the entity. When we look at an event as a clue, it has a different meaning from when we look at it as a focus. When employed as a focus, it no longer has a clue function; it now takes on a different level of meaning.

Paraphrasing Polanyi, Klein (1973) indicates that statements of purpose or meaning and principles of physiological regulation are two mutually exclusive ways of being aware of our bodily activities. The analyst can ignore the mechanistic language of physiology. For Klein "there are no such things as stimuli and responses, but only 'encounters' which have meaning" (p. 131).

As suggested by Bibring's material, the most important explanatory construct in Freud's metapsychology is the idea of an instinctual drive or *Trieb*. Holt (1976) views it as following the idea of the nervous system, which is passive, without energies of its own and functioning so as to rid itself of the noxious input via action. Holt, however, claims that neurological evidence does not support a "passive reflex model." Modern neurophysiologists say that the nervous system is not passive when tested; that not all stimulation, curiosity for example, is noxious; and that not all psychic tension is experienced as unpleasant. Further, as stimulus deprivation studies show,

> it is virtually impossible to protect a person from physiologically effective, external stimuli and keep him alive. We are bathed in a continuous sea of inescapable stimulation, and in fact our normal functioning seems to be dependent on an average expectable environment of varied stimuli [Holt, 1976, p. 165].

Experimental evidence does not support *Trieb* theory either, especially with the sex "drive." Such a drive was thought to be mediated through hormones. When these hormones were eradicated in rats by castration, sexual behavior tended to stop and then dramatically increase after injections of the hormone. This result was initially seen as support for the drive theory. However, long-term studies now indicate that the physiological capacity to engage in sexual intercourse and have orgasm can persist for 30 years after the removal of the gonads (Holt, 1976). Experiments also support the idea that sexual behavior depends on more than a biochemically based drive (see, for example, Beach, 1956).

The position that sexual behavior is more than biochemistry is also supported by another experiment with rats. "When a male has been allowed to copulate with a female to the point where he shows no further interest in her and appears 'sexually exhausted,' his capacity to perform sexually is immediately restored when a new mate is offered him" (Holt, 1976, pp. 174-175). This phenomenon is found in rats, roosters, guinea pigs, monkeys, bulls, and, anecdotally, in humans. No wonder Holt writes, "Drive is dead; long live wish! Freud's concept of *Trieb* served a useful function in his own theoretical development, but for us it is an anachronism beyond hope of rehabilitation" (p. 194).

Freud's metapsychology and his *Trieb* theory, considered pivotal in classical analysis, have not only been thoroughly and systematically critiqued by the authors just quoted (Holt 1976; Klein, 1976; Swanson, 1977) but also by Kubie (1975), Gill (1976), Peterfreund (1971), Rubinstein (1967), and Schafer (1976). Stolorow (1986a) believes the conclusions of these authors are definitive.

For those who persist in using drive theory, Michael Basch (1986), a colleague of Kohut's, has some scathing words:

> The psychoanalytic establishment is rather, a ramshackle lean-to, built by verbal sleight of hand, that hides epistemological and clinical failures that must be faced if we are to be true to Freud's vision . . . . Why does [classical analysis] continue to flourish in spite of the fact that, as I have already mentioned, adherence to that theory is essentially nominal, and no one now practices, if anyone ever did, what the theory actually mandates?
>
> We should ask those who insist on the validity and necessity of the instinct theory for psychoanalysis and who refuse to accept evidence to the contrary what evidence they need to persuade them that the instinct theory of motivation for human behavior cannot serve as an explanation for the clinical findings of psychoanalysis. If there is no answer to that question, if for our adversaries the instinct theory is a given, not subject to disproof, then, of course, we are dealing with a quasi-religious belief, not with a scientific hypothesis, and such a position speaks for itself [p. 23].

Basch (1986) sees self psychology as "bringing psychoanalysis to where it should have been, or could have been, had the imposition of instinct theory not prevented Freud and other analytic pioneers from following the lead of the transference" (p. 25).

CONFLICT THEORY

Conflict theory has always been a part of psychoanalytic thinking. In Chapter 16, we compare conflict theory and deficit theory, so we now explore briefly the nature of conflict as understood in classical theory and later as modified by ego psychology.

Initially conflict theory was based on the topographical model. In this frame, unconscious irrational impulses were in conflict with conscious rational thought. Freud (1923) eventually introduced structural theory as having greater explanatory power than the topographical model. In structural theory, the three agencies—id, ego and superego—are conceived as being in conflict. Freud had found a more technical way to describe the struggles that take place between passions, reason and conscience.

Fenichel (1945), using structural theory, defined neurosis as a conflict between the ego and the id:

> We have in psychoneurosis, first a defense of the ego against the instinct, then a conflict between the instinct striving for discharge and the defensive forces of the ego, then a state of damming up, and finally the neurotic symptoms which are distorted discharges as a consequence of the state of damming up—a compromise between the opposing forces [p. 20].

The id/ego conflict is complex because the superego is also involved. The superego sometimes sides with the ego, and sometimes with the id. With the compulsive disorders, for example, there is an ego verses id and superego conflict.

Despite the persistent critiques of drive theory, which is the underpinning of structural theory, structural theory has endured. Such endurance is understandable because it is not enough to point out the inadequacies of an old paradigm. For a paradigm shift to occur, there has to be a better alternative (Kuhn, 1962). As there was no convincing theoretical alternative to drive theory, a beleaguered classical analysis, emphasizing drive and structural theory, intrapsychic dynamics, oedipal conflicts, and strict use of the techniques of neutrality, transference regression, free association, and interpretation, continued as the predominant paradigm.

Ego psychology created a variation of the structural conflicts of classical analysis. Ego psychology, following the theoretical modifications of Hartmann, placed greater emphasis on the functions of the ego. It stressed the ego's function in helping a person adapt to the reality of the external world. Hartmann, Kris, and Loewenstein

(1946) conceived of conflict between the ego and reality in addition to the id/ego conflicts, such as with toilet training:

> First, there is the conflict between two instinctual tendencies, that of elimination and retention (instinctual conflict); second, there is the conflict between either of these tendencies, and the child's attempts to control them and to time his function: it is a conflict between the id and the ego (structural conflict); and third, there is the conflict with the external world that has made the structural conflict necessary: the mother's request for timing of elimination [p. 27].

Ego psychology also sees conflicts between the autonomous substructures of the ego. For example, "Patients seem to be emphasizing material that can best be explained in terms of ego subsystems, their integration, and how they are synchronized with each other" (Giovaccini, 1987, p. 275). Hartmann (1952), focusing on the ego, stressed the idea of ego functions: neutralization, adaptation, organizational synthesis, objectivation, anticipation, perception, thought, action, and defenses. Theoretically, once neutralized instincts are made available to autonomous ego functions, ego conflicts invested with neutralized energy are inevitable. Autonomy leads to conflict between "ego interests."

The more familiar one becomes with ego psychology, the more one realizes that Hartmann's ideas suggest many of the concepts later utilized by Kohut. For example, Hartmann (1953) referred to B. Rank's 1949 phrase "ego fragmentation" (p. 179). Kohut may have turned this term into self-fragmentation and made it one of his major constructs. Hartmann also shifted his conceptualization from ego to self in discussing several key ideas. He defined narcissism as a "libidinal cathexis of the self, not just the ego" (Hartmann, 1953, p. 179). And he stresses ego functions, not ego structures, as if they were objects. As will be seen in Chapter 14, Kohut used this Hartmann maneuver to turn the concept of a selfobject into selfobject functions to avoid the problem of reification.

Before he died, Kohut (1980) openly expressed his indebtedness to Hartmann:

> I am grateful to Hartmann because his work gave me the courage to move further along the road that his acknowledgment of the

> legitimacy of analytic interest in healthy functions had opened. And even though I know from many personal discussions with him that he could not have accepted the "psychology of the self in the broad sense" with which we are now working, I am very happy that he still read the manuscript of my *Analysis of the Self* (1971) and gave it his approval [pp. 544-545].

Kohut's desire to record self psychology's link to Hartmann is important: "It points to the historicity of self psychology within a psychoanalytic research tradition" (Stepansky, 1989, p. 65). This tradition, which was not available for Adler to appeal to, had formed by the time of Hartmann and thus prevented Freud's tactic of condemning Adler's work as a nonanalytic "ego psychology deepened by the knowledge of the psychology of the unconscience" from being used to condemn Hartmann. Kohut was implicitly appealing to this research tradition for the acceptance of self psychology as a legitimate expansion of psychoanalysis.

Besides ego psychology's theoretical modifications of psychoanalysis' idea of conflict, psychoanalysis also underwent an orthodox hardening (Lipton, 1977). For example, in the decade following Freud's death, Kris (1951) repudiated Freud's technique in the analysis of Paul Lorenz (Ernst Lanzer). This hardening is also reflected in Eissler's (1953) paper on parameters in which, while it is stated that parameters may be unavoidable in special cases, the ideal (orthodoxy) is clearly strict adherence to free association and interpretation. Lipton claimed that Eissler's work was a counterargument to Alexander and French's (1946) emphasis on experience at the expense of insight, manipulating the transference instead of analyzing it, and leaving unresolved the attachment of the patient to the therapist. Such orthodoxy was aimed at devaluing and disavowing the personal relationship between the patient and the therapist. The resolution of intrapsychic conflict occurred only through a well-timed and correct interpretation (Gill, 1954).

Brenner (1982) offers a modern view of drive theory. He does not want to drop the clinical use of the term "drive," even though he admits there is no support for its somatic source and tension-discharge elements. He proposes a psychological construct of drive that rests on a pleasure principle that is the single most dominating motivation for mental life.

Criticizing Brenner's position, Mitchell (1988) claims that this truncated "pleasure" view of drive theory so distorts the idea of pleasure that it is unnatural and obscure. In Brenner's theory, for example, it is difficult to understand "why sexual pleasures are any more central motivationally than any other forms of pleasure" (p. 85). Brenner is then forced to defend his theory with the idea "that whatever the person does, no matter how painful it feels and seems, *must* be pleasurable in terms of some unconscious wish" (p. 85). Brenner (1982) also has to claim that any wish, once activated, follows its pleasure-seeking path until it succeeds (p. 32). But once he makes this claim, argues Mitchell (1988), "Brenner portrays the mind, instead of being pleasure seeking, as being fatefully committed to whatever early wishes happen to emerge within it" (p. 85). Brenner's psychologically based pleasure theory of motivation does not hold up under scrutiny as a useful way out of the problems of drive theory.

Thus, Freud's psychoanalytic paradigm using the model of a mental machine driven by psychic energy—a paradigm that has held sway for nearly a century—is acknowledged as mobilizing much valuable clinical research and theoretical debate. Nevertheless, it is increasingly seen both within psychoanalytic circles and especially in the newer therapeutic professions of psychology and social work, as an inadequate general theory of psychotherapy. It is the theory, nevertheless, against which new paradigms are compared.

Before we examine the new self psychology paradigm, two chapters are devoted to important precursors: (1) Ferenczi and (2) the British school. Other precursor theorists such as Adler and Rank are examined elsewhere (Detrick and Detrick, 1989). We include chapters on Ferenczi and the British theorists because their ideas, in conjunction with Hartmann's, are sufficient to demonstrate that the concepts of self psychology did not suddenly emerge *ex nihilo* to challenge the drive-theory paradigm. In the next chapter we turn to the discoveries of Sandor Ferenczi.

Readings for Chapter 6: Ferenczi, 1928; Ferenczi, 1933; Gedo, 1986, Chap. 3; Rachman, 1989.

6

Ferenczi, the Dissident

The self psychology paradigm casts the work of Sandor Ferenczi in a new light. Through the eyes of classical analysis, Ferenczi was seen as becoming increasingly demented in his later life or, more generously, as courageously experimenting with an "active technique" and because of the poor results, saving the analytic movement from going down a therapeutic dead end. In the light of Kohut's work, a radically different picture emerges of a Ferenczi on the main clinical highway, too far ahead of his colleagues for his work to be appreciated. We examine Ferenczi's ideas under the following headings: (a) background, (b) character analysis, (c) active technique, (d) narcissism, (e) trauma, (f) collaborative analysis, (g) last days, and (h) precursors to self psychology.

BACKGROUND

When the analytic phase of his career began in 1907, Ferenczi had already published about 30 scholarly papers on various subjects in

Hungarian and German journals. He was 34 years old. "His predominant personal qualities were enthusiasm, warmth, tenderness, giving, optimism, and compassion" (Rachman, 1989, p. 90). As the leader of the Hungarian analytic movement, Ferenczi made his most important contribution, second only to Freud's, in building clinical theory. Freud described Ferenczi's initial theoretical and clinical contributions as "pure gold." The esteemed Ferenczi accompanied Freud to Clark University (Massachusetts) in 1909, where they walked together every morning while Ferenczi suggested the topic for Freud's lecture of the day (Freud, 1933). For the next five years, Ferenczi's published articles gained him a reputation as the outstanding contributor among Freud's early disciples.

During World War I, Freud analyzed Ferenczi. Gedo (1976) says of this analysis:

> Its partial failure must be attributed to the unavoidable historical circumstance that it was performed at a time when psychoanalytic knowledge had not yet reached the point that would have made possible the successful treatment of Ferenczi's type of pathology [pp. 358-359].

Gedo meant narcissism. Supporting Gedo's view is Rachman's (1989) belief that the Freud/Ferenczi correspondence verifies the view that Ferenczi was maternally deprived.

Torok (1979), also after studying the Freud-Ferenczi correspondence and Ferenczi's scientific diary, writes that Freud had prohibited Ferenczi's marriage to the woman Ferenczi loved. This injunction may have led Ferenczi to experience Freud as the depriving mother and retraumatizer. Ferenczi married the woman eventually in 1919 (Gedo, 1976), but the marriage led to an irredeemable bitterness in Ferenczi and guilt about it in Freud.

This hostility/guilt impasse in their relationship may explain why Ferenczi eventually came to be seen as a traitor to psychoanalysis. For example, by 1930 Ferenczi was reproaching Freud for having failed to analyze the negative transference when Ferenczi was being treated during the war. Freud (1937), on the other hand, without mentioning Ferenczi's name, described the unsatisfactory results with Ferenczi in "Analysis Terminable and Interminable." It is possible to understand Ferenczi's later clinical thinking as having resulted from his attempts at self-analysis because of the failure of his treatment with Freud. Ferenczi's most important work really consisted in the search for a suitable treatment for himself as a narcissistic character (personality) disorder.

CHARACTER ANALYSIS

Ferenczi's first step was to emphasize the difference between symptoms and character structure, and the need to treat the underlying character disorder. He was the first analyst to make this distinction (Gedo, 1988). Even though Freud, in the 25 years between 1895 and 1920, expanded diagnostic categories to include entities other than hysteria, his broadened nosology was insufficient for Ferenczi. Besides "transference neurosis" Freud (1895) had included the "anxiety neuroses," which reflected "psychical insufficiency" and "narcissistic neuroses" (Freud, 1914), which included psychoses, homosexuality, and melancholic depression. Ferenczi was also not satisfied with Freud's theories of pathology and treatment techniques. Freud laid more emphasis on the importance of genetic interpretations; Ferenczi stressed the crucial importance of affective reliving in the here and now of the analysis, a position that has become widely accepted in modern psychotherapy (Gill, 1984).

Ferenczi set down his views about character analysis in *The Development of Psychoanalysis* (Ferenczi and Rank, 1924). He pointed out that henceforth psychoanalysis could not confine its therapeutic aims to the elimination of isolated symptoms or of dynamic "complexes"; it had to address itself to personality in all its aspects. Freud's partial disagreement with the book "shattered" Ferenczi and was seemingly a failure in a twinship transference (Kohut 1971; see also Chapter 13, this volume).

ACTIVE TECHNIQUE

Although Ferenczi stressed treating character structure, he conducted "experiments" with an "active technique" after resuming his private practice in 1919. Jones (1920) reported on this technique.

Ferenczi said he was encouraged to use the active technique because of Freud's statements at the Budapest Congress in 1918 suggesting that a phobic cannot change unless induced to face his phobia and act despite it. Freud also suggested active measures with obsessional neurosis.

Federn (1933), in support of Ferenczi, said that experimentation in active methods was quite common during that period, although nobody talked about it (Lorand, 1966). Federn himself and his colleagues in Vienna had tried various methods for furthering analysis in cases that had reached an impasse. This common practice of experimentation suggests that the attack by Ferenczi's analytic colleagues on the active method was a displacement of a dissatisfaction for other reasons, perhaps the threat that Ferenczi's clinical ideas in general posed to the growing intellectual edifice built on drive and structural theories.

The central aspect of Ferenczi's active technique was to request that the patient, in addition to using free association, act or behave in a certain way, in the hope of increasing tension and thereby mobilizing unconscious material. It was used only after a stalemate occurred. He urged patients to fight certain habits. Ferenczi also cautioned that the technique could not be used with all patients. Ferenczi (1920) called attention to the fact that interpretation itself is an active interference with the patient's psychic activity because "it turns the thoughts in a given direction and facilitates the appearance of ideas that otherwise would have been prevented by the resistance from becoming conscious" (pp. 199-200).

By 1925, however, Ferenczi, ever the innovator, had discarded the commands and prohibitions of his active technique in favor of positive and negative suggestions. He also had modified his active technique in "Contraindications to the Active Psychoanalytic Technique" (Ferenczi, 1925), where he indicated the need for retreat if there were no responses to a suggestion. He particularly warned against being too emphatic or forceful lest this be experienced by the patient as a sadistic attack. As Lorand points out, Ferenczi was exploring what Eissler (1953) later referred to as "parameters." Ferenczi did so because he was probing for success with the "dried up" cases that came to him from all over the world as their last hope. Ferenczi, predating Winnicott by 40 years, experimented with adjusting the analytic situation to the patient's needs—setting up a facilitating environment. These technical experiments were later seen by Eissler (1953) as a "deviation" from analytic orthodoxy and from the true techniques of free association and interpretation.

Encouraged by the work of Ferenczi, Franz Alexander experimented with the active technique in evolving the idea of a "corrective emotional experience." In this maneuver, Alexander (1953) recommended manipulating the transference so that it was the opposite of the traumatic relationships of the patient's upbringing. Alexander's ideas were rigorously opposed in the psychoanalytic climate of the 1950s as not being psychoanalysis and therefore incapable of producing permanent structural changes in the patient. When self psychology is accused of being another version of a "corrective emotional experience," it is important to understand that it is being accused of manipulating the transference in the rejected tradition of Ferenczi and Alexander. Self psychology claims, however, that its theory does not sanction "active techniques."

NARCISSISM

With increasing clinical experience, Ferenczi's search for a way to treat character structure became more focused on the narcissistic character disorder. He called one narcissistic type involving archaic character pathology "the wise baby." Awareness of this syndrome arose from Ferenczi's self-reflection as well as from his work with patients. He describes these patients as having been traumatized by parental failures to help them with weaning, habit training, and renouncing the status of childhood in favor of more mature modes.

In the course of the development of the "wise baby," excessive strictness or deficient external controls form harsh superegos in children who have difficulty differentiating fantasy from reality. Later, as patients they cannot trust the analyst's dependability and will test him repeatedly. Thus the negative transference must be analyzed before a positive transference can blossom. These patients cannot free associate; they need unlimited time in working through.

Termination cannot be initiated by the therapist and should occur only when the mourning for the lost gratifications of childhood has been completed.

Many of these "wise baby" patients are suicidal, with an intense self-destructiveness that might exemplify the concept of the death instinct. Their oedipal problems are unresolved, and they are preoccupied with what we have come to call existential concerns. Their early traumatization acts like a constitutional adaptive defect, as if a solid "life force" has failed to come into being because of the deficiency of "good care." The personality is fragmented by multiple splits that defend against the affective recognition of infantile traumata. Ferenczi saw this pathology as similar in some ways to that of the psychoses.

The most sensitive issue for these "wise babies" is abandonment, against which they defend themselves through narcissistic withdrawal. Often, however, a precocious maturity emerges and they take on a protective role toward their parents during childhood. This precocious behavior is seen as a masochistic surrender involving an identification with an aggressor who is then unconsciously devoured. A failure of these defenses leads to a profound hopelessness and helplessness. The reality of the traumatic events is ultimately defended against by pervasive doubt or depersonalization. Ferenczi "was actually engaged in the pioneering study of borderline patients and their treatment by psychoanalysis" (Gedo, 1976, p. 373).

TRAUMA

In working with narcissistic and borderline character disorders, it did not take long for Ferenczi to recognize that sensitivity to being traumatized was a central issue. His professional interest in trauma began during World War I, when he collaborated with Abraham, Simmel, and Jones on war neuroses (trauma). He recognized that, as a result of the trauma of battle, there is regression to previously abandoned methods of adaptation. Ferenczi's interest in trauma stayed with him throughout his professional career, as evidenced by his final paper read to the Wiesbaden International Psycho-Analytic Congress in September 1932 (Masson, 1984). The paper, "Confusion of Tongues Between Adults and the Child" (Ferenczi, 1933), was presented to the Congress but was not published until Balint's persistence was rewarded in 1949.

In that paper, Ferenczi's "recent more emphatic stress [was] on the traumatic factors, which have been undeservedly neglected of late in the pathogenesis of the neuroses" (p. 156). (This emphasis on trauma was also Freud's (1896b) in "The Aetiology of Hysteria.") Ferenczi was again suggesting that many patients have been sexually molested as children. It, in effect, gave a message that psychoanalysis had been going down a blind alley by analyzing only intrapsychic fantasies. Masson (1984) concludes, "It is Ferenczi's ideas about trauma that made him unacceptable to Freud, and not his experiments with technique" (p. 166).

Masson's position may not go far enough. Ferenczi's emphasis on trauma was only one aspect of a whole new approach to psychoanalysis. Rachman (1989) wrote of Ferenczi's 1933 paper:

> It solidified the new method of humanistic psychoanalysis; reintroduced the seduction hypothesis; encouraged professional acceptance of sexual abuse of children by parents and parental surrogates; introduced the concept that analysts should retraumatize their patients in Freudian therapy; and precipitated the final disruption of Ferenczi's relationship with Freud and the analytic community [p. 95].

Ferenczi's awareness of the theoretical importance of trauma led him to believe that one of the consequences of trauma was the arrested development of the patient (Ferenczi, 1913), a concept that was taken up by Anna Freud (1965) and introduced into self psychology by Gedo (1966, 1967). (It is discussed further in chapter 16, this volume.)

COLLABORATIVE ANALYSIS

In treating character disorders, Ferenczi developed a collaborative approach to avoid fostering resistance and retraumatization in the patient. It was this collaborative approach that made Ferenczi's treatment seem more humanistic. His collaborative method is discussed under the following topics: 1. empathy, 2. retraumatization, 3. mutual analysis, 4. identification with the aggressor, and 5. lay analysis.

Empathy

Through his clinical experience, Ferenczi gradually came to devote more attention to the theory and use of empathy in conducting psychotherapy. He arrived at this construct out of a concern for resistances to the analyst's interventions.

> I recall, for instance, an uneducated, apparently quite simple, patient who brought forward objections to an interpretation of mine, which it was my immediate impulse to reject; but on reflection not I, but the patient, turned out to be right, and the result of his intervention was a much better general understanding of the matter we were dealing with [Ferenczi, 1928, p. 94].

He also saw empathy as connected to the idea of tact: "I have come to the conclusion that it is above all a question of psychological tact whether or when one should tell the patient some particular thing" (p. 89). Tact in determining when to interpret was more important than the interpretation itself. But then he goes on, "But what is tact? . . . It is the capacity for empathy" (p. 89).

Rachman (1989) points to evidence of Ferenczi's use of empathy:

> Several published resources provide examples of Ferenczi's empathic functioning as an analyst. There are Ferenczi's first case of psychoanalytic therapy (Ferenczi, 1919a), what I (Rachman, 1976) have termed Ferenczi's "Case of the Female Croatian Musician" (Ferenczi, 1920); the "Grandpa Encounter" in Ferenczi's discovery of the language of empathy (Ferenczi, 1931); and Thompson's (1964) report of "The Case of The Slovenly Soldier"

In the Croatian Musician case, Ferenczi seems to have participated in what we now call a mirror transference (chapter 11) because he encouraged a woman to sing in his presence.

Retraumatization

With his increasing emphasis on trauma and empathy, "Ferenczi was the first analyst to identify the traumatic aspects of the psychoanalytic situation" (Rachman, 1989, p. 98). Ferenczi thought that the orthodox analytic stance did not encourage empathy.

> The deliberate "restrained coolness," "professional hypocrisy," the focus on the patient's criticisms of the analyst as resistance, the clinical facade behind which an analyst hides from a genuine interpersonal encounter, all contribute to producing an ungenuine and therapeutically limited experience [and trauma akin to the patient's childhood trauma] [p.99].

Mutual Analysis

Ferenczi also advocated the idea of mutual analysis, in which the analyst shared with certain patients his own problems when they overlapped with problems of the patient. This idea, although never published, appears in Ferenczi's diary and is hinted at by Ferenczi's reference to the professional hypocrisy of not focusing on the analyst–patient relationship as an interactive process of responding. In the diary, he also talks about the analyst's admitting errors as a way of earning the trust of the patient, a point that anticipated Kohut's recommendation to interpret the patient's experience of empathic failure.

Identification With the Aggressor

Another of Ferenczi's original clinical constructs also relates to the collaborative relationship between analyst and analysand. Long before Anna Freud added "identification with the aggressor" to the list of ego defenses, Ferenczi (1927) had discussed the idea in his writings: "First we are afraid of punishment; then we identify ourselves with the punishing authority" (p. 73).

This concept of identification with the aggressor was elaborated five years later in Ferenczi's (1933) last paper:

> Gradually, then, I came to the conclusion that the patients have an exceedingly refined sensitivity for the wishes, tendencies, whims, sympathies and antipathies of their analyst, even if the analyst is completely unaware of this sensitivity. Instead of contradicting the analyst or accusing him of errors and blindness, the patients *identify themselves with him*; only in rare moments of an hysteriod excitement, i.e., in an almost unconscious state, can they pluck up enough courage to make a protest; normally they do not allow themselves to criticize us, such a criticism does not even become conscious in them unless we give them special permission or even encouragement to be so bold. That means that we must discern not only the painful events of their past from their associations, but also—and much more often than hitherto supposed—their repressed or suppressed criticism of us [pp. 157-158].

Lay Analysis

Ferenczi also supported the continuation of lay analysis. This was an understandable position in view of his growing conviction about a collaborative alliance and his fears that medicalizing the analytic profession would only reinforce an authoritarian analytic stance. Such a stance is signified by the Freudian notion of a two-tiered hierarchical view of reality in which the therapist's task is to change the patient's distorted view of reality as revealed in the transference.

In 1926, when Ferenczi visited New York at the invitation of the American Psychoanalytic Association, the New York Society was cold and distant, angry with him for his support of lay analysis. Jones (1961) indicated, wrongly, that the New York Society's coldness was due to Ferenczi's not informing the Society that he was coming. Jones also stated that Ferenczi had been completely ostracized by his colleagues, certainly an exaggeration in view of the fact that some members of the New York Society attended his lectures. There was, however, a coolness toward Ferenczi by the New York Society's leadership because of the lay analysis issue.

LAST DAYS

Despite Freud's criticism of Ferenczi's experiments in technique, Freud and Ferenczi continued to correspond. Their relationship had gradually become strained, beginning with Freud's rejection of Ferenczi's idea on the need for character analysis (Ferenczi and Rank, 1924).

The estrangement, which lasted until Ferenczi's death in 1933, became more obvious during the late 20s. Ferenczi had hoped for a renewed closeness with Freud once he abandoned his active techniques as not significantly improving therapeutic results. But the differences between Ferenczi and Freud were far more substantial than Ferenczi's experiments with an active method. Ferenczi's clinical experiences and discoveries threatened Freud's drive-structural theory long before Freud was able to acknowledge the weaknesses of his paradigm.

Ferenczi's clinical discoveries also threatened Freud's classical paradigm to a degree that even Ferenczi was not aware. He almost single-handedly attacked Freud's approach to psychoanalysis on just the clinical front, when what was needed was a broad attack on the whole paradigm. It was not until Kohut made his broad-based attempt to replace Freud's mechanistic view of the mind with the concept of the self, and to reject drive theory, that a new paradigm emerged that could successfully challenge Freud's classical one. Compared with Kohut's work, Ferenczi's was a heroic gesture. Fortunately, through Melanie Klein and Michael Balint, the seeds of many of Ferenczi's ideas later blossomed into the British school.

In 1933 Ferenczi was terminally ill with pernicious anemia. On the basis of Ferenczi's deviation from the classical technique, Jones (1961) claimed that Ferenczi had a latent psychosis and that a mental regression was apparent in Ferenczi's later writings. There does not, however, appear to be a shred of evidence that Ferenczi ever suffered from a personality impairment or mental illness, except for the last weeks of his life, when his spinal cord and brain were effected by anemia (Lorand, 1966). Michael Balint (1958) and others who were in contact with Ferenczi until his death have said that, until the last week, he remained completely lucid and alert.

Gedo (1986) takes the slightly different position that some loss of scientific rationality made its appearance in Ferenczi's writings in September 1932. Ferenczi spoke then of the possibility of an "ideal power" working magically, each telekinetic action subordinating externals to the will of "the ego" (p. 46). This regression of Ferenczi's sense of reality to a belief in the omnipotence of thoughts may have been in the service of disavowing his impending death and his sense of helplessness.

Jones thought Ferenczi was conspiring against him (Lorand, 1966). Jones harbored negative feelings toward Ferenczi, often expressed as irritation and criticism of Ferenczi even 20 years after Ferenczi's death in a conversation with Lorand. Why? Gedo suggests that the ambivalence of Jones and others toward Freud was handled through splitting. Freud was idealized, and his closest collaborator, Ferenczi, became the target of their hostility.

Pernicious anemia was Ferenczi's physical cause of death at the age of 59. If one takes an empathic stance, however, it is difficult to avoid feeling that he died of a broken heart. More accurately, he died from lack of mirroring nourishment to sustain his brilliant, creative work. The heir-apparent fell to palace intrigue. His death was a tragic waste, coming at a time in his life when his clinical experience, would have enabled him make further significant theoretical contributions to psychotherapy. But, as we can now see, his work was not fruitless. It took the perspective of time and the work of Kohut for many to appreciate fully the contribution of Ferenczi, who had the good fortune to be a collaborator with Freud but the misfortune to wait in his shadow.

PRECURSOR TO SELF PSYCHOLOGY

Ferenczi's ideas foreshadowed key clinical concepts in self psychology. For example, nearly 30 years before Winnicott's construct of the transitional object, Ferenczi (1927) discussed the same notion: "The natural tendency of the baby is to love himself and to love all those things which he regards as parts of himself, his excreta are really a part of himself, a transitional something between him and his environment, i.e. between subject and object" (p. 67). We agree with Rachman (1989, pp. 93-95), however, that Ferenczi's thinking went beyond the idea of a transitional object to something close to Kohut's general idea of a selfobject. This idea lies behind the discussion of whether the family adapts to the child, or the child to the family. Ferenczi wrote, "We are generally concerned with the adaptation of the child to the family, not that of the family to the child; but our special studies in psychoanalysis have shown that it is we who should make the first adaptation" (p. 61). In Ferenczi's thinking, the family is meant to function as a selfobject to the child and not the reverse.

Ferenczi's writings show an awareness of the reparative reverse selfobject experience (Lee, 1988), where the child acts as a selfobject to the mother in the hope that the mother will function as a selfobject for the child.

> Children have the compulsion to put to rights all disorder in the family, to burden, so to speak, their own tender shoulders with the load of all the others; of course this is not only out of pure altruism, but is in order to be able to enjoy again the lost rest and the care and attention accompanying it. A mother complaining of her constant miseries can create a nurse for life out of her child, i.e. is a real mother substitute, neglecting the true interests of the child [Ferenczi, 1933, p. 166].

Predating Kohut by many years, Ferenczi stressed introspection, advocated the empathic method, urged therapists to admit their interpretive errors, talked about the nuclear self, and was concerned about a patient's fragmentation and atomization. Kohut developed similar clinical ideas but elaborated them more fully than Ferenczi did. Kohut also offered conceptual alternatives to the outdated philosophical assumptions of the classical paradigm. We believe that Kohut, scholar as well as clinician, would not have neglected to read Ferenczi and profit from him. If Kohut was not influenced by Ferenczi, then the similarity of their ideas is a remarkable example of a convergence of independently derived theory.

It is clear, then, that Ferenczi was a pioneer in formulating theoretical ideas derived from working with severely disturbed patients. He predated the modern interest in the borderline syndrome by 50 years. Although his later clinical ideas were rejected by Freud and Ferenczi's palace rivals, who were committed to classical analysis, his influence was felt in the British school, especially through the work of Michael Balint. Unhampered by the issue of orthodoxy, members of the British school were free to explore the consequences of treatment by using explanations not tied to drive theory or the classical point of view. We turn to these British theoreticians in the next chapter.

Readings for Chapter 9: Klein, 1935; Balint, 1968; Brandchaft, 1986; Bacal, 1989; Brandchaft, 1989.

7

The British School

Following the example of Ferenczi, the theorists of the British School continued to explore the unchartered waters beyond Freud's classical theory. This school was not strictly British. Its first major thinker, Melanie Klein, and another leader, Michael Balint, were Hungarian expatriates, former students of Ferenczi. Others were Heimann, Fairbairn, Guntrip, Winnicott, Khan, Bion, Sutherland, and Bowlby. Their divergent ideas, covering 50 years, created a "school" only in a broad sense. This chapter explores the clinical and theoretical work of four members of the British School—Klein, Fairbairn, Balint, and Winnicott—and discusses how their work ultimately contributed to the development of a new psychotherapy paradigm and to ideas that were the intellectual forerunners of self psychology.

KLEIN

Melanie Klein made her initial reputation as a pioneer of child analysis. Behind her techniques was the assumption that the spontaneous play of children is equivalent to free association in adults. Following her mentor, Ferenczi, on the importance of enactments, Klein understood that children communicate through enactments rather than words (self psychology also understands enactments as efforts to communicate) and respond to interpretations with further enactments.

On the basis of her work with infants, Klein challenged Freud's idea of the centrality of the Oedipus complex in the development of psychopathology:

> Her example and her teaching influenced a whole generation of psychoanalysts outside the United States in the conviction that the key to understanding and amelioration of basic psychological disorders lay in the activation, observation, understanding, and explanation of archaic transference configurations, together with their displacements and disavowals, as entities in their own right and not simply as evasions of or regressions from too intense an oedipal rivalry . . . .
>
> She maintained that the archaic tie was foundational when she concluded from her psychoanalytic investigation and treatment of small children that the basic structures of normal and pathological development were laid down in earliest infancy. She thereby signaled her departure from Freud and the theory of the centrality for development of the oedipal conflict of the fourth and fifth year [Brandchaft, 1989, p. 232].

Observing many symptoms of depression in child patients, Klein (1935) posited the idea that, starting at 18 months, depression was the major clinical issue. This depression arose from an attempt to preserve the "good object." Stripped of concrete images, such as "devouring the breast," her thesis "that the secure establishment of a bond to a good internal object is the key to a useful, productive, creative, and generative life, can hardly now be faulted" (Brandchaft, 1986, p. 254). Manic, schizoid, and paranoid defenses are variations of this depressive problem.

Klein's concept of projective identification bears some similarity to Kohut's selfobject construct. She was referring to a child's fantasy of expelling bad parts into the mother to be rid of unwanted, aggressive elements. Projective identification was considered to be a pathological, defensive operation whereby the other person in a two-person relationship is denied independent volition because the patient's fantasies make the therapist an extension of the patient. In conjunction with the concept of projective identification, Klein wove into an elaborate theoretical narrative the technical concepts of introjects, introjective identification and splitting.

Linked as Klein's concept of projective identification was to the idea of introjects, that is, "internal objects," it depended on Freud's mechanistic and materialistic way of viewing the "mind." When the modern "mind" became viewed as an information-processing organ, Klein's concept of projective identification retained only limited theoretical value. The concept, as originally understood by Klein, nevertheless suggests that she and her mentor, Ferenczi, after experiencing patients with pregenital problems, were groping toward an idea akin to the selfobject function that Kohut made central to his thinking.

Theorists since Klein have kept the concept of projective identification theoretically useful by expanding its meaning. Malin and Grotstein (1966), for example, assert that the concept covers a "normal as well as abnormal way of relating which persists into mature adulthood" (p. 27) and see it as building ego integration as well as functioning for defensive purposes. Langs (1976) focuses on the interactional dimension of projective identification, revealing the efforts to which therapist and patient go to induce in others aspects of their own internal state. Ogden (1979), in a view similar to Kohut's, characterizes projective identification as a basic way of being with an object that is psychologically only partially separate. Tansey and Burke (1989) generalize that projective identification has "defensive, adaptive and communicative properties" (p. 44) and that projective identification cannot take place unless the recipient has a corresponding introjective identification.

Racker (1957) breaks down the idea of projective identification into two basic processes: complementary identifications, and concordant identifications. In one form of complementary identification, the patient elicits from the therapist, through interpersonal influence, critical verbal behavior; thus the therapist identifies with the sadistic experience while the patient experiences being a victim. Another form of complementary identification is with a reversal, where the therapist experiences being attacked and criticized. In the concordant identification, the patient induces in the therapist an experience similar to the one being experienced by the patient. This idea of concordant (projective) identification comes close to a primitive type of communication that Kohut conceived of as a twinship experience.

Perhaps Melanie Klein's most important, though unintended, contribution to psychotherapy was her technique of interpretation. Believing in the curative value of interpretations, Klein often made them, usually commencing with the first session, and liberally used technical imagery, such as, "devouring the breast." She was stricter about using interpretations than most of her classical colleagues were, perhaps to avoid the kind of censure Ferenczi received in experimenting with his active techniques. Interpretations, as she used them, came very close to being indoctrination. It was the counterproductive results of interpretations used this way that so clearly point to the dangers of seeking a cure through interpretations only.

Klein's dogmatic personality, if not the major reason for her doctrinaire approach to psychotherapy, certainly intensified it. Her dogmatic rigidity has been reported by many colleagues. Judith Fay (cited in Grosskurth, 1986) reports that "it was possible to criticize or quarrel with (Paula) Heimann, who would laugh it off. With Klein one would have felt in the wrong" (p. 422). Laing, for example, detested Klein's dogmatism and the way she beat her followers into submission. He saw her early interpretations as impingement, the techniques of a professional torturer (Grosskurth, 1986, p. 422). This seems like harsh criticism. Yet many who knew Klein say something similar; there is strong evidence of her indoctrinating approach to analysis. For example, Clare Winnicott, the second wife of Donald Winnicott, was analyzed by Klein. Her analysis became a battle of wills. Clare said of Klein that she was a brilliant theoretician, but not a clinician; she implanted theory. Ferenczi called such implanting "superego intropression" (Balint, 1968).

Edward Glover's view of Melanie Klein (Grosskurth, 1986) seems to have been expressed in a case he reported of a young man whose mother had a "consistent policy throughout her life of emotionally exploiting dependents, especially her children, and preventing any exhibition of resentment by making them feel guilty. She had a high opinion of herself as a mother but was, in fact, self aggrandizing, tyrannical and selfish" (p. 311). She was an emotional steamroller, glossing over environmental factors and accentuating endopsychic factors. With her, the process of preconceived theories influencing interpretation was overt. Many think this young man was really Melitta, Klein's daughter, whom Glover analyzed.

Further evidence that Klein's interpretive approach could be more of a liability than an asset in the therapeutic results comes from Melitta, and from Richard, one of Melanie Klein's child patients. Melitta, herself an analyst, said that Kleinians brainwash their patients "to believe they are incapable of making any decisions or coping with life unless they have undergone a 'thorough analysis'" (Grosskurth, 1986, p. 229). Once fully analyzed, like the true believer, they will be saved from hell and enjoy eternal bliss in the life after death.

Richard, Melanie's four-year-old patient, was interviewed 50 years after the experience. Referring to an interpretation made by Klein that his father's penis was incorporated inside his mother's body, Richard commented, "I think she could have cut this claptrap out." What he remembered as valuable was her soothing him when he cried. Klein would say, "Life is not all bad." These comments by Richard suggest that it was not the content of what Klein said, but the soothing function she served, that he found usable. Tolpin (1971) describes such soothing as an important selfobject experience without which anyone is quite vulnerable to fragmentation.

Klein's tough-minded, dogmatic personality, while it led to a countertherapeutic, doctrinaire approach to interpretation, enabled her to win one of the most important political/theoretical struggles to occur in psychoanalysis. The conflict reached its zenith in the British Psychoanalytic Society during 1942 and the London blitz (Grosskurth, 1986). The Kleinians, who had been in power for nearly 20 years, were challenged by the growing strength of the classical analysts, who were supported by an influx of continental refugee analysts. A change in leadership made the struggle overt.

Ernest Jones, a pro-Kleinian who had invited Klein to England in the 20s, was replaced by Edward Glover, an anti-Kleinian, as chairman of the British Society (Grosskurth, 1986). Anna Freud was another important ally of the classical analysts. Many Kleinians did not attend the meeting because they had left London to escape the blitz, but the classically oriented refugees, who were restricted to the London area by order of the civil authorities, were strongly represented. Glover also had the support of Melanie's daughter, Melitta, who may have used the conflict to reenact her own individuation struggle.

The power struggle centered on the training of candidates. On February 25, 1942, in an "Extraordinary Meeting," Glover accused the Kleinians of being a secret cabal and stacking the group of training analysts with those of a Kleinian viewpoint. Payne answered for the Kleinians by asserting that Glover's figures were inflated. These opening shots aroused emotions and rallied supporters to both sides. The issue was joined. The British Society then went through a very uncertain, uncomfortable period of unresolved conflict. At another meeting, four months later, however, Payne presented detailed figures clearly disproving Glover's charge and dissipating tensions. Glover's attempt to undermine the influence of Melanie Klein had failed.

The Kleinian–Classical power struggle in London reflected a major policy issue for psychoanalysis. The issue was forced by the growth of Nazism, which had eradicated most of the analytic societies in Europe; the death of Freud three years earlier; the ravages of World War II; and the problem of reestablishing the analytic emigrés in England and America. Was the next step for the analytic survivors to be growth or retrenchment? Clearly the Kleinians wanted to continue breaking new theoretical ground. The orthodox group, particularly the newcomers, were naturally more concerned about establishing new practices and about the cohesiveness and continuity of psychoanalysis. They wanted the movement to consolidate around the classical approach, even to the extent of resisting the modifications to structural theory by the ego psychology of Hartmann and Anna Freud.

Ironically, Klein very strictly adhered to the techniques of classical theory, more, possibly, than the classical analysts did. She stressed heavily the importance of interpretation, intrapsychic factors, and drive theory. For example, she, more than other theorists, accepted Freud's dual drive theory, emphasizing the importance of the death instinct as well as the libido. On structural theory, while she still utilized the concepts of id, ego, and superego, Klein's seemingly "minor" modification of the superego as being formed by an infant of 18 months rather than in the oedipal period, began a process that under Fairbairn intellectually dismantled structural theory.

Klein's discarding of the centrality of the Oedipus complex was a clear break with classical theory. Under her strong leadership, acceptance that the mother-infant bond was crucial for the growth of a healthy child—the concept of the "depressive position"—legitimated the exploration of, and theorizing about, pregenital character disorders. She paved the way for a number of British theorists to build on and expand her hard-won bridgehead of the centrality of the mother-infant bond. The first of these was W. R. D. Fairbairn.

FAIRBAIRN

Fairbairn pioneered in the treatment of schizoid personalities. He described their characteristics as follows: "(1) an attitude of omnipotence, (2) an attitude of isolation and detachment, and (3) a preoccupation with inner reality" (Fairbairn, 1940, p. 6). He saw that schizoid behavior was not possible without a "split in the ego." Fairbairn appears to have been using Klein's concept of splitting, but when he referred to splitting as "resulting in all degrees of integration of the ego" (p. 9), he obviously was using it more broadly than the archaic form used by Klein. Fairbairn's meaning is close to Kohut's idea of fragmentation and lack of cohesiveness (Brandchaft, 1986). Also, with Fairbairn, splitting took place in the ego as well as between the good and bad internalized objects of Klein's thinking. Fairbairn differed from Kohut in that he sought to heal the "splits in the ego" in order to develop in the patient the capacity for object relations, whereas Kohut sought the opposite: object relations to consolidate the nuclear self (Brandchaft, 1986).

These differences indicate a move away from Klein, who was still wedded to drive theory. Fairbairn's major accomplishment was to shift theoretical concerns from drive theory toward the idea of a depressed, or hungry, ego. This word ego, as Fairbairn used it, was no longer a technical part of structural theory, but the self in a broad sense. Similarly, Fairbairn still used the term libido, but it no longer consisted of a drive or drives biologically based, urgently seeking a target of discharge. For Fairbairn, the libido was the self in a state of longing to be bonded to a nourishing source ("object"). With the schizoid, there was a calm, detached surface self, repressed affect, and a well-defended, hungry internal self that emerged eventually in the therapeutic transference.

Fairbairn's object relations theory was the first major attempt in psychoanalysis to explain psychotherapy without referring to drive theory. Fairbairn (1944) still spoke of an id, but of an id "impulse" that "cannot be considered apart from objects, whether external or internal" (p. 88). For this reason, he saw no further metapsychological use to claiming a distinction between the id and the ego:

> Freud's conception of the *origin* of the ego as a structure which develops on the surface of the psyche for the purpose of regulating id-impulses in relation to reality will thus give place to a conception of the ego as the source of impulse-tension from the beginning [p. 88].

This was a significant theoretical leap. The ego, that is, self-structures, not the id, comes first. It took many years for infant studies to build up substantial observational data to support Fairbairn's position.

Several other matters need to be considered in this brief discussion of Fairbairn's underrated, often ignored, contribution to psychotherapy theory. First, Fairbairn used the diagnosis of schizoid to cover a broad range of character disorders, many of which would now be diagnosed as narcissistic or borderline. Second, Fairbairn was the first theorist to challenge Freud's developmental theory of growth from narcissism to maturity, that is, from dependence to independence.

To Fairbairn (1951), the self grew from an infantile dependence through a period of transition to mature dependence (p. 163). The stage of infantile dependence was characterized predominantly by an attitude of taking. The transitional stage saw the use of paranoid, obsessional, hysterical, and phobic techniques. The stage of mature dependence had an attitude of giving, with accepted or rejected objects exteriorized (Fairbairn, 1941, p. 39). Fairbairn saw dependence on its own separate line of development years before Kohut adopted a similar position.

A third issue was Fairbairn's changes in technique. In working with schizoid personalities he came to appreciate that a schizoid's major strategy was to avoid meaningful emotional engagement with people and especially with the therapist. Fairbairn then realized that using the couch strengthened the very character defenses that needed changing, so he saw analytic patients seated and face to face. This change in technique led him to question the value of traditional analytic procedures.

Such a brief review barely does justice to Fairbairn, whose work has influenced many modern theorists, such as Mitchell (1988).

BALINT

Michael Balint's major contribution to a new therapeutic paradigm consisted of a challenge to the classical theory of intrapsychic processes and fantasies. Following his mentor, Ferenczi, Balint believed that Freud had taken a wrong turn in stressing intrapsychic at the expense of environmental influences and in neglecting to develop an adequate theory of trauma. He thought that Freud, with his original seduction theory of neurosis, and Ferenczi (1933) with his "Confusion of Tongues Between Adults and the Child" paper, which reopened the incest issue, had both been portraying trauma in a specific form. That is, incest is the experience of one type of psychological trauma, which also includes rape, torture, significant personal losses, and other injurious "events."

Balint's view of trauma, however, went much further than wounding or stressful events. Not only did he see a broad list of potentially traumatic situations, he also thought that two other factors effected how a person subjectively experiences a stressful event: (1) the character of the person being stressed and (2) the degree of psychological support received from emotionally significant persons (selfobjects). Thus, Balint's theory of trauma is a combination of what happens and how a person experiences what happens. That is, the theory includes the "external" and "internal" dimensions of the experience that are discussed in the theory of trauma. (See chapter 22, this volume).

Balint (1968) also refined the theory of interpretation. He not only rejected Klein's indoctrinating style, he clearly saw interpretation as being of only limited value for psychotherapy:

> Our technique was worked out for patients who experience the interpretation as interpretation and whose ego is strong enough to enable them to "take in" the interpretation and perform what Freud called the process of "working through" [p. 10].

Interpretation was developed, according to Balint, for the oedipal level, where there is an agreed upon, conventional use of language. He then went on to develop the idea of the preoedipal level, the level of the "basic fault," where the patient does not experience interpretation as interpretation, but as narcissistic wounding. Therefore, interpretation cannot be the primary method for preoedipal character disorders.

Anticipating Kohut's empathic-introspective mode of observation, Balint (1952, chapters 3, 5, 8, and 9) developed this methodological principle in a series of papers. He saw the preoedipal period as involving a two-person system where satisfaction comes from the relational "fit." When this fit takes place, the preoedipal person has a quiet, tranquil sense of well-being. When this meshing is missing, the subjective experience is one of emptiness, loss, deadness, futility, and lifeless acceptance of everything that has been offered. Another response to the absence of a personal fit is a sense of persecutory anxiety, where bad things are perceived as not happening by chance. For persons with a "basic fault," the key question is the fit of the therapeutic relationship, not interpretation.

Once Balint's major focus became the therapeutic relationship, he saw the need for a "new beginning." This new beginning involves regressing to a point before the faulty development started and "discovering a new, better-suited, way which amounts to a progression." Thus the therapeutic process enables "regression for the sake of progression" (Balint, 1968, p. 132). He uses the example of a 30-year-old woman who, since earliest childhood, could never do a somersault, although at various periods she tried desperately to do one. In response Balint said, "What about now?—whereupon she got up from the couch and to her great amazement, did a perfect somersault without any difficulty" (pp. 128-129). This act signaled her new beginning.

Such a constructive view of "acting out," as reflected in the idea of a new beginning and in Ferenczi's and Klein's view of enactment, involves an understanding that therapeutic regression can be beneficial. Balint also recognized that it could be malignant, as was the regression of Breuer's Anna O (Breuer and Freud, 1893-95). With malignant regression, the patient seeks an external event, a gratifying action. In the benign form, the patient seeks consent to use the external world to solve an internal problem. That is, malignant regression is regression aimed at gratification, whereas benign regression is aimed at recognition. To Balint, these benign regressions never had the qualities of despair and passion that characterize the malignant type. So it was that Balint expanded on Ferenczi's (1913) idea of repairing deficits from arrested development.

Balint, like Kohut, rejected Freud's idea of primary narcissism, where the infant was incapable of attachment. For him, the concept of primary narcissism was an unsupported theoretical extrapolation, whereas secondary narcissism was clinically observable. This secondary narcissism was largely a response to a disturbed infant relationship with the mothering "environment." Instead of experiencing an early state of primary narcissism, an infant experiences "primary love," that is, a state of intense, harmonious relatedness to the mother-environment. Like Kohut, Balint saw aggression as a behavior emerging when disjunctures and discontinuities occurred between the participants in primary love.

Like Fairbairn, Balint saw a person's development as moving from archaic dependence to mature dependence. He saw object relations as developing from a passive, archaic type to a mature interdependent form of love. Beginning with the earliest stage, the "work of conquest" transforms the object relationship to one of mutuality in which the object can no longer be taken for granted and its own independent and interdependent needs must be recognized and respected. To achieve such growth and mutuality, an infant needs a "co-operative partner" (Brandchaft, 1986).

Balint also took an important step in delineating the nature of pathogenic influence on the development of a person. He not only recognized the effects of insufficient selfobject responding, but also realized that the use of an infant or child to satisfy a parent's unconscious needs can have a devastatingly noxious effect on the child (Brandchaft, 1986). Brandchaft, reviewing the work of Michael Balint and his wife, Alice, pays the high tribute of crediting their work for "originality, courage and creativeness" (p. 255).

WINNICOTT

Donald Winnicott may be the most quoted theorist of the British school. He idealized Ernest Jones, was analyzed first by James Strachey and then by Joan Riviere, and was supervised by Melanie Klein. Such analytic training initially shackled him to a biologically based, innate-forces approach to psychoanalysis. It is not difficult to see how, with his pediatric background, the creative Winnicott eventually balanced his analytic training with an increasing focus on the contribution of environmental factors, especially the environment of the therapeutic relationship. The mother is the infant's environment. Thus "his declarations that 'there is no such thing as a baby' and that 'infant and mother together form an indivisible unit' (Winnicott, 1960, p. 39) were the most emphatic challenges to the edifice Klein built that an unshackled mind could proclaim" (Brandchaft, 1986, p. 269). In comparison, Klein saw the mother as bonded to the infant rather than as one part of a larger mother/infant system, as did Winnicott.

In 1962 Winnicott moved decisively away from Klein on the subject of transference. He made the distinction between the therapist as a displacement target for parents and the therapist as a modern representative of the parents (Winnicott, 1962, p. 167). Brandchaft (1986) sees Kohut's position as closely resembling Winnicott's: "Here analysis is not the screen for the projection of internal structure (transference), but the direct continuation of an early reality that was too distant, too rejecting, or too unreliable to be transformed into solid psychological structures" (Kohut, 1978, pp. 218-219).

Early experience with the doctrinaire Klein may have influenced Winnicott also on the issue of moving from a false self to a more singular, unique, and creative true self. Here he seems to reflect ideas close to Kierkegaard's concepts of the authentic and unauthentic modes of existence. Unauthentic existence is the modality of the person who lives under the tyranny of the "plebs," that is, anonymous collectivity. Under authentic existence a person accepts responsibility for his own existence and suffers a great deal of anxiety as a consequence (May, 1958).

Winnicott's main goal in psychotherapy was to enable the patient to experience growth of the true self. His major technique was to establish what he called a "holding environment," which enabled a controlled regression to take place. What helped in the holding environment was not interpretation, but flexibility in technique such as hand holding, which he sometimes did, and extending sessions to an hour and a half or more. Winnicott, more than any other major psychoanalytic thinker, tried to use the therapeutic arrangements to facilitate the emergence of the true self.

Winnicott allowed just about anything in a session, including "play, silence, re-living, acting-in or acting-out, teasing, mourning, and *all* feeling and its expression, whether by patient or analyst" (Anderson, 1985, p. 7). Margaret Little, who was analyzed by Winnicott, said that Winnicott would go to sleep and she would yell at him to wake up (Anderson, 1985, p. 8). She was able to acknowledge how boring it must have been for him to listen when she just talked and talked. What is interesting about Little's acceptance of Winnicott's falling asleep is her response to Ella Sharpe, her analyst prior to Winnicott. Sharpe, who was authoritarian and gave stereotypical interpretations, irritated Little. Little says of Sharpe, "She didn't touch my illness, and I knew it." She did not resent Winnicott's "error" in falling asleep, because he had created the overall environment that she needed, so any single piece of behavior did not matter.

Margaret Little, who developed an excellent reputation as an analyst, summarized her experience of Winnicott: "If I hadn't been helped by Winnicott, I would have committed suicide or I would have become a chronic mental patient" (Anderson, 1985, p. 2). Her statement, and those made by other analysands of Winnicott, such as Enid Balint and Masud Khan, create the impression that Winnicott was a masterful and gifted clinician. What shines through the accounts of Winnicott's work is his humanness. He did not hesitate to go to the toilet during a session; he had a sense of humor; and he always wanted the patient to teach him. He did not attempt to "mother" his patients by infantilizing them, yet he gave them great attention, caring, and security. He managed to make patients like Margaret Little believe that he cared intensely for them. One gains the impression that this caring was authentic, because it placed great demands on Winnicott's strength and stamina. This intense caring, however, achieved significant results with patients who were beyond the scope of classical treatment.

Winnicott's major theoretical contribution was in flexibility in technique. Not only did he shatter the classical position of neutrality, regression neurosis, and interpretation (Gill, 1954), he demonstrated the value of intense caring and commitment. In so doing, he rediscovered what religious counselors and general medical practitioners (including pediatricians) had known for a long time and what Freud practiced. It may be a blessing that Winnicott was trained as a pediatrician before he went through his analytic training.

Bacal (1989) writes:

> There is, in fact, compelling evidence that Winnicott understood the idea of early selfobject functioning in much the same sense as Kohut did, but did not, so to speak, organize the idea so precisely. The caring functions of the mother are facilitated by the infant's capacity to experience her as a *subjective object* . . . . For Winnicott . . . the subjective object was "the first object, the object *not yet repudiated as a not-me phenomenon*," that is, an object that is experienced as an extension of the self [p. 261].

In summarizing the common contribution of these four British theorists, Brandchaft (1989) writes, "They shared the determination to continue the tradition of Freud not by the celebration and reaffirmation necessarily of his concepts, but of his ideals" (p. 256). Together with others, such as Ferenczi and Hartmann, they developed ideas that were the major precursors to self psychology.

Having now completed the first phase of this text covering the preparers of self psychology, we next explore a basic philosophical stance that is consonant with self psychology—postempiricism. Influenced generally by postempiricism, self psychology was able to accept the ideas of a major philosophical shift that had occurred while Freud was undertaking his clinical investigations. This postempiricist philosophy, and its influence on the development of self psychology, is covered in the next chapter.

Readings for Chapter 10: Kuhn, 1962; Goldberg, 1988, chapters 1-4.

8

Metatheory: Theory About Psychotherapy Theory

After World War II, a growing disenchantment with Freud's classical theory fostered a depreciation of the value of theory in the practice of psychotherapy. This depreciating attitude, widespread outside psychoanalytic circles, was also represented within them. It led some people to emphasize the primacy of clinical observation over theory and an empiricist philosophy, as adopted for example, by Waelder (1962).

Waelder "suggested that we observe single facts, which then become arranged in patterns in ascending order up to our generalizations, theories, values and even our view of the world" (Goldberg, 1988, p. 92). His idea of building from simple facts to complex configurations used the basic position of logical positivism that facts can be validated or disproved. Commencing with this theory/observational issue, what follows examines (a) empiricism and the inductive method, (b) the postempiricists, and (c) postempiricism in self psychology.

EMPIRICISM AND THE INDUCTIVE METHOD

In their attempt to deemphasize theory, the clinical observationists represent the theoretical position of the 16th-century English scientist Francis Bacon. He stressed the inductive method as the starting point of knowledge. Using this inductive method, a clinician open-mindedly accumulates observations, watches for emerging patterns, forms hypotheses, and seeks further information based on these hypotheses.

This inductive method of knowing has been thoroughly discredited and abandoned by modern philosophers of science. They say that science does not and cannot operate in this fashion. Their "postempiricist" position is supported by four arguments: (1) theory influences the perception and selection of facts, (2) subject and object lack a clear division, (3) words fail to refer adequately to the objects they denote, and (4) objectivity denies natural selection of ideas. The cogency of these arguments means that empiricism is an unrealizable ideal. We now look at these criticisms of inductive theory in more detail.

Theory Influences the Perception and Selection of Facts

Self psychology accepts the postempiricist position of modern philosophy that ideas influence what are considered facts (Basch, 1988b). Kohut (1984), for example, states that "an observer needs theories in order to observe" (p. 67). Goldberg (1988) takes the same position with his "theory impregnation of facts" (p. 7). Once it is accepted that theory precedes observation, then clinical effectiveness depends on the outcome of the struggles among a host of competing theories.

Basch (1988b) once demonstrated the power of theory over observation by asking a woman student, who had just become a mother, to describe the psychological life of an infant. She effortlessly described Locke's *tabula rasa* theory of egolessness. Then, when asked to describe her own baby, she talked about its affective responses from day one, "givens" already present and shaping what is experienced.

Subject and Object Lack a Clear Division

This problem is evident in the area of measurement with complex instruments or with the process of observation. In a famous address before the 1927 International Congress of Physics, the atomic physicist Niels Bohr discussed this problem (Chessick, 1979). He said that in the atomic particle domain, the only way the observer (and his equipment) can be uninvolved is if he observes nothing at all. As soon as the observer sets up the observation tools on his workbench, the system he has chosen to put under observation and his measuring instruments for doing the job form an inseparable whole. Therefore, the results depend heavily on the apparatus.

Bohr, illustrating what is known as Heisenberg's uncertainty principle, showed that any apparatus designed to measure position at the level of atomic particles with ideal precision cannot provide any information about momentum, and vice versa. Measuring a particle's position changes its velocity and measuring its velocity changes its position. Two mutually exclusive experiments are needed to obtain full information about the mechanical state, each complementing the other. So, he conceived of methods as "complementary descriptions" of that being studied. To him, theories are complementary descriptions of an area of knowledge.

John Archibald Wheeler, a colleague of Albert Einstein, said:

> What is so hard is to give up thinking of nature as a machine that goes on independent of the observer. What we conceive of as reality is a few iron posts of observation with papier-mache construction between them that is but the elaborate work of our imagination [Quoted in Schwaber, 1983a, p. 273].

Similarly, there is no clear distinction in psychotherapy between subject and object. The therapist (subject) uses theories of psychotherapy as instruments of observation and selects what of the patient (object) is observed and therefore what influences the interaction between them. Conversely, a patient (subject) views the therapist (object) from a personal set of beliefs and this observing also influences the interaction. Such interaction makes it difficult to conceive of subject and object; there are two subjects. Object represents a point of view, not a thing.

Words Fail to Refer Adequately to the Objects They Denote

In its model of building from simple facts, the inductive method assumes that words have simple, clear-cut definitions, as commonly used and agreed upon. This simply is not so! No word can stand alone outside a dictionary (Goldberg, 1988). It is only in the usage of a word that we can say what it means. For example, even though children begin to speak by using single words, these invariably imply a sentence. The child's word blanket (with idiosyncratic pronunciation), stands for "I want my blanket." Moreover, words may have many meanings. The word "star," for instance, may refer to a terrestrial body, a movie idol, or a shaped sticker on a child's school assignment. Only by the way the word is used in a sentence can it be determined what the word denotes. Words are not atomized, discrete entities. They are always in relationship with other words in a narrative. The relationship of words to each other, more than the words themselves, tells the story.

Behaviorism, once considered the hallmark of scientific psychology because of its inductive method, was clearly shown by Chomsky (1959), a linguist, merely to lend the appearance of scientific rigor to the study of human verbal behavior. Chomsky noted, for example, that while the terms stimulus, response, and reinforcement can be used with logical consistency and coherence in the tightly controlled environment of the laboratory, they lose all meaning, and therefore explanatory usefulness, when applied to normal human social interaction and verbal behavior. Further, such constructs, when used to describe events as discrete as a human eye blink and as broad as an exchange between nations, lack the specificity to provide the clarity and precision necessary for understanding meaningful relationships between events.

Campbell (1969), arguing for "anchorless knowledge," states that only in context do words have meaning:

> In linguistic epitomes of knowledge, the same principle holds: the smaller the fragment the more equivocal the meaning. Somehow, with long continuities, relatively precise meanings are recorded and communicated, but this achievement is not to be attributed in any manner to the incorrigibility or unequivocality of its elements, be they words or sentences. As a statement of knowledge or a communicative act, an isolated letter is more equivocal than a syllable, a syllable than a word, a word than a sentence, a sentence than a paragraph, a paragraph than a chapter. Alternatively stated, a word is most equivocal in isolation, less so when embedded in a paragraph . . . a word is but an intermediate stage in a hierarchy of equivocalities, and no effort at clarification nor improvement of definition will make it a firm foundation for knowing [p. 44].

As Chomsky pointed out, it is only in the isolated context of the laboratory that the words stimulus, response, and reinforcement have any specificity of meaning. Such terms have little clinical usefulness or scientific value if they cannot be meaningfully used in the broader world as experienced by the clinician and his patient. This world is usually best described by a narrative. As Goldberg (1988) states, "Apparently random open systems need to be described differently from hypothetico-deductive systems" (p. 10). A narrative or a story has been proposed as a meaningful way to describe open systems (Sherwood, 1969; Ricoeur, 1984).

Objectivity Denies Natural Selection of Ideas

Modern philosophers of the postempiricist position have conceded that there is no rock-solid anchor upon which all knowledge can be built. Plato assumed the world of "forms" as immutable. And Descartes built his on the assumption *cogito ergo sum* ("I think, therefore I am"), to which Brinton (1963), somewhat tongue-in-cheek responded, "Why not 'I sweat, therefore I am'?" Every supposedly irrefutable starting point has been thoroughly refuted by postempiricist philosophy.

"suspension of memory & desire"
Bion — no presupposition

In agreement with both Kuhn (1962) and Popper (1959), Goldberg (1988) states, "The heart of the scientific attitude toward knowledge [is] that no concept, no idea, no truth is immune to change. "Goldberg (1988) points to the shifting, evolutionary state of knowledge:

> Thus, when a community of scholars says, "let us agree that loss means . . . ," they always parenthetically note "until we agree otherwise." This becomes tantamount to change by consensus and truth by agreement rather than the correspondence theories that are so appealing to us. We would rather point to the data to prove our point instead of asking for a vote. However, we seem always to return to some agreed upon or negotiated "reality" to which our facts correspond. Truth is also hermeneutic since it is a product of our understanding and interpretation, and so is not a "given" [p. 15].

Although it is an ad hominem argument, it would appear that the reluctance to accept this postempiricist position has more to do with a discomfort with conflict and uncertainty inherent in the position than it does with a lack of cogency of the postempiricist position. Campbell (1969) describes the equivocal state of knowledge:

> In science we are like sailors who must repair a rotting ship while it is afloat at sea. We depend on the relative soundness of all the other planks while we replace a particularly weak one. Each of the planks we now depend on we will in turn have to replace. No one of them is a foundation, nor a point of certainty, no one of them is incorrigible [p. 43].

The inductive method and empirical philosophy cater to the wish for objectivity. By objectivity, the empiricists mean the observer should observe without bias, that is, be theory neutral. Such a hope for theory-neutral observations, however, may be a naïve wish for a community of investigators who are like-minded enough to agree on what they see. If so, the inductive method could be associated with a deep-seated desire to avoid conflict and to deny a Darwinian type of natural selection among ideas.

THE POSTEMPIRICISTS

If the inductive method is not the mainstay of science today, how then is scientific knowledge gained? To understand the postempiricist position in science, we shall explore the ideas of philosophers Karl Popper, Thomas Kuhn and Mary Hesse. Popper (1963), for example, saw bold conjectures as the starting point of science. These conjectures are then subjected to rigorous, critical discussion, with the goal of discrediting them! The process is an attempt to eliminate error. Those conjectures which survive such a process are then submitted, where possible, to experimental investigation.

Even when our conjectures survive vigorous efforts to discredit them, they are not knowledge (episteme), according to Popper. These opinions are not Truth; they are simply guesses about the truth, approximations that enable our lives to be more adaptable. To Popper, the history of philosophy is not simply a record of past errors, but a running argument, a chain of linked problems and their tentative solutions.

Popper stressed falsifiability as a criterion of demarcation between science and non-science. By this criterion, Marx and Freud did not have scientific constructs. Although their theories are nonfalsifiable and hence, not scientific, they are valuable. This process of falsifying does not produce truth—just a greater approximation of truth. It indicates a degree of verisimilitude. Verisimilitude has three requirements: 1) that the new theory explain the same facts the earlier theory explained; 2) that the new theory unify new parts and suggest new connections and 3) that the new theory pass a new test.

What Popper referred to as conjectures, Kuhn (1962) saw as beliefs that cohered to form paradigms. To Kuhn, scientific knowledge changed through a natural selection among competing paradigms. Disagreeing with Bacon, he said that there was no such thing as research in the absence of paradigms. For example, a paradigm shift occurred when Newton's 18th-century corpuscular theory of light was challenged by Einstein's 20th-century wave theory.

Reasons for a paradigm shift lie in the function of paradigms. Paradigms gain status by solving problems, making predictions, and developing communities of practitioners with shared beliefs. Paradigm change occurs when there are too many anomalies to the old paradigm and when there is a workable alternative to the reigning one that promises a better, broader range of problem solving.

Unlike Popper, Kuhn thought falsifiability was not the sine qua non of a scientific theory. Rather, it was the "coherence" of a theory and its ability to "best fit" experience that determined its usefulness and therefore whether it is better than another theory. The tenure of one theory ends when a better theory comes along. To Kuhn, testing was not the mark of science because experiments can be challenged, and theories remain essentially unmodified because of ad hoc adjustments.

Mary Hesse (1980), summarizes the postempiricist position as follows:

> 1. Data are not detachable from theory, and so facts are to be reconstructed in the light of interpretation.
> 2. Theories are not models externally compared to nature in a hypothetico-deductive schema but are the way the facts themselves are seen.
> 3. The law-like relations are internal because what count as facts are constituted by what the theory says about interrelations with one another.
> 4. The language of natural science is metaphorical and inexact, and formalizable only at the cost of distortion.
> 5. Meanings are determined by theory and are understood by theoretical coherence rather than by correspondence with facts [p. 7].

POSTEMPIRICISM IN SELF PSYCHOLOGY.

The postempiricist philosophy of science helps explain self psychology's heavy attention to theory. Stern (1985) says that "science advances by shifting paradigms about how things are to be seen. These paradigms are ultimately belief systems" (p. 17). Self psychology involves a full-scale attempt to replace the classical analytic paradigm with a new one. It sees any advance in the science of understanding and changing human personality as coming from a major paradigm shift. Grotstein (1983) agrees:

> In the span of just a few years the school of self psychology has emerged as representing perhaps the most important paradigmatic shift in psychoanalytic theory and practice in decades. Its deceptive simplicity belies its conceptual sweep as a major *systematized* alternative to classical theory [p. 165].

The postempiricist position that theory predominates over fact surfaced in self psychology through the concepts of "experience-near" and "experience-distant" theory. The term experience-near was popularized by Kohut (1959) in his discussion of therapeutic methodology. Empathy was deemed the way to explore a patient's inner experiences and develop a personal explanatory theory as a subjective narrative. By experience-distant theory, Kohut was referring to generalizations. He had in mind, among other things, Freud's metapsychology and such constructs as id and superego.

What is the self psychology paradigm? Commencing with empathy as a method of observation, it uses the narcissistic transferences (mirror, idealizing, twinship, and merger) to transform therapeutically a patient's archaic narcissism through microinternalization, into a new personality structure. This therapeutic transformation is possible because the self–selfobject relationship is reenacted in the treatment. Hence, self psychology would be better described as selfobject psychology, or a selfobject theory of motivation.

Self psychology takes seriously the postempiricist emphasis on the power of ideas to determine facts, as shown by the efforts made to keep its theorizing as experience-near (clinically anchored) as possible. Its one major metaphysical construct, the self, is openly acknowledged as experience-distant. Even if ideas influence facts, facts ought to be at least clinically demonstrable. For example, infants have some kind of genetically derived predispositions. These dispositions then act as primitive organizers of experience. Popper anticipated this with his idea of a testable conjecture. Stern (1985) now cites experimental evidence to support the notion that infants are primed to look for regularities, to expect them, from day one. Infants are born with invariance as an organizing principle already in place.

> From birth on, there appears to be a central tendency to form and test hypotheses about what is occurring in the world (Bruner,

> 1977). Infants are also constantly "evaluating," in the sense of asking, is this different from or the same as that? How discrepant is what I have just encountered from what I have previously encountered (Kagen et al. , 1978)? It is clear that this central tendency of mind, with constant application, will rapidly categorize the social world into conforming and contrasting patterns, events, sets, and experiences. The infant will readily discover which features of an experience are invariant and which are variant—that is, which features "belong" to the experience (J. Gibson 1950, 1979; E. Gibson 1969). The infant will apply these same processes to whatever sensations and perceptions are available, from the simplest to the ultimately most complex—that is, thoughts about thoughts [p. 42].

non-changing -

These invariants become organizing principles. They become more complex with experience, determining what will be seen as important and perceived as facts. An infant's bad experiences, consistent enough to be seen as an invariant, will lead to a radically different set of beliefs about the nature of reality than will an infant's basically good experiences.

Once the idea of a newborn's general organizing principle is accepted, Freud's concept of transference takes on a fresh significance. The therapeutic experience of a patient's distortion of "reality" arises from his or her subjectively organized belief world, which determines both perception of facts and the meaning of these facts. This position is described by Stolorow and his colleagues (1987):

> Transference is neither a regression to nor a displacement from the past, but rather an expression of the *continuing influence* of organizing principles and imagery that crystallized out of the patient's early formative experiences [p. 36].

So it is that the postempiricist position, the primacy of theory over fact, and self psychology's understanding of transference support each other.

Postempiricist views of science also suggest a new way to understand interpretation as an interactive process. Chessick (1977) writes, for example, that Popper's view of science as conjectures we try to invalidate "is (unintentionally) an *excellent characterization* of the process of interpretation and subsequent rejection or confirmation that goes on in the everyday work of psychoanalytically informed uncovering psychotherapy" (p. 321).

Such a process view of interpretation is not new to, nor exclusive to, psychotherapy. Self psychology theorists such as Atwood and Stolorow (1984) link it to the "hermeneutic circle," a method familiar to biblical scholars and historians:

> In textual interpretation, the meaning of a particular passage is established primarily by considerations relating the passage to the structure of the text as a whole; parts of the work are thus assessed in relation to an understanding of the totality while knowledge of the whole is constituted by study of the parts. Dilthy characterized historical inquiry as involving a similarly circular movement between focus on particular events and a view of the total meaning-context in which those events participate [p. 3].

The postempiricist philosophy, with its understanding of the inability of facts, words, or even objects to be discrete, atomized entities, is utilized in self psychology's view of the self. To Kohut, the self was never a completely individuated, absolutely independent being, functioning in emotional isolation. The self is always in need of selfobjects. For Kohut, the issue of personal growth and maturity was one of transforming the nature of a self's selfobject relationships from archaic to more mature forms. Stated differently, the issue of selfobject needs is whether these are met exclusively with one person in their archaic form, or whether they can be met in a diversity of ways and relationships, even intermittently. Under no condition, according to Kohut, can a self exist for any extended period without needing some form of selfobject relationship.

Self psychology's success as a new psychotherapeutic paradigm can be assessed by using Popper's concept of verisimilitude. The self psychology paradigm makes a reasonable claim to meeting, to some degree, his three requirements: 1) the new theory explains the same facts that earlier theory explains; 2) the new theory unifies new parts and suggests new connections; and 3) the new theory passes some new test. In more detail:

1. Self psychology's new theory is able to explain neurotic conflicts, not in terms of drive theory, but as signs of fragmentation in the self.

2. Kohut widened the scope of psychoanalysis to include a theoretical understanding of narcissism, enabling the successful treatment of that disorder. Some of the post-Kohutians have expanded self psychology theory to include an understanding of the treatment of severe character disorders, including the borderline syndrome and even the treatment of psychotic disorders.

3. The results of the use of self psychology theory in treatment have been very encouraging. The claim that self psychology passes Popper's test of verisimilitude for a scientific theory evokes criticism from those of other theoretical positions. These criticisms echo those described by William James, that there are "three phases through which every new theory passes: its critics first condemn it as absurd, then dismiss it as trivial and obvious, and finally claim it as their own discovery" (Quoted in Goldberg, 1974, p. 254). It is a major sign of the acceptance of the self psychology paradigm that many theoreticians are now claiming that self psychology's ideas are not really new. Perhaps the greatest testimony to the scientific status of self psychology, however, is that it still presents itself as an open system, in the process of changing—until a paradigm of "better fit" comes along.

Although Stolorow (1986a) works from a self psychology framework, he reminds us that theories are ultimately judged by their ability to enhance therapeutic effectiveness:

> The point is that *all* psychological theories are to some degree imbalanced and reductionistic, they *all* aim at ordering and therefore simplifying the staggering complexity of clinical data, and they *all* embody theoretical preconceptions and philosophical assumptions. These are not meaningful criteria for evaluating the superiority of one theory over another. The clinically valid criteria are whether theoretical frameworks enlarge or constrict our capacity to gain empathic access to patients' inner lives and

whether they therefore enhance or diminish our therapeutic effectiveness [p. 44].

Accepting the limitations of an empiricist philosophy, Kohut made empathy the method of self psychology. With this empathic method of observation, Kohut was able to explore the workings of the subjective self. He was not the first to use the concept of empathy—Freud, Ferenczi, and Balint had discussed it—but Kohut gave the term a precision and clarity it had not had before. He constantly emphasized its place as the starting point of his theory. We explore self psychology's concept of empathic understanding in the next chapter.

Readings for Chapter 11: Kohut, 1959; Wolf, 1983b; Basch, 1983b; Chessick, 1985, chapter 18.

9

Empathic Understanding

In July 1957, Heinz Kohut delivered a brief version of his paper "Introspection, Empathy, and Psychoanalysis" (Kohut, 1959) to a meeting of the International Psycho-Analytic Association in Paris. It was the first public notice of what was to evolve into the new major paradigm of self psychology. In this paper, empathy was declared to be the methodological door to this new theory. In what follows we explore Kohut's ideas on empathy under the following headings: (a) vicarious introspection, (b) the process of knowing, (c) attenuated knowing, (d) identification, (e) projection, (f) attunement, and (g) cure.

VICARIOUS INTROSPECTION

In defining his therapeutic method, Kohut turned to the concept of introspection. He believed that through introspection a person could observe his own inner world and that of another person if there was also the capacity to introspect vicariously. Such vicarious introspection he called empathy. Introspection and empathy were the perceptual tools for the exploration of the world of the subjective. They were means of observation, of gathering subjective data. Basch (1986) adds that empathy is a "readiness to experience what it is the patient is experiencing in the patient's terms" (p. 25).

Kohut (1959) cited the example of a tall man to describe what he meant by "vicarious introspection:"

> Only when we think ourselves into his place, only when we, by vicarious introspection, begin to feel his unusual size as if it were our own and thus revive inner experiences in which we had been unusual or conspicuous, only then do we begin to appreciate the meaning that the unusual size may have for this person and only then have we observed a psychological fact [pp. 207-208].

This concept of introspective (and vicarious introspective) data is in contrast to the idea of objective data in the physical and biological sciences. Wolf (1983a) says that these data represent two types of perception, introspective and extrospective. Thus we live in two worlds, an objective one based on extrospective schemata and a subjective one, organized around introspective data. Wolf elucidates with the example of a hand. Looked at extrospectively, the hand is an object in the world; experienced introspectively, it is a part of the self. Introspective and extrospective data are different modes of experience. In arguing for the acceptance of introspective data as being valid for the subjective world as extrospective data is for the world of objects, Kohut says they are really two different approaches to reality. Using Niels Bohr's concept of complementarity, Kohut saw two complementary ways of measuring reality, which neither represents fully because of their limitations as perceptual instruments.

Brain studies support this notion of two distinct ways of perceiving reality. As Grotstein (1983) indicates, only recently have brain laterality studies revealed that duality of consciousness is a neurological fact (Gazzaniga and Le Doux, 1978). In the terminology of these studies, empathy can be considered as right-brain con-

right brain — left brain
empathy, detached observation, data
feeling

Empathic Understanding 107

sciousness, whereas detached observation is a method pertinent to left-brain consciousness—approximately.

When it comes to understanding the subjective self, Kohut (1959) sees the introspective and extrospective methods as unequal in value. The subjective is not yet graspable by extrospection. Kohut concedes that one day it may be possible to measure subjective reality through some physical data, such as brain waves. At present, however, the psychological approach to subjective experience is the only useful one. Even so, Kohut's openness to the possibility that the extrospective mode may assist the introspective method and vice versa suggests the need for further thinking about the relationship of these two methods. For example, in the following instance Wolf (1983b) used introspection to gain a vicarious view of the extrospective world.

An analysand told Wolf about the large crowd at the Mass celebrated by the Pope on his visit to Chicago, and Wolf imagined the noise of all those people. In fact, as he learned, it was remarkably quiet. This process is an example of vicarious extrospection, erroneous at first but quickly corrected through feedback. Similarly, extrospective case history data, such as birth order, or other objective data, such as personality tests available to the psychotherapist, may act as a starting point for the empathic method of gaining introspective data. In fact, extrospective clues may reduce the amount of hermeneutic circling and the length of time before a psychotherapist's attempts at vicarious introspection are experienced by the patient as being "tuned in."

Our position on the introspective/extrospective issue is very close to that of Stolorow and his colleagues (1987). They claim that "psychoanalytic investigation is *always* from a perspective within a subjective world (patient's or analyst's); it is always empathic or introspective" (P. 5). For self psychology, this subjective perspective is clearly the aim. Yet, Wolf (1983b) and the Shanes (1986) hold open the door for some extrospective role in psychotherapeutic work. Wolf proposes that "we oscillate between extrospective and introspective modes of gathering data" (p. 685). The Shanes argue that some analytic understanding comes from "objective knowledge of the patient's life" (p. 148). These authors include the extrospective, but their thinking leaves unresolved the issue of which takes precedence in therapeutic work. Kohut (1959) saw introspection and empathy as "linked and amalgamated with other methods and observation. The final and decisive observational act, however, is introspective or empathic" (pp. 209-210). We believe that when extrospective data is viewed as a possible starting point, it is given a useful role without undermining the primacy of the empathic method.

By embracing empathy as his method, Kohut rejected the classical analytic primacy of insight through interpretation. He favored the empathic side in the running battle between cognitive insight and empathic responding in the history of psychoanalysis, a conflict which can be discerned first in the thinking of Freud where insight and empathy were two separate strands. Whatever Freud said about insight has to be balanced by his use of the term *Einfuhlung* (empathic understanding) 15 times in his writings, thus indicating its importance to him (Wolf, 1983b, p. 310). Even so, as important as the concept of empathy was to Freud, it never featured centrally in his thinking as it did with Kohut.

Others in the history of psychoanalysis also saw the importance of empathy. Ferenczi (1928) developed the concept of empathy through the idea of "tact" in giving interpretations. Balint (1952) also developed the idea of an empathic methodology in a series of papers. Basch (1988b) thinks that Glover's term "inexact interpretation" is evidence that many in the previous generations of therapists "became empathic with their patients and responded accordingly" (p. 56). Friedman (1978), in assessing this insight/empathy struggle throughout the history of psychoanalysis, sees insight as nearly, but never really, in the ascendancy. He thinks that the patient's positive attachment to the therapist has been viewed as the more important therapeutic agent. For example, by 1938 Freud's (1940) position was similar to that of the 1936 Marienbad Symposium, which accepted Strachey's (1934) paper about the patient's introjecting the benign attitudes of the analyst. This formulation implies the importance of an affective bond and its internalization by the patient, not interpretation.

Other analysts gave primacy to a patient's attachment behavior and focused on empathy. Reik (1937), for example, defined empathy as the analyst's sharing the experience of the patient as if it were his own. Murray (1938) referred to the process of recipathy (reciprocal empathy), while Schafer (1959) used the phrase "generative empathy." And Fliess (1942) described a "trial identification" in which the analyst affectively reacts to the analysand's material by "tasting" or introjecting it. The skill of the therapist depends on the ability "to step into [the patient's] shoes, and to obtain in this way an inside knowledge that is almost first hand. The common name for such a procedure is empathy" (pp. 212-213).

In contrast to these theorists, Kohut made empathy central to his theoretical system, and, initially anyway, used the term far more precisely than did his predecessors. Once empathy lost Kohut's initial precision of meaning as an observational, data-gathering process, the theoretical waters became muddied and thinking about empathy became unclear.

Many issues arise when empathy is used as a broad, overinclusive, idealized concept. One danger is the expectation of a cure based on the magical covenant, often disavowed. Such idealization of empathy surfaces where a person cannot tolerate any criticism of the concept of empathy, nor consider empathy as having limitations in any process of cure. The idealization is also revealed by the belief that no amount of evidence can refute the fact that "true" empathy always produces a therapeutic cure. If there is no cure, then the therapist was ipso facto unempathic. Now, while the absence of a positive therapeutic result *may* arise from lack of attunement by the therapist, the empathic idealist sees this lack as always the reason. Conversely, it is impossible to imagine a situation where empathy is not the reason for a cure. This linking of empathy and cure is not falsifiable (Popper, 1963) and hence is an unscientific proposition, no longer useful as an explanatory construct. The idealized version of empathy belongs to the realm of faith, religion, and magic.

The dangers of directly linking an idealized version of empathy and cure are obvious from the thinking of Mitchell (1988):

> It is often not the experience of "empathic failure," but the experience of empathic success that precipitates withdrawal, devaluation, and fragmentation. For someone who has experienced repeated failure of meaningful connection, whose essential attachments are to constricted and painful relationships (in actuality or in fantasy), hope is a very dangerous feeling. It may

> be precisely the sense of meaningful connection that precipitates the analysand's withdrawal, because the possibility of such a connection calls into question the basic premises of the analysand's painfully constricted subjective world [pp. 160-161].

THE PROCESS OF KNOWING

Kohut initially saw empathy as the process of coming to know. This understanding can be put to a variety of practical uses. For example, empathy can be used by a corporation's personnel department to gather information from employees for management. Information gained in this way then influences decisions made primarily for the benefit of the corporation. Such an intelligence-gathering function can be viewed as an abuse of the empathic method only if empathy is assumed to be exclusively a therapeutic method. When empathy is understood theoretically as data gathering for a variety of uses, including but not limited to psychotherapy, much confused thinking is avoided.

That empathy is not exclusively a therapeutic method is evident in the empathic method of intelligence-gathering that has long been a part of military tradition. For example, in World War II, a few days after Rear Admiral Chester Nimitz became Commander-in-Chief of the Pacific Fleet, he gave Commander Edwin Layton, the Fleet intelligence officer, his new assignment:

> I want you to be the Admiral Nagumo [Commander of the Japanese First Air Fleet that attacked Pearl Harbor] of my staff. I want your every thought, every instinct as you believe Admiral Nagumo might have them. You are to see the war, their operations, their aims, from the Japanese viewpoint and keep me advised what you are thinking about, what you are doing, and what purpose, what strategy, motivates your operations. If you can do this, you will give me the kind of information needed to win this war [Layton, Pineau, and Costello, 1985, p. 357].

The eventual result of Layton's efforts, including codebreaking, was the ambushing and defeat of the Japanese carrier force at the battle of Midway, considered the turning point in the Pacific war.

The military use of empathy to gather intelligence illustrates its potential advantage in any struggle for power. Marriage raises a similar issue. Is empathy used by a spouse in the service of understanding, communication, and intimacy; or does empathic data gathering, in the guise of intimacy, serve as a weapon in a marital struggle for power? Sometimes a breakdown in marital communication occurs because one or both spouses are unable to communicate. More often, however, the lack of communication occurs because empathy has been consistently used by one spouse as a means of gaining control, and the other spouse is refusing to be manipulated by this maneuver.

If empathy is a process of knowing, and no more, other theoretical constructs are needed to explain how psychotherapy works. A major issue in psychotherapy is a therapist's capacity to care, that is, to invest in the long-term interests of the patient. Psychotherapy places the client's needs first, not those of the corporation, the military, or the marriage. Stated another way, it is not just empathic data gathering, but the use to which it is put, that determines whether a patient changes in psychotherapy.

ATTENUATED KNOWING

Kohut also recognized that while empathy was a data-gathering process, it inevitably stimulated affects. Such affects could be negative ones, such as anger, distress, and disgust, or positive ones such as interest and joy (Tomkins, 1962-63). By 1984, Kohut not only was defining empathy as "the capacity to think and feel oneself into the inner life of another person," but also he added the idea of empathic attenuation: "It [empathy] is our lifelong ability to experience what another person experiences, though usually, and appropriately, to an attenuated degree" (p. 82). Such a notion of attenuation suggests that too much empathic understanding can traumatize. This capacity for empathy to traumatize needs further theoretical understanding and elaboration.

Kohut called the patient's overstimulated experience of being empathized with "empathic flooding." Would not empathic overstimulation indicate the therapist really was not being empathic? It would if empathy were considered an intuitive gift of instantaneous knowing. But Kohut carefully defined empathy as not being intuitive. On the contrary, it is a trial-and-error process of coming to understand how the patient feels and thinks. It involves the "feedback" of the hermeneutic method. Only by reading the signs of overstimulation can the therapist make adjustments. Of course, if the therapist avoids the hermeneutic process and ignores the signs of a patient's overstimulation for any length of time, the therapist is being unempathic and the patient will experience an empathic failure. Empathy is not the capacity to set up a perfect relationship where there is no overstimulation, but the ability to perceive, through vicarious introspection, overstimulated patient responses as they occur.

The idea of empathic attenuation assumes a quantitative dimension. Is the amount of empathy experienced by the patient critical to therapeutic change, or is the experience itself the key factor? Thought of quantitatively, empathy can be conceived as a powerful magical force as if it were an emotional medication. If a little is good, a lot must speed up the process. Empathy then takes on a similarity to a religious, sacramental agent (see chapter 2, this volume) and not just a data-gathering function. Yet, if empathy is not a byproduct of the magical covenant and is the means whereby one person knows the subjective self of another, then the amount of empathy is not as important as the experience of being empathically known. If this is so, the patients get well not because the therapist is "more empathic," but as a result of other processes not adequately covered by the concept of empathy as vicarious introspection.

IDENTIFICATION

Kohut also indicated that empathy is not identification and hence is not sycophancy. The problem of unempathic identification is illustrated by an incident involving Adolf Hitler. In 1933, the Germans opened the British diplomatic pouch and discovered that Sir Eric Phipps, the British Ambassador to Germany, viewed Hitler as "a fanatic who would be satisfied with nothing less than the dominance of Europe" (Manchester, 1988, p. 89). Hitler, enraged, demanded a "'more modern' diplomat who showed at least some understanding of the changes taking place in Germany" (p. 90). So Phipps was replaced by Sir Neville Henderson who could "enter with sympathetic interest into Hitler's aspirations," and who quickly became a friend of Herman Goring (p. 90).

In view of subsequent historical evidence, it is clear that through identification with and idealization of the Nazis, Henderson accepted at face value German propaganda to the effect that they wanted nothing more than peace and self-respect, and thus he moved close to becoming a Nazi sycophant. He identified with the false, peripheral group-self that the German government presented to the world. In hindsight, Phipps was empathic in his understanding of how Hitler and the Nazi leaders thought and felt. He correctly perceived that the core German self, as represented by the Nazis, was intent on revenge and gaining domination of the world to erase the shame of defeat in World War I.

PROJECTION

Kohut (1971) made it clear that empathy is not projection (p. 65). In classical theory, projection is first and foremost a defense against drives, but it is also a defense against self-understanding. In contrast to projection, by vicarious introspection a person tries to imagine what it is like to be in another person's shoes. With projection, the focus is the self; with empathy the motivation is to understand the other person. Projection as understood classically not only interferes with understanding another person but is experienced by the patient as unempathic rejection because there is no obvious effort to understand.

A second reason empathy is not projection is that empathy involves the hermeneutic circle; projection does not want such "feedback." Trainee therapists, who frequently defensively project because of fear, are unable to describe clues in support of their "hunches," especially those that may indicate what the patient is feeling. They also miss all but the grossest signs of patient fragmentation as a result of their unempathic projective stance. It is not just that the projecting therapist misses the clues; there is a basic resistance to the need for the clues themselves. Those who project their intrapsychic dynamics tend to be self-righteous personalities to whom the idea of a mistake is anathema (Lax, 1975). Their first priority is to protect the grandiose state of their self by remaining invulnerable and not responding to the empathic needs of patients.

ATTUNEMENT

Although empathy was a data-gathering process in Kohut's early writings (1959, 1966, 1971), by 1975 he had expanded its meaning in three ways: 1) empathy is the recognition of the self in the other and is an indispensable tool of observation, without which vast areas of human life, including man's behavior in the social field, remain unintelligible; 2) empathy is the expansion of the self to include the other and constitutes a powerful psychological bond between individuals, a bond that—more perhaps even than love, the expression and sublimation of the sexual drive—counteracts human kind's destructiveness against fellow creatures; and 3), empathy is the accepting, confirming, and understanding human echo evoked by the self and is an essential psychological nutrient without which human life as we know and cherish it could not be sustained. To summarize, by 1975 Kohut was using the term empathy to describe (a) an observational tool, (b) a bond, and (c) a necessary precondition for psychological health.

In conceptualizing the idea that empathy formed a bond, Kohut had moved from the empathic process of knowing to the goal of this process, the state of being in an empathic bond. The aim of empathy, the process of coming to know a subjective self, became subordinate to a higher goal of being "in-tune." This bond consists of an "empathic resonance between self and selfobject" (Kohut, 1984, p. 76). From this and other passages, it is very clear that "empathic resonance" means a good deal more than "empathic knowing" or "empathic understanding."

As with empathy, so with attunement—Kohut was not the first analyst or psychotherapist to use the construct. Loewald (1960) wrote that a parent ideally is "in-tune" with the shifting levels of a child's particular stage of development. When Balint (1968) failed to work "in-tune" with his patients, they reacted with noisy, aggressive symptoms or with despair.

The formulation of the concept of empathic resonance, or attunement, as the goal of empathic understanding, coincides with an increased interest in attunement behavior in mother–infant studies. For example, Stern (1985) refers to affect attunement as a series of steps whereby (1) the parent reads the infant's feeling state from the infant's overt behavior, (2) the parent performs some "corresponding" behavior, and (3) the infant reads this corresponding behavior as reflecting the infant's experience.

Such attunement is more than imitation. Imitation mechanically copies form, whereas attunement never copies exactly and always involves feelings! These feelings consist of both categorical and vitality affects (see chapter 21, this volume). Attunement is more than empathy, that is, more than the cognitive form of vicarious introspection. It is more like communion, where one shares another's experience without attempting to change that person. The most important obstacles interfering with the use of such empathic communion, especially for prolonged periods, are the narcissistic difficulties in the therapist (Chessick, 1985).

Most investigators of mother–infant behavior have described in detail chains and sequences of reciprocal behaviors that make up "dialogues" during the infant's first nine months. The mother constantly initiates imitations of the infant's behavior, but always with slight modifications, in a manner similar to a classical piece of music, which repeats a theme, but with countless variations. Thus, in the mother–infant pattern there is a reinforcement of the experience of a basic invariance and structure to life, but with minor variations.

Beebe and Lachmann (1988), who have closely observed the mother–infant dyad, talk about the various kinds of sharing, matching, "tuning in" and "being on the same wavelength" experiences that exist in the mutual influence structures of the first six months of life. These constitute precursors to the more cognitively formed empathic understanding that Kohut used as his method of psychotherapy.

The essence of a healthy empathic matrix for the growing self of the child is a mature, cohesive parental self that is in tune with the changing needs of the child. It can, with a glow of shared joy, mirror the child's grandiose display one minute. Yet, perhaps a minute later, should the child become anxious and overstimulated by its exhibitionism, it will curb the display by adopting a realistic attitude vis-à-vis the child's limitations. Such optimal frustrations of the child's need to be mirrored and merged into an idealized selfobject, go hand in hand with optimal gratifications and generate the appropriate growth-facilitating matrix for the self (Chessick, 1985).

CURE

By 1984, Kohut had placed greater stress on the role of empathy in a therapeutic cure. In his book, *How Does Analysis Cure?*, he devoted a chapter to "The Role of Empathy in Psychoanalytic Cure" but did not state that empathy alone effects a cure. Empathy has an important role, but there are other factors necessary for a cure. In fact, Kohut indicated that the analytic cure is a three-step process. The first is "defense analysis", the second, the "unfolding of the transference"; while only the third opens "a path of empathy between self and selfobject" (p. 66).

Elaborating the third point, Kohut wrote about the "establishment of empathic in-tuneness between self and selfobject on mature adult levels" (p. 66). That is, through the process of vicarious introspection, a self and a selfobject eventually become "in-tune," but only if this "in-tune" state is maintained over a considerable period of time can a cure occur. A lengthy process of sustained in-tuneness is especially necessary if the nature of the bond is archaic, in order for the bond to be transformed gradually into more mature one. To Kohut, the essence of an analytic cure is the gradual acquisition of structure through an empathic contact with a mature selfobject, accompanied by explanations that follow the understanding phase of treatment. Cure is not the expansion of the self, although expansion often occurs. And cure is not the ability to express verbally an understanding of former personal pathology, although this also frequently occurs after a cure.

With the new emphasis on the role of empathy in a cure, Kohut focused more on an empathic milieu, because "in such a[n] [empty] world it is human empathy that forms an enclave of human meaning" (Chessick, 1985, p. 138). Kohut took a therapeutic stance that stressed the legitimacy of the patient's claim on caretakers. His was a special nurture psychology. By 1984, Kohut had shifted further from Freud's truth-and-reality morality to empathy, from pride of clear vision and uncompromising rationality toward pride in the scientifically controlled expansion of the self.

In summary, much has been written about empathy during the last decade. Once the concept gained acceptance, a major struggle developed to prevent it from becoming so inclusive that it was used to explain everything and thereby nothing. The whole of the psychotherapeutic process cannot be adequately explained by the single concept of empathy. When the meaning of empathy was held to its precise, initial meaning as a process of understanding the subjective self through vicarious introspection, pressure arose for other, more precise theoretical constructs to describe aspects of psychotherapy. The concept of empathy, for example, pointed the way to attunement, that special bond between therapist and client. The nature of that bond needed further exploration, which occurred around the issue of the narcissistic transferences (see chapters 11-13, this volume).

The inadequacy of empathy as an idealized curative construct can be seen in an example from Kohut (1984): "If the mother's empathic ability has remained infantile, that is, if she tends to respond with panic to the baby's anxiety, then a deleterious chain of events will be set in motion" (p. 83). In such a situation the mother empathically knows how the child feels. She knows, through empathy, that the child is anxious. But this empathic understanding is not enough. Her ability to respond is faulty, not her capacity to be empathic. This inability to respond invites us to examine selfobject functions. As later chapters show, these functions play at least as important a role in a therapeutic cure as empathy does. But before turning to the subjects of narcissistic transferences and selfobject functions, we explore the concept of narcissism in the next chapter.

Readings for Chapter 10: Freud, 1914; Kohut, 1966.

10

Narcissism

Having chosen empathy as his method for understanding the subjective self, Kohut used it to undertake a major clinical study of narcissism. He published this study as "Forms and Transformations of Narcissism" (Kohut, 1966). He had many reasons for studying narcissism. First, he was experiencing an increasing number of patients in his practice with disorders reflecting narcissistic needs rather than neurotic conflicts. Second, his experience of growing to young adulthood in Germany during the Nazi era raised questions about the pathologically narcissistic Nazi core of Germany. Third, he was concerned with his own narcissistic needs as a creative thinker. In this chapter we explore (a) the definition of narcissism, (b) the adaptive value of narcissism, (c) transformed narcissism, and (d) narcissism and the autonomous self.

THE DEFINITION OF NARCISSISM

Self psychology redefines narcissism. Hartmann represented the old view clearly when he said that narcissism is the cathexis of the self

(Kohut, 1971, p. xiii). He was following Freud's (1914) view of narcissism, represented in the polemical paper "On Narcissism." When Freud wrote this paper, he was "fuming with rage" (Chessick, 1980a). The defections of Jung and Adler not only had troubled him, they forced him to define more precisely his theory of instincts. Using his famous U-tube analogy, Freud (1914) defined narcissism as the flowing of energy back into the ego. He cited paranoid schizophrenia as an example of "secondary narcissism," in which most of the libido is directed to the self. In object love the energy flows outward; the state of being in love exemplifies the libido cathected to an object. A phase of autoerotic primary narcissism, where the infant blissfully experiences the world as being itself, is postulated at the beginning of life. "All major psychoanalytic contributions to the concept of narcissism since Freud have largely remained locked into the 1914 model" (P. Ornstein, 1974, p. 128).

Kohut (1966) challenged Freud's notions of object libido and narcissistic libido. According to Freud, there is a totally narcissistic libido in the newborn, and as the infant becomes a child and then an adult, there is a shift toward all libido being invested in objects and none in the self. Using Freud's theory, the therapist tries to replace the patient's narcissism with object love, an aim Kohut thought not only difficult—if not impossible—but very undesirable. Kohut challenged the assumption that narcissism had to be eradicated. Such an eradicating solution, he argued, is itself influenced by the absolute ideas of an archaic grandiose self and hence is narcissistic. Kohut conceived of object libido and narcissistic libido as developing along separate but parallel lines. They are not on the opposite ends of the same continuum, as Freud contended, but move along two separate continua from archaic to more mature forms.

Although the term narcissistic was first used by Freud in a 1910 footnote to "Three Essays on the Theory of Sexuality" (Freud, 1905a), Rank actually wrote the first paper on narcissism in 1911 (Chessick, 1985). Nonetheless, Freud stamped these disorders with the implication of a poor prognosis for psychoanalytic psychotherapy when he distinguished them from the transference neuroses. The DSM-III description characterizes the narcissistic person as manifesting a sense of self-importance, an exhibitionistic need for attention and admiration, feelings of entitlement, lack of empathy for others, and interpersonal exploitativeness. Chessick points out that the DSM-III diagnosis describes an extremely unlikable person, obviously maladapted, and headed for trouble, obviously an extreme view. In practice, clinicians treat patients with narcissistic symptoms ranging from minimal to extreme, such as the sexual perversions.

Kohut's initial challenge to Freud's view of narcissism used the thinking and language of drive theory. In the evolution of Kohut's thought, however, once drive theory was dropped as an explanatory tool, his idea of narcissism became clearer. Although he never defined narcissism in a single, clear, and simple definition, he described it through his understanding of the narcissistic transferences and their later form as selfobject functions. Self psychology now sees narcissism as pertaining "to the maintenance, restoration, and transformation of self experiences" (Stolorow et al., 1987, p. 16). In Hartmann's language, narcissism is viewed as essential to the cohesion (not cathexis) of the self. Mitchell (1988) sees narcissism as a set of illusions. These illusions are not merely defenses against internal drives, as Kernberg believes, or as growth enhancing as Kohut held, "but most fundamentally . . . a form of interaction, of participation with others" (p. 204).

THE ADAPTIVE VALUE OF NARCISSISM

Kohut (1966) expressed the conviction that the modern view of narcissism was prejudiced toward always seeing it as pathological. Hence, it was seen as completely undesirable, devoid of any redeeming features, and deserving of eradication. Kohut believed to the contrary.

For Kohut, narcissism, which can take archaic, pathologically destructive forms, has adaptive value, and the potential to make a significant contribution to modern life. Wolf (1988a) wrote, "Mature selfishness is really the expansion of the self and its selfobjects to take in the whole world" (p. 130). If this is so, the central question for Kohut was understanding how to harness narcissism for constructive purposes, not how to get rid of it. He was interested in the "transformation" of archaic narcissism to mature forms.

By asserting that narcissism can have adaptive value, Kohut (1966) recognized that he was paddling upstream against the prevailing "altruistic value system of Western civilization" (p. 98). Such a value system was reinforced by the teaching and preaching of the major religious bodies against the sin of being selfish. But, to Kohut, most lamentable was the reinforcement given by Freud's theory to this negative bias against narcissism. In supporting narcissism's adaptive value, Kohut found himself in conflict with Freud's views. In discarding Freud's views on narcissism, Kohut eventually rejected Freud's drive theory, the keystone of classical analysis.

By diagnosing pathological narcissism, Kohut (1966) avoided the behavioral symptoms outlined in DSM III and focused on "the painful affect of embarrassment or shame which accompanies them and by their ideational elaboration which is known as inferiority feeling or hurt pride" (p. 98). Following clues from Freud, Kohut saw shame as arising from "exhibitionistic aspects of pregenital drives" (p. 98) At this stage in his thinking, Kohut was still using the language of drive theory to explain his new ideas. Narcissistic tension also occurs as the self strives to live up to its ideal. He saw the affective byproducts of narcissism as pointing to both the ambitions and the ideals sectors of the self.

As early as 1966 Kohut had formulated the bipolar theory of the self. The two poles of the self, ambitions and ideals, develop as a differentiation from primary narcissism. Kohut reminds us that primary narcissism is a psychological state:

> The baby originally experiences the mother and her ministrations not as a you and its actions but within a view of the world in which the I-you differentiation has not yet been established. Thus the expected control over the mother and her ministrations is closer to the concept which a grownup has of himself and of the control which he expects over his own body and mind than to the grownup's experience of others and of his control over them [pp. 99-100].

Kohut referred initially to the ambitions pole as the "narcissistic self" and the ideals pole as the "idealized parent imago." These are "new systems of perfection" that arise from disturbances to the primary narcissism because of inevitable imperfections in the mother's ministrations. The baby attempts to maintain the original perfection and omnipotence either by imbuing the rudimentary self or the rudimentary "you," the adult, with absolute perfection and power.

To Kohut, the establishment of a narcissistic self or an idealized parent imago is not pathological per se. These subjective states represent significant developmental achievements. Problems arise only if traumatic experiences lead to fixations at these maturation points and to an inability to internalize these idealized parents as ideals. For example, "premature interference with the narcissistic [grandiose] self leads to later narcissistic vulnerability because the grandiose fantasy becomes repressed and inaccessible to modifying influences" (Kohut, 1966, p. 104). When narcissistic forms of arrested development occur, these patients present with a great deal of grandiosity, expressed in a variety of ways, most often as unrealistic expectations of the self shown through self-criticism or condemnation for their not achieving impossible goals. This grandiosity is transformed only with difficulty because the patient is constantly overwhelmed by feelings of shame for failing to fulfill unattainable expectations. An example of a fixation at the ideals pole is seen when there is a failure to reach these ideals and the self experiences a deep longing for connection with an idealized parental imago.

TRANSFORMED NARCISSISM

If not traumatized, the grandiose and idealizing poles of the self develop from archaic to more mature forms. Kohut evaluated both poles as measures of the patient's level of narcissistic development from archaic to useful forms. On the grandiose line of development, ambitions become more realistic and goal oriented, and energy is released "for ego activities" (P. Ornstein, 1974, p. 135). On the idealizing line of development, ideals act as guides rather than as absolute controls and may be transformed into such forms of as: "(i) man's creativity; (ii) his ability to be empathic; (iii) his capacity to contemplate his own impermanence (death); (iv) his sense of humor; and (v) his wisdom" (Kohut, 1966, P. 111).

Creative Activity

That creative activity is a transformation of narcissism can be seen in the creator's idealized relationship to his work. Work functions for the creative person as a transitional object (Winnicott, 1951). It is similar to a mother's love for her unborn fetus or newborn baby or the single-minded devotion to the child who is taken into her expanded self. Kohut placed heavy stress on creativity not autonomy (Chessick, 1985, p. 225).

The creative individual is less separated from his surroundings than is the uncreative person. The I–You barrier is not clearly defined. The "external" is experienced more as a part of the internal and, therefore, with far greater intensity and sensitivity. The creative person is trying to recreate a perfection that was formally a part of the self. During the creative act, the creative person does not relate to work with the give-and-take mutuality that characterizes object love. Once underway, creativity takes precedence over interpersonal relationships.

Empathy

A second way narcissism is transformed is through the capacity for empathy in adult life. Empathy (as discussed in chapter 9, this volume), is a mode of gathering subjective data about another self through vicarious introspection. It is the process of exploring what another thinks and feels by placing oneself in another's shoes. At birth babies have a built-in capacity for attunement with their mothers (Stern, 1985). Beebe and Lachmann (1988) call this capacity for mutual influencing (see chapter 23, this volume), a precursor to empathy. The educational processes of Western culture are designed to replace this "inferior" narcissistic capacity with unempathic forms of cognition that foster an objective, materialistic, and mechanical view of life. In Kohut's mature person, the primitive capacity for attunement has not been expunged but is transformed into vicarious introspection for appropriate utilization in adult personal relationships.

Acceptance of Transience

The acceptance of transience, that is, of finiteness and death, is a third way in which narcissism is transformed. Freud (1916) pointed out most people's reluctance to accept the impermanence of objects whether people or cherished values (P. 305). The acceptance of our own impermanence—that the self is finite in time—is even more difficult. Kohut (1966) believed that the ability to accept transience "rests not simply on a victory of autonomous reason and supreme objectivity over the claims of narcissism, but on the creation of a higher form of narcissism" (p. 118). Those who genuinely accept death face it with a quiet pride rather than a sense of resignation and hopelessness. Such people share with Goethe the insight that the acceptance of death leads to a richer feeling of being alive. Most people, who, for example, are given a short time to live for medical reasons, set about packing as much as they can into each precious moment. Under such circumstances, death adds to rather than detracts from the quality of life. Such a heightened sense of living results in a cosmic narcissism that transcends the limits of the individual and leads to a new awareness and interest in the broadest issues of existence.

Capacity for Humor

The fourth sign of transformed narcissism is a capacity for humor. Although affirming Freud by quoting him, Kohut had a different view of humor. Freud (1927) said that "humor has something liberating about it; but it also has something of grandeur and elevation . . . [and] the triumph of narcissism, the victorious assertion of the ego's invulnerability" (p. 162). Freud was describing grandiosity that disavows the meaning of events. By contrast, Kohut (1966) described a genuinely transformed narcissism that does not deny events; it is the ability of the self to deflect a wound, to achieve a mastery that also accepts the unalterable realities that limit the assertions of the narcissistic self.

> Humor and cosmic narcissism . . . permit us to face death without having to resort to denial . . . [and] are metapsychologically based not on a decathexis of the self through a frantic hypercathexis of objects . . . . A genuine decathexis of the self can only be achieved slowly by an intact, well-functioning ego; and it is accompanied by sadness as the cathexis is transferred from the cherished self upon the supraindividual ideals and upon the world with which one identifies. The profoundest forms of human and cosmic narcissism therefore do not present a picture of grandiosity and elation but that of a quiet inner triumph with an admixture of undenied melancholy [p. 121].

Wisdom

A quality of wisdom is a fifth indication of transformed narcissism. Wisdom derives from the acceptance of limitations in one's physical, intellectual, and emotional powers. There is a recognition that the grandiose self needs to compromise with time by rating priorities and discovering what is truly important to be accomplished and what can be left for others. Wisdom is reflected in a sense of balance and proportion that takes into account the broad picture. It is generally achieved, if at all, in a person's more advanced years.

Kohut (1966) believed these five dimensions of experience to be invaluable in evaluating psychoanalytic therapy:

> The reshaping of the narcissistic structures and their integration into the personality—the strengthening of ideals, and the achievement, even to a modest degree, of such wholesome transformations of narcissism as humor, creativity, empathy and wisdom—must be rated as a more genuine and valid result of therapy than the patient's precarious compliance with demands for a change of his narcissism into object love [p. 123].

NARCISSISM AND THE AUTONOMOUS SELF

Kohut accepted a healthy, adaptive function for transformed narcissism and rejected the goal of a completely autonomous self. He rejected the concept of dependence altogether because on introspective-empathic inspection it turned out to be a "further reducible psychic state" (Ornstein, 1978, p. 31). As Grotstein (1983) says, "Kohut eschews the traditional notion of the increasing independence of the self from its objects" (p. 176). It is a manifestation of nontransformed archaic narcissism for a person to value absolute autonomy and perfect freedom.

To Kohut, a person's striving for complete independence not only sets an impossible goal, but disavows legitimate narcissistic needs. These persons are "counterdependent" rather than maturely adaptive in their behavior. The apparent "nonnarcissism" of the completely autonomous person is a covert form of archaic but disavowed narcissism. It is possible that the goal of classical psychoanalysis, the complete autonomy of the patient, encourages the disavowal of narcissism.

In addition to the classical goals of complete autonomy, another traditional concern is strong ego (self) boundaries. It was deemed that a narcissistic person had "weak ego boundaries," whereas an autonomous person had strong ones. But the focus on boundaries does not address the issue of narcissism. It is possible to argue that strong boundaries are necessary if there is a weak empty core; that is, a person needs a strong outer ("false") self to protect a weak inner self. Kohut placed the emphasis not on boundaries, but on the cohesion of the whole self. A self's cohesion, or lack of it, is the issue in narcissism.

With a strong cohesive self, boundary issues are not critical. A boundary can be "penetrated" by the psychological presence of another functioning as a selfobject (see chapter 14, this volume) and the cohesive self is not imperiled or triggered into a state of collapse. In fact, the presence of an empathic person functioning as a selfobject is not experienced subjectively as an intrusion into self boundaries, but as a cohesive presence. To Kohut, the self's cohesion, not boundary strength, was the critical issue.

In taking this stand against the disavowal of legitimate dependency needs, Kohut was not alone. He joined, for instance, the English poet John Donne, who said, "No man is an island, intire of it selfe." He also joined British analysts who, commencing with Fairbairn, and including Balint, Winnicott, and Bion, suggested that an infant grows from infantile dependence into mature dependence (Grotstein, 1983). These British analysts understood that a person feels autonomous by being properly "dependent-connected" to someone who provides support. In making this same point, Kohut used the concept of a selfobject function. To keep the self cohered, a person needs others to function as selfobjects, which are objects we experience as part of our self (Kohut and Wolf, 1978, p. 414). To Kohut, then, the selfobject function never disappears, it only undergoes transformation and maturation.

Kohut arrived at the idea of a selfobject function through an understanding of the narcissistic transference. In the neurotic transference, the therapist becomes a screen for displacements and projections of actual past experiences with parents or significant others. In the narcissistic transference, the longing for missed experiences is relived with the therapist. In other words, neurotic transferences involve experiences that have taken place; narcissistic transferences, those which have not. Obviously, some patients present with both types of transferences; nonetheless, the distinction between these two transferences is useful.

The use of the term transference for the therapist's relationship with both narcissistic and neurotic patients created confusion. It forced constant clarification of the type being referred to, whether classical, or narcissistic as defined by Kohut. And because Kohut initially also referred to two types of narcissistic transferences, the idealizing and the mirroring (before he added twinship as a third), the term narcissistic transference began to be replaced by the term selfobject function. Kohut saw idealizing, mirroring, and twinship selfobject functions as being ways to describe specifically the needs of the narcissistic transference.

In the next three chapters we see in detail how the needs for these mirroring, idealizing, and twinship selfobject functions manifest themselves, and the problems of managing psychotherapy when these transferences are present so that growth occurs along the narcissistic line of development. The mirror transference is explored in the next chapter.

Readings for Chapter 11: Kohut, 1971, chapters 5-7.

11

Mirror Transference

The mirror transference takes us to the heart of Kohut's ideas about the transformation of narcissism. It was Kohut's understanding that narcissistic transferences represented arrested developmental needs, not pathological aberrations, that opened the door to their being utilized to bring about growth. This was especially so for the mirror transference. Using these transferences is not easy or simple; nevertheless, therapists can now achieve with narcissistic persons good results that previously were accidental or virtually impossible before Kohut published his ideas. In this chapter we cover the mirror transference as (a) definition, (b) clinical example, (c) responding, (d) the grandiose state, and (e) conforming and creative states.

DEFINITION

Kohut (1971) defined a mirror transference as

> the therapeutic reinstatement of that normal phase of the development of the grandiose self in which the gleam in the mother's

> eye, which mirrors the child's exhibitionistic display, and other forms of maternal participation in and response to the child's narcissistic-exhibitionistic enjoyment confirm the child's self-esteem and, by gradually increasing selectivity of these responses, begin to channel it into realistic directions [p. 116].

A mirror transference represents a therapeutic revival of the grandiose self (Chessick, 1985), which awakens a demand for validation (Basch, 1988a) from a responsive selfobject (Goldberg, 1988) who recognizes, admires, and appropriately praises the patient.

"what a good boy!"

A patient whose exhibitionistic needs have been adequately validated by parents does not develop a mirror transference during psychotherapy. When a parent's self-confidence is secure, then the proud exhibitionism of the budding self of a child will be responded to with acceptance. However grave the blows may be to which the child's grandiosity is exposed by the realities of life, the proud smile of the parents will keep alive a bit of the original omnipotence (Kohut and Wolf, 1978). Faulty mirroring by the parents leads to arrested development and a yearning for a significant growth-producing mirroring experience.

In 1971 Kohut postulated three ways that the mirror transference could express a patient's exhibitionistic grandiosity. In the archaic merger, the patient, who thinks the therapist knows what is on his mind, demands total control, as if the therapist were an arm or a leg. In the alter-ego/twinship type of merger, the patient insists that he and the therapist are alike. With the mirroring type, the mirror transference proper, the therapist has the task of praising, echoing, and mirroring the patient's performances.

By 1984, Kohut had changed his thinking. Instead of seeing the alter-ego/twinship type as a subentity of the mirror transference, he conceived of it as a separate transference, considerably different from the mirror transference. (It is discussed in chapter 13, this volume, as is the archaic merger transference, which Kohut left unseparated from the mirror transference.)

Patients who seek a mirror transference with a therapist are searching for the means to transform a primitive grandiosity into wholesome pride in performance (Goldberg, 1974). Such archaic grandiosity creates the illusion of being very powerful; it also makes unrealistic demands. When these grandiose demands are transformed, they change into self-regulation and self-discipline (Chessick, 1985). When mirroring focuses on genuine achievements, the transference may shift to an idealizing one in which the grandiose self gradually turns into an enthusiastic, realistically ambitious, cohesive self.

CLINICAL EXAMPLE

Mr. I was a 25-year-old single male, mentioned by Kohut (1971, 1977) and written up in Goldberg (1978). Mr. I presented for treatment because of his inability to perform on the job adequately and because of a failure to establish an enduring relationship with a woman, despite much dating.

After two years of treatment involving an idealizing transference, the patient's need turned into mirroring. This mirror transference could be anticipated from his case material. The evidence is as follows: He enjoyed masturbating in his girlfriend's presence because he liked "an audience"; he spent a great deal of time looking at himself in a mirror; his hobby was photographing nude women; he wanted the best analyst ever to think his sexual exploits were great; his case was "the greatest"; and he wanted to show off his pictures, records, and poems to his analyst. All this points to a grandiose self in need of transformation!

As further evidence of the grandiose state of his self, Mr. I acted Like a Don Juan with women, conquering them and making them participate in sadistic and bizarre sexual exploits. Goldberg writes:

> He could be cruelly demanding of each one [of his girlfriends]: showing up unannounced, leaving abruptly in the middle of the night when expected to stay over, and, on the way home suddenly deciding to spend the rest of the night with another. "If you treat them badly, they'll do everything you want them to do" [p. 22].

For example, with one of them, they urinated on each other and then wallowed in the warmth of the urine.

Another indication of a mirror transference was Mr. I's wanting to be admired for the changes he had reported, yet he bemoaned the fact that he needed recognition for every little accomplishment. "He tried to attract the attention of the analyst's applause at every turn" (Goldberg, 1978, p. 35). He said of his sister, "Her admiration had always made him feel great and powerful, and he has desperately sought such admiration (for his 'big penis' and 'great mind') from sister-figures ever since his sister married" (p. 43).

One of the important themes to emerge in Mr. I's treatment was the risk of his becoming "overstimulated." He said that an early memory was of a lake where "getting a strike on every cast had a personal pleasure connected with it" (p. 56). He also wanted his father to be there, to witness and admire his success, but he wondered why all these exciting activities in this memory had anxieties connected to them. Mr. I then associated to wanting the analyst's praise and approval, but he was afraid that the analyst might debunk the activities that kept him (patient) calm, or on an even keel. After one analytic session he said, "a great hour, good communication—really putting it together—makes me almost ecstatic and I began to feel overstimulated" (p. 62). It is also clear from the material (p.83) that being understood was overstimulating.

There is also evidence that when Mr. I sought a mirroring response from his analyst, and did not get it, he was wounded. This happened when he brought in some diaries, possibly a sign of sharing some of his old, isolated, secret grandiose self. The analyst made the mistake of focusing too much on the content of the diaries. This mistake came out the next morning when Mr. I reported a two-part dream (Goldberg, 1978):

[The first part:]

> On a dock fishing, caught a big fish still on the pole, carried it into the cottage to show it to Dad, and probably to Mom too. Expected him to say, 'Good fish.' He said, you can clean it. I didn't want to; just wanted to show it. The fish then shriveled up a bit as a result of the conversation [p. 75].

[The second part:]

> The government has crucified one of my friends, G.C., for some un-American behavior. I saw him on the cross, hugging a statue of Jesus. Then it was Jesus on the cross; he was so

> big, splendid, great, the downfall of this man on the cross added to the splendor of the occasion. He was suddenly slumping, the muscles suddenly relaxing, and he was dying [pp. 75-76].

In associating to these dreams, Mr. I complained that the analyst had asked a lot of questions about the content of the diaries, instead of saying "very interesting" and admiring them. Then he mused, "No sense in bringing these in; you didn't admire them."

From this dream material, it is evident that when Mr. I became wounded by the analyst's lack of empathic responding to the diaries (first part) he retreated into a merger transference (second part). Combine with this retreat from mirror to merger transference the two years of an idealizing transference before the mirror transference emerged, and there is the suggestion of a narcissistic line of retreat (regression) from idealizing through mirroring to merger, as wounding occurs and inadequate repairs are made.

MIRRORING AS RESPONSE

As can be seen from the foregoing illustration, it is one thing for a therapist to recognize the emergence of a mirror transference; it is another matter to respond in such a way as to help transform the grandiose self. For some self psychologists it is sufficient to affirm the patient's need for mirroring without in any other way responding directly to the need. This position is another expression of "its wrong to gratify" the client because gratification produces the "malignant regression" described by Balint (1968). Bacal (1985) points out that a malignant regression, called fragmentation in self psychology, occurs as a result of a catastrophic selfobject failure, not as a result of gratifying.

Also in response to the "interpret the need for mirroring" position, self psychologists experienced with mirror transferences suggest that while affirming the need is sometimes sufficient to shift the transference to an idealizing one, frequently it is not. In fact, the actual interpretation of the mirroring need alone may be experienced by the patient as withholding and hence a form of rejection that results in an empathic break that needs repairing. on the other hand, active mirroring may overstimulate patients, especially those who have the greatest need for mirroring. Empathic monitoring of the patient's level of stimulation is necessary if the therapist actively mirrors; and active mirroring should take place only after interpretation of the need for mirroring has failed to reduce symptoms of fragmentation. Because of the danger of overstimulation, active mirroring is best introduced only tentatively.

Whatever the active response of the therapist, it is undesirable to reduce mirroring to a therapeutic technique. First, a technique implies a mechanical model of psychotherapy and thus a way of avoiding involvement rather than being engaged in a bond with the client. Second, the mirror transference is based on the client's subjective experience of being mirrored rather than any single thing the therapist actively does. And, third, the nature of what is experienced as mirroring is very much determined by the developmental need. Thus, at one stage mirroring may be more like the experience of "show and tell" in front of an obviously pleased teacher or proud parents. At an earlier stage, it may be centered on the fleeting but special look of the mother. At a later stage, the mirroring experience may be part of an elaborate ceremony that rewards and celebrates a significant accomplishment.

Mirroring also involves a process of mutual responding, referred to as attunement. This attunement is analogous to the idea of feedback loops, but because feedback as a concept is too easily linked with computers and mechanistic thinking, the idea of corrective mutual responding is preferred. Take, for example, the case of Miss E. When she brought home her high school report card, her preoccupied mother responded tersely with "That's very nice." Superficially the mother gave a mirroring response, but its mechanical, ritualistic quality failed the subjective expectations of Miss E. She did not experience her mother's response as the deeply satisfying and vitalizing form of mirroring she needed. So Miss E countered with, "I get all As and all I get is 'That's very nice'?" Her mother, adjusting her mirroring response, then said, "No, let me give you a hug, its wonderful!"

THE GRANDIOSE SELF

The idea of the mirror transference is linked to that of a grandiose self. For the grandiose self, successes achieved are never enough; because, imbued with perfectionism, the grandiose self is never satisfied. It will brook no limits; its greed knows no bounds. Its ideas are perfect; its control, absolute. It acts dangerously to prove its omnipotence. Lying and name dropping are attempts to live up to its expectations (Chessick, 1985).

If we heed the warnings of Schafer (1976) and others about the dangers of reified thinking, we need to avoid using the term grandiose self and speak instead of the self being in a grandiose state. Otherwise we risk thinking of the grandiose self as a center of initiative, separate from other parts of the self, and then self psychology finds itself in the same reified position as classical analysis, with its structural theory agents (id, superego, ego). Initially self psychology's discussions of the grandiose self reflected this reifying tendency, but the issue of the reification of the grandiose self faded as the theoretical emphasis shifted away from the narcissistic transferences towards the selfobject experience (see chapter 14, this volume).

A major concern among therapists is to avoid inflating the grandiose self. There is a fear that actively mirroring the grandiose self in a mirror transference may simply encourage more grandiosity. And it may. If increased grandiosity is a possibility, thought needs to be given to the circumstances under which mirroring will enhance the transformation of narcissism and those under which it will only reinforce a grandiose state.

Circumstances that promote a grandiose state of the self are (1) countertransference rejection, (2) mirroring without achievement, (3) achievement without appropriate effort, and (4) excessive mirroring even with appropriate success.

Countertransference Rejection

Countertransference rejection takes many forms. Grandiosity irritates others, so invites rejection, and fosters the feeling that the person "needs to be cut down to size." Efforts aimed at puncturing a person's grandiose state by pointing out reality inevitably wound and only increase narcissistic dynamics; if anything, they foster the continuance or exacerbation of the grandiose state. Another way that countertransference rejection emerges with patients who seek a mirror transference is in the need of the therapist to compete with the patient. A tendency to lecture the patient arises out of the therapist's counterexhibitionistic dynamics (Chessick, 1985). So does the need to control the patient by using exhortation and persuasion. Yet another type of countertransference occurs when the therapist actively mirrors the patient because the patient's case history indicates a need for mirroring, rather than waiting for the mirror need to manifest itself in the transference. The problem is further compounded if an adequate idealizing bond has not had time to develop.

All these countertransference-based behaviors wound the patient, reinforce the grandiose state, and result in the emergence of symptoms of a crumbling (fragmenting) self. Hypochondria, compulsive sexuality, or sexual perversions are defenses against such a crumbling self and the deadness felt within. They are attempts magically to revitalize the self (Chessick, 1985). The patient may also respond to the rejection of the mirroring needs by gross identification with the therapist. Such an identification is a magical attempt to solve the problem of the fragmenting self. Like anything magical, it is impermanent. Yet another way a patient may respond to rejection of mirroring is through yearnings for merger. Such a merger, with its surrender of much of the self's organization, produces intense narcissistic rage, covertly expressed through the demands and control of the merger transference.

Mirroring Without Achievement

If a therapist mirrors a patient's wishes and fantasies or gives "false mirroring," that is, actively engages in praise and flattery of a patient where no achievement is involved, the grandiose state of the self can indeed be enhanced. Historical examples of monarchs, prelates, presidents, military commanders and corporate chief executives, who developed a more grandiose self when surrounded by a coterie of sycophants supports this notion. Such leaders, who become isolated, also become more grandiose and more out of touch with what is practically useful. Further, because false mirroring raises false hopes, the grandiose self is susceptible to more severe wounding and symptoms of fragmentation when trauma inevitably occurs. Such trauma also increases the amplitude of the oscillations between irrational overestimation and feelings of inferiority when ambitions are thwarted. Such large oscillations are manifestations of a person in a grandiose self-state.

A solution to the problem of a patient's seeking flattery or mirroring of wishes and fantasies during psychotherapy is to focus on the patient's real achievements, however small.

Achievement Without Appropriate Effort

Grandiosity is also strengthened by the failure of the social system to enforce laws and gain respect. It is, for example, a criminal's belief in his ability to beat the consequences of his behavior that reinforces his sense of omnipotence. Of course, if such a person is also admired and affirmed by a reference group for being able to break laws with impunity, this kind of mirroring adds further reinforcement to the grandiose self. Such a person was described in The New York Times (March 22, 1989). Willie Bosket, a self-proclaimed "monster," had committed 2,000 crimes between the ages of 9 and 15, including 25 stabbings. Silvia Honig, a social worker who first met him at the age of 12, said that reformatories let him conduct a reign of terror: attacking staff members with clubs, smashing windows, stealing, sodomizing other inmates, escaping in state vehicles. "After a while, he got the impression he was omnipotent," said Miss Honig, who became his closest friend. Clearly, allowing persons to behave in whatever ways they like without being answerable for their behavior reinforces their already formed grandiose state of the self.

The military moves of the Nazis leading up to World War II also exemplify the expansion of the grandiose self because of achievement through bluff. Encouraged by feeble Allied responses to his earlier moves, Hitler, on Saturday, March 7, 1936, sent a few thousand German troops to occupy the demilitarized zone of the Rhineland, a move that broke agreements signed after World War I. Two years later, emboldened by an Allied policy of appeasement, Hitler ordered 100,000 German troops into Austria. The Sudeten crisis followed, and a year later, encouraged by Chamberlain's

Munich agreement, Hitler invaded Czechoslovakia. Then, encouraged by the lack of any significant Allied response to the Czech takeover, Hitler made his next move, which was into Poland (Manchester, 1988).

When clients encounter good news, congratulations on the good fortune are appropriate. The grandiose ideas that sometimes accompany such good fortune are not mirrored. The patient needs calming, soothing responses for the overstimulation the good fortune engenders.

Excessive Mirroring Even with Appropriate Success

Even where mirroring reflects real achievements, a person's self can become overstimulated from an excessive state of grandiosity. Such a person may have hungered for success for so long that when it comes it is overwhelming despite selfobject mirroring. Dreams of a hostile environment or a swarm of dangerous hornets (Kohut and Wolf, 1978) can be signs of just such stimulation, which undermines any possibility of the transformation of the grandiose self into healthy ambition. When a child achieves without experiencing mirroring, the experience of success in adult life may not leave a residue of enjoyment. On the contrary, success to such a person is as much a problem as a failure. Success means being flooded by unrealistic archaic greatness fantasies which produce painful tension and anxiety. Persons who are unduly shy after a very successful accomplishment, may be defending against such retraumatization.

MIRRORING THE CONFORMING AND CREATIVE STATES OF SELF

As indicated earlier, what is mirrored is as important as the mirroring responsiveness of the therapist. Mirroring wishes and fantasies can reinforce the grandiose state of the self rather than transform it. To avoid such reinforcement, mirroring needs to target the significant achievements of the patient. Such achievements, however, will vary significantly, depending on whether they fulfill the expectations of others or whether they are spontaneous creations.

What the therapist mirrors can determine whether a conforming or creative state of the self is strengthened. One boy, for example, was taken by his mother to swimming, skating tennis and piano lessons each week. As small, significant progress was made in these areas, she praised and affirmed him for the increased skill. When, however, using pillows, cushions and blankets, he created his own cubby house within the living room of his home and sought his mother's praise, it was not forthcoming. He was, in fact, rejected for "making a mess." Thus, what is mirrored by parents helps make and shape who we are and how conforming or creative the self will become.

The need for mirroring is only one way that a narcissistic transference emerges during psychotherapy. We explore another, a need to idealize the therapist, in the next chapter.

Readings for Chapter 12: Kohut, 1971, chapters 2 - 4; Tolpin, P., 1983a.

12

Idealizing Transference

For thousands of years, high-status religious leaders and counselors were idealized by persons seeking help. Freud recognized the importance of idealization, maybe because he had sought a relationship with a succession of idealized persons in the first part of his own life (Gay, 1988). He also believed that much of the temporary improvement in his early analytic cases had occurred because they sought to please him as the idealized analyst. Balint (1936) noted that the prospect of termination often triggered a patient's renewed yearning for the sustenance of an idealized analyst.

Classical analysis, however, relegated the idealizing analytic experience to the status of a pathological defense in need of purging. Classical analysts see idealization not as a manifestation of transference, but as a defense against libidinal drives. Their technique is to interpret the defensive purpose of idealization to the patient so that underlying primitive drives, especially aggression, emerge in the relationship. This is a move strongly advocated by the neo-Kleinian Kernberg (1975).

In contrast, Kohut (1971) viewed idealization as a transference not in the classical sense of a repetition with the therapist of key experiences in the past, but as a narcissistic transference in which the patient seeks to overcome arrested, unmet developmental needs. Kohut seems to have been influenced in his view by Aichorn (1951), his own analyst. Aichorn had facilitated the formation of idealizing transferences in his adolescent patients through his intuitive skills as a therapist and his charismatic personality (Kohut, 1971, pp. 161-164). This idealizing transference, one type of narcissistic transference, has its own "line of development" from archaic to mature forms. This chapter covers (a) definition, (b) etiology, (c) signs, (d) countertransference, and (e) a clinical illustration of an idealizing transference.

DEFINITION

Kohut (1971) viewed the idealizing transference as an attempt to save "a part of the lost experience of global narcissistic perfection by assigning it to an archaic, rudimentary (transitional) selfobject, the idealized parental imago" (p. 37). Chessick (1985) sees the idealized parent imago as a magical figure to be controlled and with which to be fused. Wolf (1988) makes an idealizing transference the "re-establishment of the need for an experience of merging with a calm, strong, wise, and good selfobject" (p. 126). And Basch (1988a) defines the idealizing transference as

> one's unrequited longing to be strengthened and protected when necessary by an alliance with an admired, powerful figure . . . . It is the need to be united with someone one looks up to, and who can lend one the inspiration, the strength, and whatever else it takes to maintain the stability of the self system when one is endangered, frustrated, or in search of meaning [p. 141].

Kohut (1971) described Mr. A as an example of the idealizing transference. Mr. A had a "tendency toward feeling vaguely depressed, drained of energy, and lacking in zest (with an associated drop in his work capacity and creativity during periods when this mood had overtaken him)" (p. 57). His self-esteem was vulnerable, as

> manifested by his sensitivity to criticism, to lack of interest in him, or to the absence of praise from the people whom he experienced as his elders or superiors. Thus, although he was a man of considerable intelligence who performed his tasks with skill and creative ability, he was forever in search of guidance and approval; from the head of the research laboratory where he was employed, from a number of senior colleagues, and from the fathers of the girls whom he dated. He was sensitively aware of these men and of their opinion of him, attempted to get their help and approbation, and tried to create situations in which he would be supported by them. So long as he felt accepted and counseled and guided by such men, so long as he felt they approved of him, he experienced himself as whole, acceptable, and capable; and under such circumstances he was indeed able to do well in his work and to be creative and successful. At slight signs of disapproval of him, however, or of lack of understanding for him, or loss of interest in him, he would feel drained and depressed, would tend to become first enraged and then cold, haughty, and isolated, and his creativeness and work capacity deteriorated [pp. 57-58].

In summing up this case Kohut said:

> What he lacked, however, was the ability to feel more than a fleeting sense of satisfaction when living up to his standards or reaching his goals. He was able to obtain a sense of heightened self-esteem only by attaching himself to strong, admired figures whose acceptance he craved and by whom he needed to feel supported [p. 62].

Vase w/ hole in bottom √ water

Etiology

Under optimal development the child idealizes the father (or another person) and then, through a succession of minor disappointments with him, experiences a slow diminution of the idealization. At the same time, there is internalization, that is, "the acquisition of permanent psychological structures which continue, endopsychically, the functions which the idealized self-object had previously fulfilled" (Kohut, 1971, p. 45).

Not all disappointment with an idealizing transference is gradual. For example, "the parents' unempathic modesty . . . may traumatically frustrate the child's phase-appropriate need to glorify him" (p. 43). Where the disappointment is traumatic, the idealized parent imago is retained in its unaltered form, is not transformed into a tension-regulating psychic structure, and remains an archaic, transitional selfobject that is required for the maintenance of narcissistic homeostasis. These people constantly seek an approving relationship with someone they admire and look up to.

Even when some structuralization has taken place, it may be so precariously established that a child's disappointment with the idealized selfobject may lead to a renewed insistence on, and search for, an external object of perfection (Kohut, 1971, p. 44). An idealized parent imago, not internalized gradually, is repressed as an archaic structure. The patient, forever searching for an omnipotently powerful person to merge with and from whose support and approval the individual may gain magical strength and protection, becomes unconsciously fixed on a yearning for an external idealized selfobject (Chessick, 1985).

Transmuting internalization occurs only after sufficient idealizing (mirroring, twinship, or all) experiences have taken place. It is a consequence of the minor, nontraumatic failures in the response of the idealized selfobjects that there is a gradual replacement of the selfobjects and their functions by an expanded self and its functions. While gross identification with selfobjects and their functions may temporarily and transitionally occur, the ultimately wholesome result, the autonomous self, is not a replica of the selfobject. The analogy of the intake of foreign protein in order to build up one's own protein is very serviceable here—even as regards the detail of the splitting up and arrangement of the material that was ingested (Kohut and Wolf, 1978).

To Kohut, transmuting internalizations take place through interpretations. These are not classical interpretations focused on drives and their defenses, but interpretations focused on the inevitable empathic failures of the therapist. Such interpretations are most meaningful after the therapist has failed to understand the patient and then linked these failures to a parent's shortcomings by not empathically comprehending the needs of the patient as a child. No attempt is made to soothe or comfort the agitated and angry patient for empathic failures; only an interpretation after the fact is indicated (Goldberg, 1974).

Contrary to Balint's (1968) experience of interpretations failing to take effect with preoedipal patients, interpreting the therapist's empathic failure to a narcissistic patient can make for a noticeable improvement. And such an interpretation does not wound, because it is focused on the empathic lapse of the therapist and not on the patient and thus avoids shaming the patient. Such an interpretation also allows the patient to experience the therapist as being humane.

SIGNS

Silent Idealization

Silent idealization seems to be the most authentic idealizing transference (Gedo, 1975, 1981). In contrast to the defensive idealization, the silent idealizing transference repeats a more archaic experience where the selfobject's availability and perfection are taken for granted; thus the idealizing transference tends to be silent. Its focus will be on functional abilities of the idealized parental imago rather than a specific person. If it becomes explicit, objectified, it is spoiled. Therefore, the silent idealization is not interpreted to the patient. This uninterpreted silent idealization leads the patient to experience increased energy and a sense of vitality in his day-to-day life. This kind of idealization is frequently expressed in a patient's referring friends to the therapist.

Open Admiration of Therapist

The open admiration of a therapist's character and values often reflects a defensive idealization (Wolf, 1988). Such defensive idealizations usually involve a gross identification with a person who is acknowledged as an independent source of initiative even if the qualities attributed to him are illusory (Gedo, 1981).

The open admiration of the therapist may also be conceived as an attempt to mirror the therapist, that is, a reverse selfobject function (Lee, 1988), where the patient functions as a selfobject for the therapist. Eventually this attempt by the patient to serve the therapist needs to be interpreted, not just accepted as is the case with a silent, true idealizing transference. Mirroring the therapist may be one of the most mistaken misrepresentations of the idealizing transference made by those who use the jargon of self psychology without studying it or reading case material presented from a self psychology point of view.

Resistance to Idealization

Resistance to idealization may be seen as a prolonged and bitter depreciation of the analyst (Wolf, 1958). Overt hostility toward the analyst can be regarded as a resistance against the establishment of an idealizing transference (Tylim, 1978). Fear of the loss of ego boundaries and a wish to merge can be sources of such resistance (Chessick, 1985).

Once an idealizing transference has formed, swings from the therapeutic activation of the idealizing transference to a transient need for a mirroring transference as the patient feels more grandiose are among the most common resistances in the analysis of narcissistic personalities (Kohut, 1971). Other clinical signs of a disturbance of the idealizing transference are cold, aloof, angry, raging withdrawal, which also represents a swing to the grandiose self, and feelings of fragmentation and hypochondria due to separation and creation of eroticized replacements, especially voyeurism (Chessick, 1985).

Defensive Idealization

Kohut's thinking includes the idea of defensive idealization. He believed that such defensive idealization is directed against oedipal rivalries, and not aggressive drives. Thus, Kohut (1971, p. 75) spoke about such idealization as buttressing secondarily repressions of, reaction formation against, or denials of structurally deeper underlying hostility. Where defensive idealizations occur, reactions to disappointments in the selfobject are expressed through anger and intensified longings for it. These defensive idealizations are best not interpreted, yet are useful in alerting the therapist to explore with the patient in what ways the patient is experiencing empathic failure.

To illustrate: Miss S developed a defensive idealization to cope with an older, competitive, and punitive sister. As a result of such defensive idealization, Miss S felt inferior. These inferiority feelings could be a sign of a defensive idealization reenacted in the transference. A frequent comment by Miss S in the initial stages treatment was, "I feel so stupid." She also reported many situations during the first 50 sessions that she said "proved how stupid she was." These expressions decreased dramatically after the therapist gave careful attention to appropriate mirroring responses.

These defensive idealizations are best called "pseudoidealizations" (Gedo, 1981) following Segal's (1974) terminology. Pseudoidealizing transferences are reaction formations after the traumatic destruction of childhood idealizations. Pseudoidealizations are often only partially successful so that pseudoidealizations and disillusionment are maintained at the same time through disavowal. Gedo recommends interpreting such disavowal.

Where the predominant psychopathology involves arrested developmental needs, interpretation of the transference idealization as a defense will be largely incorrect. The patient's expectable reaction in such circumstances will still be primarily hostile; that is, he will respond with appropriate outrage to the disappointment of having been misunderstood. If the therapist wishes to disclaim responsibility for such an iatrogenic impasse, he may be tempted to compound his errors by further interpreting the patient's anger as confirmation of his hypothesis that the main issue is a defense against aggressive drives.

Kohut's ideas reflect a basic difference with Kernberg over responding to rageful patients. Kohut (1975) stressed the rage-assuaging properties of correct empathy and insisted that Kernberg's neo-Kleinian focus on the primary envy–hostility complex was unempathic and provocative. Patients experience such interpretations as a repetition of the unempathic behavior of parents in early childhood. They respond not only with hostility, but with renewed disillusionment and its accompanying depressive affect.

Avoiding premature interpretation of the meaning of idealization within the transference is tantamount to the indefinite acceptance of the transference and its potential to enhance a patient's adaptive behavior (Goldberg, 1978). The establishment of a stable idealizing transference often leads patients into unprecedented states of well-being, contingent on the availability and continued "perfection" of the analyst.

Those who would exploit an idealizing transference to promote direct adaptive changes are in fact reverting to the psychotherapeutic methods developed by Aichhorn (1951) for the management of delinquent youths. To gain therapeutic leverage, Aichhorn advocated the unimpeded unfolding of the transference with delinquents who would otherwise fail to develop a meaningful contact with him.

Idealization and Line of Development

Idealization has its own separate line of development. Kohut (1971) wrote of both the archaic and the comparatively mature stages of development of the idealized parent imago (p. 74). Mr. A suffered interference with the internalization process during the latent period of development. He is an example of a more mature idealizing transference at a relatively late stage of development. Kohut cited hypomania as an example of an archaic idealizing transference. Chessick (1985) notes that it is the failure of idealizing the mother that leads to the more archaic type of transference that seeks an ecstatic merger and mystical union with the godlike, idealized parent.

COUNTERTRANSFERENCE

The idealizing transference can lead to the analyst's resentment at feeling belittled when a patient's idealization begins to wane (Kohut, 1971). This reaction occurs when the analyst looks upon idealization as a realistic response to his actual qualities. A more common countertransference problem in an idealizing transference lies in the therapist's being unable to tolerate the stimulated, covert grandiosity.

In another form of countertransference, therapists show signs of rejecting clients planning to terminate. This seems to be some kind of reenactment of a mother's attack on a child when the child tries to idealize the father (Gedo, 1975). Such mothers often succeed in making the child feel guilty for wanting to individuate. This attack reflects the parent's overuse of the child as a selfobject; that is, it is a traumatic reverse selfobject experience (Lee, 1988).

Encouraging idealization is a form of countertransference that reflects the therapist's need, not the client's. Kohut advocated neither encouraging idealization nor preventing it by automatically interpreting its emergence as a resistance (Gedo, 1975).

Shame also can be a source of countertransference. Kohut and Wolf (1978) use the example of a little boy eager to idealize his father. The boy wants his father to tell him about his life, the battles he engaged in and won, but instead of joyfully acting in accordance with his son's need, the father is embarrassed by the request.

Yet another form of countertransference to the idealizing transference is an embarrassed, defensive response by the therapist in which he denies the patient's idealization, jokes about it, or tries vigorously to interpret it away. This countertransference generally produces a retreat by the patient into the grandiose self (Chessick, 1985).

There is also a countertransference fear that an idealizing transference will foster and reinforce an addictionlike need for it. However, the very core of Kohut's (1971) technical recommendation is the inevitable, spontaneous, recurrent disruption—through empathic failures—of the narcissistic equilibrium achieved in these transferences. Such empathic failures enable reconstructions of the traumatic effects of childhood disillusionments with idealized parental objects. By means of such genetic interpretations, the patient may understand and master his need for continuing idealization of omnipotent others. The indefinite acceptance of the patient's idealizations is therefore the exact antithesis of Kohut's technical recommendations.

CLINICAL ILLUSTRATION

Tolpin (1983a) presents the case of Mrs. A, a divorced woman in her early 40s who was in analysis for four years. "While the most prominent transference that emerged in the analysis was an idealizing father transference, elements of other selfobject transferences were also apparent" (p. 461). Mrs. A had been in treatment with three psychotherapists for approximately a year each before they terminated, one with the therapist's death, the others when they moved away.

The patient was the second of two children born to a successful middle-aged businessman. Her older brother, haughty and depreciating of her, was never close to her. Lacking a strong need to nurture, her mother gave over major care of her children to Miss D, a governess. Mrs. A experienced the wonderful Miss D as being devoted to and belonging to her. Miss D was

> a lively person who, as Mrs. A recalled, bathed her, dressed her, took her for walks, looked after her while she played with other children in the park, and took her to her church where Mrs. A was fascinated by chants and exotic rituals. Miss D told her stories, read to her and helped her with difficult words in books. Mrs. A loved her deeply. Then one day without warning, Miss D was gone [p. 463].

Mrs. A's loss of Miss D was a traumatic experience. Miss D, who had gone to her native country for a year, returned to visit Mrs. A's household and brought a gift of a beautiful dress, but Mrs. A would not put it on. What's more, she treated Miss D as if she were a total stranger. After Miss D made a few more visits, the family lost contact with her. Many nursemaids came and went, but none won Mrs. A's affections.

When she was nine, a second major traumatic event occurred when her father died of a heart attack in the street. Mrs. A had experienced her father as a somewhat distant, remote, and mysterious figure who lived in a world apart, a world of business and travel and absences from the home. Yet she was attached to him in an awed kind of way. She recalled two pleasurable experiences with her father. One occurred when the two of them were to go into the house but did so secretly by ducking down beneath the kitchen window so that no one in the house would see them returning. The second occasion was when she went with her father to visit old cronies, who made a great fuss over her. They said she was beautiful and intelligent and were delighted with how sweet she was.

Mrs. A's response to the loss of her father also suggests the extent of her trauma. After it,

> she was frequently truant from school. She would leave the house in the morning as if on her way to her classes but instead would get on a bus, ride from one end of the line to the other, transfer from one bus to the other, and at last after several hours return home. Then she would go to her room and read. She felt like a zombie. Sometimes she would begin to cry—on the bus, or walking on the street. Once she was so self-absorbed that she walked into a lamp post and bloodied her face [p. 464].

In her beginning year of high school Mrs. A developed a reverence for a male science teacher who gave her a ride home in his car on a cold, rainy day after she had locked herself out of her locker. She took his class in science the next year; and although she had never been interested in the hard sciences, she found herself fascinated with the material and earned an A in the course. Once she finished the course she utterly lost interest in the subject and in him.

In her early 20s Mrs. A married a former neighborhood boy she had known since grammar school. He was sincere and stable but did not have the "magic" of her father and later, of her charismatic lover. After her two children were born, Mrs. A found herself needing her husband merely to be available, to be around, to be present. During this period, there were episodes of kleptomania and depression. Then she fell madly in love with an older man at her place of work, who soon reciprocated her feelings. She was enthralled by his intelligence and wisdom. She loved him to read aloud the newspaper accounts of current political events on which he commented wisely and to which she listened with rapt attention.

Despite their plans to marry, years of high hopes and repeated promises extinguished the fires of her passion for him.

As idealization faded, it was replaced by an archaic need to be physically close.

> Several years into their relationship, when for a variety of reasons they could not spend the night together, Mrs. A sometimes could not fall asleep. In an effort to induce sleepiness she would read late into the night until she was exhausted. Sometimes she resorted to sedatives, which often did not work, and at times, in desperation, she would rush to her lover's apartment, climb into bed with him, and lying close to his body, immediately fall asleep [p. 466].

Mrs A sought treatment for recurrent depressive states, insomnia, overuse of sleeping medication, and occasional kleptomania. Her most painful problem was the love affair with this older man who would not marry her. The analyst perceived these symptoms as reflecting a basic need to reexperience an idealized transference.

On the basis of Mrs. A's idealizing relationships with her governess, father, lover, and former therapists, especially the second one, it is relatively easy to anticipate the eventual unfolding of an idealizing transference. For her, idealizing was not an unknown experience. Rather, her pattern was to form an idealizing bond, but, once it formed, to lose it.

After the analysis commenced at four times a week, Mrs. A almost immediately demonstrated an intense bond with the analyst. Her dreams reflected a sexualization of the transference, and she became supersensitive to the analyst's being away on vacation or even for short absences. She became extremely anxious lest she be retraumatized by losing the analyst for any reason. Even weekends were difficult to tolerate without seeing her analyst.

For a long time this idealizing transference was of the silent kind, always in the background. There were no overt expressions of admiration of the analyst. Such overt idealizing points to a reverse selfobject experience (Lee, 1988) in which the patient mirrors the therapist as a means of retaining the bond. After two years, Mrs. A was able to say, "In some way I have the feeling —you're perfect. Oh, I don't mean perfect, but I mean perfect for

idealizing vs. admiration
if idealiz, may lack their own quality

me here. Nothing was like this before" (p. 477). Early in the treatment, however, the idealizing transference was revealed by an increased sense of vitality, which was turned off during vacations and short breaks in treatment.

There is evidence also of both a twinship and a mirror transference, but these are more fleeting than the more "dominant" idealizing one. In an example of a twinship transference, Mrs. A said, "If I were not to leave at the end of the hour, I'd not be lying here, but I'd sit and read and you'd read and we'd be in the same room. That was the only thing I did with father—except for taking walks with him. He'd read and I'd read and there'd be no talking but I knew he was there" (p. 471). In an example of a mirror transference, she related how she watched a farmer's son jump from box to box and look to see if she was watching. Then she said, "I need to be looked at, I want to be watched the way he wants to be watched" (p. 471).

While Tolpin's case does not cover the working through and termination phases of treatment, its excellent material reflects the intense process through which patients often pass in overcoming the shame of wanting an idealized bond to the therapist.

In summary, the ubiquitous idealizing transference is one way a self with insufficient narcissistic capacities can feel cohered and energized and can seek to repair the "basic fault." Other ways are to form mirror, twinship, or merger transferences or some variation of all four. Kohut left relatively undeveloped the constructs of the twinship and merger transferences. These are explored in the next chapter.

Readings for Chapter 13: Kohut, 1979; Detrick, 1985, 1986.

13

Twinship and Merger Transferences

The twinship and merger transferences represent unfinished business in Kohut's attempt to conceptualize the narcissistic transferences. They were both originally seen as special forms of the mirror transference, but as Kohut's thinking evolved, he saw the need to give the twinship transference separate and equal status with the idealizing and mirror transferences. What follows (a) describes the twinship transference, (b) explores the merger transference, and (c) examines Kohut's case of Mr. Z as an example of the merger transference.

TWINSHIP TRANSFERENCE

Kohut (1984) described how he discovered the twinship transference. One of his patients had a fantasy of a genie in a bottle. This genie was experienced as a twin, an essential likeness of the patient to whom she could relate whenever she felt unsupported and alone. This patient also remembered a time when as a little girl, perhaps four years old, she had stood in the kitchen alongside her grandma, kneading dough (p. 196).

She remembered that at age six her cold and unresponsive parents had moved away from the grandparent, and, as a consequence, she had experienced terrible feelings of loneliness. She had replaced the self-validating experiences of the grandmother with a genie in a bottle to whom she talked. She did not accept Kohut's conclusion that he was the genie in the bottle in view of his just-announced long vacation plans. She claimed that the captive in the bottle was a twin, just like herself, and understood by her. The patient's need was for a silent presence; she would talk to the twin, but the twin did not have to respond to her. "Just being together with the twin in silent communion was often the most satisfactory state" (p. 196). Kohut then saw the significance of so many of the long silences that had occurred in the treatment: they were not resistances but a beneficial twinship experience the patient was ashamed of needing.

To Kohut, the twinship transference is the "third chance" for a cohesive nuclear self, because in it the experience of sameness or likeness serves the function of acquiring skills and "tools."

> Within the context of the transference, an outline will gradually come to light of a person for whom the patient's early existence and actions were a source of genuine joy; the significance of this person as a silent presence, as an alter ego or twin next to whom the child felt alive (the little girl doing chores in the kitchen next to her mother or grandmother; the little boy working in the basement next to his father or grandfather) will gradually become clear [p. 204].

White and Weiner (1986), extending the idea of twinship transference to twinship relationships (outside therapy), write: "The essence of the twinship selfobject relationship is similarity in interests and talents, along with the sense of being understood by someone like oneself" (p. 103). They cite the example of John, who had a twinship relationship with his writer grandfather. He felt accepted and sustained by his grandfather's warm response to his budding literary interests. John eventually became a successful editor. Culturally, twinship is referred to as a mentor or apprentice relationship. It carries with it the experience of doing something with another who is seen as basically the same as oneself.

While Kohut's experience of a twinship transference has been clinically validated by other therapists, twinship transference seldom, if ever, occurs unless accompanied by the other narcissistic transferences. Although Kohut raised it to the state of a separate transference in association with developing a tripartite concept of the self focused on ideals, ambitions and skills, the twinship transference has had a peripheral role in self psychology theory. Yet, by adding the twinship transference to the idealizing and mirror transferences, Kohut was, in effect, expanding his theory of motivation. No longer driven by Freud's biologically based *Trieb*, Kohut's self is motivated to act because of ideals, ambitions, and the need to develop competency in skills and talents.

As conceived by Kohut, the twinship transference represented a major piece of underdeveloped theory in self psychology. Yet the self psychology literature of the 80s reveals surprisingly little research or writing on the subject, except for two articles by Detrick (1985; 1986). The direction of self psychology during the 80s has been, unwittingly perhaps, toward an exploration of the archaic dimensions of the twinship transference. For example, investigations into the attunement involved in an early mother–infant bond lead to the idea of a mutual influence theory (see chapter 23, this volume). Without the "dance" that takes place between mother and child, growth and development are constricted. Such a mutual-influence experience, especially involving synchronicity, suggests that some form of primitive twinship is necessary from day one of an infant's life.

Brandchaft's (1988) psychotherapy with a case of intractable depression demonstrates that some difficult character disorder patients are able to change only after they have experienced the therapist as sharing their feelings in an archaic form of twinship. On the other hand, where psychotherapy has been based on hierarchical views of reality (Schwaber, 1983a), it has been cluttered with the wreckage of many failures.

Seen in the light of the post-Kohutian exploration of archaic twinship transferences, Ferenczi's work in the 1920s takes on new meaning. In his attempt at collaborative analysis (see chapter 6, this volume), Ferenczi can be viewed as offering some kind of twinship experience. Moreover, Winnicott's flexible, nonauthoritarian approach, and his willingness to enter into a twinship experience with his patients, made him both successful clinically and popular with his students.

Once the importance of a primitive twinship experience is accepted, the animal behavior that Lorenz (1966) observed can be reinterpreted as a form of twinship. By connecting the dance of the Greylag goose to drive theory, namely aggression, Lorenz interpreted the female's joining of her mate's dance of triumph as ritualized behavior to curb the male goose's aggression toward her. Once drive theory is rejected, the dance can be seen as an expression of a twinship bond in which the female goose imitates the male goose's behavior in a process similar to the infant's "reading" the mother's feelings from her facial muscles (see chapter 21, this volume). That is, when the infant imitates the mother's facial expression, his own facial muscles stimulate his autonomic nervous system and he thus feels what she is feeling. Clinical experience and the imprinting studies of Lorenz point to the conclusion that whatever the shape of self psychology in the future, it needs a greater understanding of the function of archaic twinship experiences.

Further, in view of the increasing realization of the pervasiveness of the archaic twinship experience, the issue of shared values and beliefs, (raised originally in chapter 2, this volume) can be understood in a new way. As Torrey (1972) notes, much of the efficacy of religious healing and the magical covenant rests on the powerful bond that comes from participating in a community of shared values. With the breakdown of such totemic systems (Lee, 1979) in an urban/industrial society, the ability to form transactional and personal relationships with those who do not share the same basic beliefs has become an adaptive necessity. The price paid for such an adaptation is the loss of common values as a major source of narcissistic cohesiveness.

Freud's free association, as a method to explore across the boundaries of values, solved one problem of the breakdown of shared values, but left unresolved the need for twinship affirmation that had formerly been taken care of through sibling relationships and membership in an extended family or tribal structure. The basic human need for twinship, that is, the experience of sameness, becomes exacerbated in a society that stresses autonomy and individualism. Self psychology's increasing emphasis on the twinship selfobject function arises from treating patients with neglected childhood needs that manifest themselves in the transference because of arrested development.

The more archaic the twinship transference, the more it approaches a merger transference (Kohut, 1984). In clinical practice, however, it is useful, even if somewhat artificial, to distinguish between the two. There is in the twinship experience a great deal of perceived concordance between the thoughts feelings and behaviors of the two partners, but there is not a complete, overlapping correspondence. In the merger transference, the one needing the merger experience expects a total and complete concordance, and any kind of difference or individuation not only is intolerable to the patient, but is experienced as wounding. Such merger transferences are much more archaic and difficult for the therapist to manage than is the twinship transference.

THE MERGER TRANSFERENCE

In 1971 Kohut conceived of both the twinship transference and the merger transference as subentities of the mirror transference. They were potential candidates for eventually being considered separate narcissistic transferences. By 1984, the twinship transference joined the idealizing and mirror transferences as a full narcissistic transference, but the merger transference did not. The idea of merger was broadened to a process that takes place in each of the three narcissistic transferences. Kohut (1984) then posited the self's shift from relying on archaic modes of nutrient to being sustained by empathic resonances from the selfobjects of adult life. This shift involves transformation of the mergers of the archaic dimension of all three narcissistic transferences, that is, "mergers with the mirroring selfobject, mergers with the idealized selfobject, and twinship mergers" (p. 70).

A merger experience, then, was at the beginning of a line of development for each of the narcissistic transferences, rather than at the starting point of a general narcissistic line of development through mirroring to idealizing and then to twinship. This means that a merger regression can occur any time a therapist loses empathic resonance during a narcissistic transference (idealizing, mirror, twinship). For example, if there is an empathic failure, it is not necessary for a regression to occur from an idealizing transference to a mirror transference and then, if empathic failure persists, to a merger transference. There is no longer the concept of a narcissistic line of regression with twinship at the mature end, idealizing and mirror in the middle, and merger at the archaic end. They are not conceived of as being on a continuum. The twinship, idealizing, and mirror transferences become different routes through which archaic selfobject merger experiences are transformed into mature selfobject needs.

Kohut's (1971) clearest definition of a merger transference is as the extension of the patient's grandiose self to include the therapist:

> In metapsychological terms, the relationship to the analyst is one of (primary) identity. From the sociological (or sociobiological) point of view we may call it a merger (or a symbiosis) if we keep in mind that it is not the merger with an idealized object (as striven for and temporarily established in the idealizing transference) but an experience of the grandiose self which first regressively diffuses its borders to include the analyst and then, after this expansion of its limits has been established, uses the security of this new comprehensive structure for the performance of certain therapeutic tasks [p. 114].

An example of the merger transference in literature comes from Eugene O'Neill's play *The Great God Brown*, "which portrays a lifelong struggle of a protagonist against fragmentation of the self. The cold unrelatedness of the father and the joyless pathological merger with the mother lead to a never-ending search for 'glue' to hold the self together" (Chessick, 1985, p. 135). Kohut (1977) remarked of this play, "nowhere in art have I encountered a more accurately pointed description of man's yearning to achieve the restoration of his self than that contained in three terse sentences

. . . 'Man is born broken. He lives by mending. The grace of God is glue'" (p. 287).

This idea of a merger transference as an extension of the grandiose self is useful in understanding what happens when a patient experiences a breakdown of the illusion of control over the therapist. Merger-hungry personalities need to control their therapists in an enactment of their need for structure. "Because they experience the other as their own self, they feel intolerant of his independence: they are very sensitive to separations from him and they demand—indeed they expect without question—the selfobject's continuous presence" (Kohut and Wolf, 1978, p. 422). Those with a merger transference are often very upset when a therapist is away on a vacation or has to cancel a session for some legitimate reason.

Another way to recognize a merger transference is by the sleepiness or boredom of the therapist. For example, one of the authors diagnosed a merger transference when he could hardly keep himself awake during the sixth session with a new patient. After a good night's sleep, he had no problem keeping alert in sessions with patients who preceded or followed that patient. That a merger transference existed was substantiated by the main topic of the session, which was that the patient's mother still clung pathologically to her, an only child in her mid 30s. The mother phoned every day, sometimes two or three times, and would be most upset if she could not talk with the patient. As Wolf (1983b) explains, feelings of boredom and a sleepy response may be "the consequences of a defensive withdrawal of the analyst's self from the engulfing propensities of the analysand's merger transference" (p. 322).

As noted, the key to understanding both the mirror transference and the merger transference is the grandiose state of the self. One difference between them is that in the merger transference the grandiose state of the self is more archaic, more engulfing, and more controlling of the therapist than in the mirror transference. Another is that the mirror and merger transferences represent two different ways of nourishing the self and keeping it cohered. In the mirror transference, a person uses the therapist's mirroring responses to experience an alive sense of self. In the merger transference, the person has abandoned hope of being mirrored and so uses a sense of being in control to achieve the same end.

Both transferences involve a risk of being wounded, but the mirror transference seems more dangerous to the patient because it depends on more overt cooperation and responsiveness from the therapist. "Objectively" the merger transference also needs the cooperation of the therapist, yet subjectively it is not experienced this way. Under the condition of an archaic grandiose state of the self, the person in a merger transference has the illusion of more control and less danger of being wounded than is actually so.

The issues previously conceived of as sadism and masochism are covered, partially at least, by Kohut's concept of the merger transference. In 1971, when Kohut was trying to conceptualize his new insights into narcissism within drive theory metapsychology, he referred to the "heightening of oral-sadistic and anal-sadistic drive elements" under the tyranny and possessiveness of the merger transference (p. 124). Sadism here means taking pleasure in inflicting pain or humiliation, whereas masochism takes pleasure from receiving pain or being humiliated.

By 1984, drive theory had been discarded, but not the merger transference. Also dropped from the lexicon of self psychology were the terms sadism and masochism. Such persons are now understood self-psychologically as merger-prone personalities. They maintain an important sense of self-coherence through a merger in which they subjectively experience control. In self psychology theory, the feeling of being in control replaces drive theory's feelings of pleasure in inflicting or receiving pain in a sadomasochistic dyad.

The "sadist" and the "masochist" experience control in different ways. The sadist seems to be the dominant person in any "sadomasochistic" merger relationship. As understood by self psychology, a narcissistic transference cannot be imposed; it is the subjective experience of the patient. Thus, when Kohut's notion of merger as the extension of the grandiose state of the self is applied, the issue of who is dominant or subservient, who is active or passive, becomes irrelevant. Such constructs, which come from social and interpersonal psychology, do not reflect underlying selfobject needs or experiences of the merger-prone person. The "sadomasochistic" relationship is seen in self psychology as a mutual merger relationship in which both persons extend their grandiose state to include the other, and both perceive themselves in control of the other, for different reasons.

The mutual merging explains the sticky enmeshment generally encountered in such a relationship. The "sadist's" experience of being in control is obvious. The "masochist's" more covert, subjective sense of control can be seen in an ability to get the "sadist" enraged any time it is necessary for the masochist to affirm the sense of being in control and hence feel cohesive. Kohut's theory also satisfactorily explains why both the "sadist" and "masochist" stay locked in such a mutual control arrangement; a subjective sense of control is necessary for maintaining a sense of self-cohesion in each of the participants in mutual merging.

The clinical observation of the frequent presence of pain in merger-prone persons is an accurate one. Further, it is easy to understand why the prevailing pre-Kohutian interpretation was that the sadist enjoyed inflicting pain and humiliation and that the masochist took pleasure from such pain and humiliation, since both persons so actively contribute to the pattern. While there seems to be a "payoff" for the pain and humiliation of a masochistic recipient, it is not in a pleasure but as a defense against fragmentation. Physical pain may be provoked when the fantasy of control is lost and fragmentation feared and when masochistically sought pain is needed to overcome the feelings of inner deadness. Pain under these circumstances is an example of the process of concretization. It is a concrete, external response to an inner experience of fragmentation.

Many patients develop an archaic merger transference in psychotherapy. The prime requirement of such a transference is that the therapist accept this merger and all the behaviors that accompany it that test out the patient's experience of being in control. As Chessick (1985) says,

> patients want us to respond as if we belong one hundred percent to them; a benign view of this desire, rather than an angry retort or harsh criticism, detoxifies patient's attitudes towards themselves and prevents withdrawal into arrogant grandiosity [p. 160].

For merger-prone persons enactments may serve a special function. When such patients act dramatically, they are usually asserting some form of control, even temporarily. Generally, such enactments are a response to the therapist, who in some way has made the patient feel helpless. Enactments, particularly dangerous acting out, such as persistently driving a car while blind drunk, may be to reinforce a conviction of omnipotence and grandiosity.

During a merger transference, a gross identification with the therapist may take place in which the patient tries to be an absolute replica of the therapist. Such a gross identification is a quick way to gain a sense of control by magically and instantly gaining the power and skill of the therapist. The difficulty of such a solution is that this form of identification is not internalized and hence does not last. It is a good sign, however, when a patient shows interest in understanding what is happening. The quest for such understanding and the demand for explanation is the search for the type of control that promotes growth and not regression.

Most persons who seek psychotherapy while needing a merger transference do so because they have recently been traumatized by the loss of control of some important relationship. One male patient, an executive who managed many employees, presented for treatment full of rage. His wife of 18 years had asked him for a divorce and demanded that he leave the house immediately. Initially he sought the therapist's help to regain control of his wife. When the therapist indicated that this was beyond his power, the patient developed an intense merger transference that enabled him to tolerate the divorce proceedings.

Another patient sought psychotherapy when she determined to break off an enmeshed, 12-year courtship that "was going nowhere and would never develop further." The merger transference enabled her to terminate with the boyfriend without experiencing symptoms of fragmentation. She was then able to develop a new courting relationship that eventually resulted in a happy marriage.

At a minimum, merger cases such as these involve a transitional merger transference with the therapist, which allows time for a new merger experience to develop socially after an old, crucial, self-cohering merger experience has been lost or is about to be lost. Merger transference cases can achieve more than this.

Once a merger transference develops, although the initial intent of the patient was to use the therapist as a transitional source of glue, the transference may grow beyond the need for merger. A major reason persons become locked into a permanent merger/enmeshment is that their need for control is not accepted by a significant selfobject. Under conditions of nonacceptance, even though they may experience being in control, merger-prone persons' sense of control is precarious. They can never relax their vigilance to celebrate the power they have achieved. On the other hand, once secure in their sense of control, merger-prone people naturally seek recognition and celebration, that is, mirroring, for the significant achievement they experience gaining control to be. It is the therapist's calm, consistent acceptance of the patient's experience of control, over a significant period of time, that leads to the emergence of a mirror transference or one of the other narcissistic transferences and the potential to transform the grandiose state of the self.

Kohut's (1979) case of Mr. Z is reported in the literature as a case of a mirror transference. However, it more accurately illustrates the treatment of the merger transference.

The Case of Mr. Z

Mr. Z's analysis took place in two installments, each conducted five times a week and lasting about four years and separated by an interval of five and one half years. During the first installment, Kohut interpreted the material from a classical analytic position. During the second installment, which began while he was writing his "Forms and Transformations of Narcissism" (1966) and ended while he was immersed in writing *The Analysis of Self* (1971), he viewed the patient's material differently, from a self psychology perspective.

When Mr. Z began treatment, he was a graduate student in his mid-20s. His father had died four years before, and he lived with his widowed mother. A few months before Mr. Z consulted with Kohut, an unmarried friend with whom he had been close since high school formed a relationship with an older woman. This friend not only excluded the patient from the relationship with this woman, he also became less interested in seeing Mr. Z.

Mr. Z's masturbation fantasies were masochistic. In these he performed menial tasks submissively for a domineering woman. He always reached sexual climax after imagining being forced into the sexual act by a woman who was strong, demanding, and insatiable. At the moment of ejaculation he typically experienced a feeling of desperately straining to perform in accordance with the woman's commands, similar, as he explained, to a horse that is made to pull a load that is too heavy for its powers and that is driven on by the coachman's whip to give its last ounce of strength, or similar to galley slaves whipped on by their overseer during a sea battle.

The theme most conspicuous during the first year of analysis was a regressive mother transference. Kohut saw this transference as unrealistic, deluded by grandiosity, and full of demands that the psychoanalytic situation should reinstate the position of exclusive control where Mr. Z was admired and catered to by a doting mother. When Kohut interpreted the absence of sibling and oedipal rivalries, these evoked intense rage in the patient. The rages became worse when Kohut interpreted Mr. Z's narcissistic demands and his arrogant feelings of entitlement. They also increased with weekend interruptions, occasional irregularities in the schedule, and especially during the therapist's vacations.

In the childhood fantasies that Mr. Z reported, he imagined himself a slave, being bought and sold, like cattle, by women for the use of women. He was an object that had no initiative, no will of its own. He was ordered about, treated with great strictness, had to clean up his mistress' excrement and urine. In one often repeated fantasy, a woman urinated into his mouth, forcing him to serve her as an inanimate vessel, as a toilet bowl.

As a result of the first installment of analysis, Mr. Z's masochistic preoccupations disappeared gradually until they were almost nonexistent at the end. He moved out of his mother's house to an apartment on his own, and he began to date and become sexually active with several girlfriends. During the second analysis, Kohut saw these behavioral changes of the first analysis as evidence of a transference cure in which Mr. Z conformed to what he thought would please Kohut, and hence, this first analysis had been a reinforcement of a false self.

The second installment began with an idealizing transference, manifested in a dream in which a male figure is portrayed as having an impressive appearance and a proud bearing. The patient was proud of Kohut. This initial phase of idealization was of a short duration, however. It was replaced by a merger transference in which the patient became self-centered and demanding, insisted on perfect empathy, and was inclined to react with rage at the slightest lack of attunement with his psychological states or at the slightest misunderstanding of his communications. During this second analysis, Kohut no longer saw Mr. Z as resisting change or opposing maturation because he did not want to relinquish childhood gratifications. Instead, he saw Mr. Z as desperately struggling to disentangle himself from the noxious selfobject relationship with his mother.

The description of Mr. Z's relationship to his mother filled many hours of the second installment of his analysis. In the first installment, Mr. Z had presented a defensively idealized version of his mother. This time, she was depicted as a person with intense, unshakable convictions that translated into attitudes and actions that emotionally enslaved those around her and stifled their independent existence. She had enjoyed Mr. Z and mirrored him, but only if he submitted to total domination by her and did not have significant relationships with others. Mr. Z's mother was pathologically jealous; father, son, servants were all strictly dominated by her.

The second installment of Mr. Z's analysis saw a gradual recognition of just how pathological a relationship his mother had had with him during childhood. This awakening seems to have been spurred on by his mother's psychosis a few months prior to his seeking the second treatment. He feared that it was his leaving home that had disrupted his mother's merger with him and had, therefore, precipitated the psychotic breakdown. He also felt a threat of self-fragmentation because his mother's illness had brought about a loss not only of her archaic merger with him, but of his merger with her.

The mother's pathology showed up in three areas; her interest in his feces, her involvement with his possessions, and her preoccupation with small blemishes in his skin. These behaviors reflected an ineradicable and unmodifiable need to retain her son as a permanent selfobject. For example, she had insisted on inspecting each of Mr. Z's bowel movements until he was six. When she abruptly ceased these inspections, she simultaneously became preoccupied with his skin, particularly the skin on his face. Mr. Z experienced his mother as not being interested in him personally. She approached her inspections of him with a self-righteous certainty that allowed no protest and created almost total submission. She also was passionately involved with collecting furniture, art objects, and bric-a-brac. This obsessional behavior covered over a feeling of internal emptiness and the tight control of a merger transference, which she needed to shore up her fragmentation-prone self.

The second treatment consisted of diminishing the merger-enmeshment relationship of Mr. Z with his mother. During this period, he discovered that to be separate from his mother was neither evil nor dangerous but the appropriate assertion of health. He also became aware of long-disavowed yearnings for a relationship with an idealized father. As he became aware of this need, he also discovered a pride in his father and a source of masculine strength. Without any merger propensity, he could acknowledge that despite his mother's obvious pathology, she had given him a great deal. His masochistic compliance was replaced by the joyful activities of an independent self.

The case of Mr. Z not only exemplifies a merger transference, it also raises the issue of defensive idealization. Mr. Z's idealization of his noxious, merger-prone mother was clearly defensive. This defensiveness, however, was not a reaction-formed aggressive drive. It functioned to protect the cohesive function the mother-merger provided to the self. Any attack by the therapist on the idealization of the mother in the name of individuation is a therapeutic blunder, which only provokes the patient to defend the idealized person as a way of preserving the merger function that is vital to self-cohesion. Further, the strength of the defensive idealization measures the archaic quality of the merger. Hence, a clue to Mr. Z's growth out of the merger with his mother was a decline in the idealization of her.

Persons who present with merger transference needs are not always casualties from a broken mutual-merger relationship. Sometimes they seek help because of a regression after a severe wound to the grandiose state of the self. Such wounding occurs with an unexpected blocking of grandiose aspirations. Not only does this blocking produce narcissistic rage, it also creates a yearning for merger. When these efforts to merge are frustrated by a person's friends, resulting fragmentation symptoms encourage the seeking of professional therapeutic help.

The merger transference may be a more important clinical experience to understand than are the other narcissistic transferences (idealizing, mirror, twinship); Kohut, in fact, made the merger transference the archaic beginning of all the narcissistic transferences. Moreover, the merger transference takes us beyond narcissism, as defined by Kohut, into the borderline and severe personality disorders and into psychosis itself. The archaic merger transference emerges, then, as a transitional experience and as a potential gateway through which more disturbed patients can grow into more functional narcissistic disorders and eventually even into mature adaptive functioning.

The four transferences explored in this and the two preceding chapters are conceived of as functions that maintain, restore, or transform the self. Generalized, these narcissistic functions are called *selfobject experiences*. In the next chapter we shall explore the concept of a selfobject experience, one of Kohut's major contributions to self psychology.

Readings for Chapter 16: Kohut, 1971, chapter 4; Grotstein, 1983; Atwood and Stolorow, 1984, chapters 2 and 3.

Self-object experience = transference

transference may serve as
a self-object experience.

14

Selfobject Experiences

Kohut (Kohut and Wolf, 1978) defined selfobjects as follows:

> *Selfobjects* are objects which we experience as part of our self; the expected control over them is, therefore, closer to the concept of the control which a grownup expects to have over his own body and mind than to the concept of the control which he expects to have over others [p. 414].

With this definition, Kohut appears to build on the idea of object hunger first expressed by Fairbairn (1944) and elaborated by Guntrip (1969).

Fairbairn said that the ego needed object relationships. He saw "multiple egos (by which he meant selves) in intimate union with repressed objects" (cited in Grotstein, 1983, p. 186). Kohut, moving beyond the language of structural theory, saw the self as needing not just objects, but selfobjects. These selfobjects are seen as less differentiated than objects and more essential for the functioning of the self. Kohut realized that the self, to remain adaptive and cohesive, always needed selfobjects.

Grotstein's claim (1983) that "the subject of selfobjects has a long history" (p. 186) alerts us to the fact that Kohut's idea was not entirely original. Not only did Klein and Fairbairn have a similar idea, but Freud's concept of secondary identification was close to it. Terman (1980) also points out that "there is a great similarity between the experience which they [Balints] describe as primary love and Kohut's description of a selfobject relationship" (p. 354). Further, Boyer and Giovacchini (1967) came close to the idea of a selfobject by acknowledging the analyst's function as an "adjunctive ego" or "alter ego" in borderline and schizophrenic cases.

Notwithstanding that Kohut's idea of a selfobject was foreshadowed, no one else placed the construct at the center of a theory of psychotherapy. Nor did anyone give it the specificity, with clinical examples of idealizing, mirroring, twinship and merger that Kohut did. Further, the ideas of others never led to sweeping changes in the theory and practice of psychotherapy or to the prospects of even further change, that Kohut's emphasis on the selfobject achieved.

Kohut's interest in the selfobject needs evident in the narcissistic transferences eventually culminated in *The Analysis of the Self* (1971), in which he said, "The subject matter . . . is the study of certain transference or transferencelike phenomena in the psychoanalysis of narcissistic personalities, and the analyst's reaction to them" (p. 1). Kohut's clinical experience with patients who had idealizing or mirroring transferences led him to see, initially, that there are two kinds of selfobjects:

> those who respond to and confirm the child's innate sense of vigor, greatness, and perfection [i.e., mirroring]; and those to whom the child can look up and with whom he can merge as an image of calmness, infallibility, and omnipotence [i.e., idealizing] [Kohut and Wolf, 1978, p. 414].

To these selfobjects he added twinship in 1984. Kohut had arrived at the concept of the selfobject by generalizing that each narcissistic transference reflected a different kind of selfobject need.

With the evolution of the concept of selfobject from the narcissistic transferences, the idea of a "line of development" was retained. Each of the narcissistic transferences was conceived as developing from archaic to mature forms. Similarly, then, selfobjects can take archaic or mature forms. It is the mature forms that are considered to be necessary in order for the self to function in healthy and adaptive ways. Hence, as adults, we develop empathic matrices, with others functioning as mature selfobjects of idealization, mirroring, or twinship or as a combination of them.

Understandably, the idea of a selfobject led to some immediate theoretical difficulties. These resulted from the selfobject being conceived either as an object with substance, a reified "thing," or as a whole person. Neither view accurately portrays Kohut's selfobject. To avoid viewing a selfobject as if it were a billiard ball of Newtonian atomic theory, Kohut and other self psychology theorists emphasized the selfobject as a function. This stress on selfobject function also clearly indicates that the infant is not responding to parents as objects, but to the mirroring or idealizing supplied by the parent or surrogate. As Stolorow (1986b) says, "'Selfobject' does not refer to an environmental entity or caregiving agent. Rather, it designates a class of psychological *functions* pertaining to the maintenance, restoration, and transformation of self experience" (p. 274).

Elucidating further, Kohut saw that allowing the whole therapist to be perceived as a selfobject encourages therapeutic failure. It fosters an archaic identification with the therapist and a therapeutic regression in which a massive emotional surrender takes place. Such a surrender by a patient, defensive in nature, actually prevents experiencing the selfobject functions that foster growth and vitality.

The evolution of the concept of selfobject did not stop with selfobject functions. Far from it. For while the emphasis on function avoided the dangers of objectification, it opened the door to another major problem. It placed too much responsibility in the hands of the therapist and encouraged an active search for the correct selfobject function to bring about a therapeutic effect on the patient. Hence, the concept of selfobject function can be wrongly used to justify a thinly disguised intrusive therapy and an overeager attempt by the therapist to bring about a "corrective emotional experience."

To counter the problems engendered by the idea of selfobject functions, the stress in self psychology soon moved from selfobject functions toward the concept of a selfobject experience. As Lichtenberg (1988) expresses it, "the overarching concept that conveys the mutual relationship of self-regulation and regulation between self and environment is of a 'selfobject experience'" (p. 61). Rotenberg (1988) also indicates that "we use the term 'selfobject' to refer to an object *experienced subjectively* as serving selfobject functions" (p. 197).

With the concept of selfobject experience, it becomes clear that parenting and psychotherapy are a lot more than technique. It is not what the parent does or says that counts, but how the infant experiences what the parent says or does, or does not say or do, that determines if the infant's selfobject needs are met. This means that a parent or therapist has to listen carefully for communications from the infant or patient and make adjustments accordingly. One therapist's attempt at mirroring by the use of praise and affirmation may be experienced by a patient as meaningless; another therapist's casual comment may be felt by the patient as deeply satisfying.

Atwood and Stolorow (1984) describe a serendipitous casual comment that helped alleviate a patient's paranoid transference psychosis which had persisted for weeks.

> The patient inquired about a day hospital program with which he knew the analyst was familiar. The therapist responded spontaneously and non analytically, saying that he felt that the patient was "too together" for this particular program. The patient became utterly elated and revealed that he experienced the analyst's comments as an unexpected vote of confidence, a longed for expression of approval [p. 58].

They go on to report that the patient's improvement was sustained by the analyst's growing ability to make use of Kohut's understanding of archaic narcissism. Ultimately, only a pattern of mutual responsiveness guides the therapy and assures that a therapist will be experienced as the needed selfobject function.

By placing the idea of selfobject experiences at the center of his thought, Kohut was, in effect, refining the concept of empathy. Empathy, to him, still remained vicarious introspection, but the goal of empathy became understanding the selfobject experiences for which the patient hungered. As self psychology has evolved, empathy is no longer "the central shibboleth" as Curtis (1986, p. 9) claims. Thus, it is possible for a therapist to be unempathic in many areas of a patient's life, but empathic about selfobject needs and hence enable significant therapeutic change. It is also possible for a therapist to be empathic about many facets of a patient's life, yet not understand the patient's disavowed selfobject needs, and hence foster therapeutic stagnation and failure. The importance of making selfobject needs the empathic focus is reflected in the following case illustration.

Case Illustration

A patient who eventually manifested a deep hunger for mirroring during psychotherapy could not understand this need because he had experienced both his parents as affirming, mirroring persons. The therapist, however, suggested that the mirroring function had been defective in some way, even though the nature of this defect was not obvious. Progress toward understanding the defect eventually occurred after several empathic failures. These were detected through a pattern of behavior where the patient would be late and then have nothing to report. Exploration of the session that preceded one of these unproductive sessions revealed that the patient had not experienced the therapist as excited by the material presented, material the patient felt was original.

The therapist had missed the importance of the patient's insights because they were not particularly new or fresh to him. He had slipped out of the empathic mode and made an "objective" evaluation of the originality of these insights. When the therapist asked the patient what was new about the insight, the patient experienced the therapist as belittling his subjective discovery and felt wounded. This wounding led to an impasse for the rest of the session that was resolved next session when the therapist, by exploring the nature of his empathic failure in response to the lateness/lack of association clues, realized that for the client, the shared insight had been experienced as a creative thought. The client had presented his discovery to the therapist in the hope of receiving a joyful mirroring response.

After the therapist took responsibility for the impasse, indicating his realization that the patient had sought joyous affirmation, not an objective evaluation, for his self-discovery the patient was able to recall many incidents when his mother had insufficiently recognized his creative efforts. She mirrored the obvious achievements of getting a good report card, or his performance in the school play, but such mirroring took place around her expectations, not the original discoveries of her child. Hence, the patient experienced mirroring as reinforcement of patterns of expected behavior in the service of conformity, not personal growth. Such parental mirroring fostered a false self and a walled-off, hungry part of the core self.

Once Kohut had defined the concept of selfobject experience by using the three narcissistic transferences of mirroring, idealizing and twinship as examples and accepted it as central to self psychology theory, ideas for other selfobject functions emerged. For example, Wolf (1988) lists adversary, merger, and efficacy selfobject needs, in addition to the needs of mirroring, idealizing, and alterego (twinship). Discovering additional selfobject functions was encouraged by Kohut (1983): "This task of arriving at an optimum number of explanatory clusters of specific selfobject failures with their respective self pathologies still lies largely ahead of us" (p. 402).

Marian Tolpin (1986), in response to Kohut's challenge, takes a developmental point of view. She believes that "there are phase-appropriate selfobjects at all subsequent stages of life" (p. 120, n.2). Lichtenberg (1988) concurs. He sees that "for each of the five motivational systems at each period of life [physiological, attachment, assertion, aversive and sensual], there are specific needs and that when these needs are met the result is a selfobject experience" (p. 61).

In stressing developmental stages, Tolpin (1986) indirectly challenged the idea that each of the three narcissistic selfobject functions develops from the archaic to the mature. To her, "the term 'archaic,' used developmentally, is a misnomer," carrying pejorative overtones. She sees "simply phase appropriate selfobjects of infancy" (p. 120).

Following Tolpin's reasoning, we take the position that selfobjects can be grossly categorized as prenarcissistic and narcissistic. Tolpin's (1971) selfobject experience of infantile soothing can be considered an example of a prenarcissistic selfobject function. Encouraged by Kohut, Tolpin wrote about an overstimulated infant's need for soothing selfobject experiences. She saw this in the way mothers sooth infants overcome by stranger anxiety or when infants use what Winnicott (1951) called a transitional object—a favorite blanket or teddy bear—to soothe themselves. Tolpin suggests that selfobject experiences are broader than those associated with narcissistic disorders, even though many self psychologists see soothing needs as a manifestation of mirroring or idealizing selfobject experiences.

When idealizing, mirroring, or twinship selfobject needs emerge during intensive psychotherapy, they support a diagnosis of a narcissistic personality. But what is the diagnosis of a person who presents full of rage? If the patient calms down in a few sessions in response to the therapist's attempt to understand the source of the wound, the need for narcissistic selfobjects often emerges. If the rage is prolonged, or eventually deepens, however, a transference is being sought that is akin to one manifested by a borderline personality, where soothing is a major selfobject need. Gedo (1979) too sees soothing as a selfobject function separate from Kohut's three narcissistic functions when he talks about pacification. In addition, he sees unification and optimal disillusionment as other needed functions for a therapist working with character disorders.

Grotstein (1983), conceptualizing prenarcissistic selfobjects, uses the idea of a "background selfobject of primary identification" (p. 187). He elaborates:

> There is a considerable difference phenomenologically between background objects and interpersonal objects which are impressed into service as selfobjects. The concept of selfobject, I strongly maintain, transcends far more than just simply the mother or father. It includes tradition, heredity, the mother country, the neighborhood, etc. [p. 185].

The idea of a selfobject is reflected in the use of the possessive pronoun "our" when a person talks about "our flag," "our village," "our church"; he or she may be referring to important background selfobjects.

Background selfobject → safety

After making this distinction between a background selfobject and a narcissistic selfobject as Kohut conceived it, Grotstein suggests its major function. The background selfobject promotes in an infant

> a sense of *being* and *safety*, to be followed later by the achievement of self-affirmation. It corresponds to Winnicott's (1963) concept of the environmental mother, Sandler's (1960) concept of the background of safety, and Freud's (1909) concept of idealized parents of family romance [p. 187].

Such a view of the background selfobject is in contrast to the narcissistic selfobject experiences that vitalize a depleted self and decrease the risk of implosive collapses that are experienced as fragmentation.

Grotstein's background selfobject concept may be a useful way to conceive of many prenarcissistic selfobject functions that surface in the literature. Marian Tolpin (1986) for example, talks about a carrying selfobject function with early infants (p. 118). Maybe the functions of carrying, holding (Winnicott, 1960), soothing (Tolpin, 1971), feeding, and the other functions of what Winnicott (1966) refers to as "good-enough" mothering, are all background selfobjects fostering a sense of safety. These background selfobjects are gradually expanded to include mother earth, mother country, and mother church. Perhaps, too, Winnicott's (1951) idea of a transitional object can be considered as an example of a selfobject experience that contains aspects of both background selfobjects and narcissistic selfobjects.

The concept of background selfobject raises the question of the major needs of an infant in the prenarcissistic period. The narcissistic stage presupposes that a self has formed, however fragile or inadequate, and that selfobject functions are now necessary to vitalize, maintain, or expand it. On the other hand, in the prenarcissistic stage of development, the task of self-formation, using an imprinting-like process partly genetically triggered, needed invariant background selfobjects. Through such a process, and by establishing a bond with background selfobjects, four crucial elements of the core self are able to emerge. These are a sense of agency, of coherence, of affectivity and of history (continuity) (Stern, 1985). These experiences of the core self, partially illusory in nature, are given a certainty and absoluteness by the security afforded by the presence of background selfobjects and a person's attachment to these.

The exploration of prenarcissistic selfobject functions was one way of expanding the concept of the selfobject. Another way was to investigate the nature of the "interaction between the self and selfobject" (Wolf, 1980a, p. 119). Conceptually, this interaction came to be expressed as the "self–selfobject unit" (M. Tolpin, 1983, p. 375) or the "self–selfobject experience" (P. Tolpin, 1983b, p. 262). Referring to this interaction as a self–selfobject relationship, Goldberg (1980a) writes: "The self becomes the idea one has of one's relationships with others, with those who continue to sustain and support and satisfy" (p. 5). Basch (1986), however, stresses "self–selfobject experience, not selfobject relations or relationships to indicate that we are dealing with endopsychic processes" (p. 27).

Once the idea of a self–selfobject unit is accepted, a dyadic relationship between two persons is no longer seen as between two "objects." It is now conceived as being between two self–selfobject units. Following this line of thought, a therapeutic relationship can be described by the cumbersome expression "the self–selfobject/self–selfobject relationship." This relationship suggests that not only may the therapist serve as a selfobject experience for the patient, the patient may serve as a selfobject experience for the therapist—but, one hopes, not excessively.

One solution to such a cumbersome description may be to use Atwood and Stolorow's (1984) concept of the "intersubjective field":

> The conceptualization of an intersubjective field is, in part, an attempt to lift the selfobject concept to a higher, more inclusive level of generality. It is our view that the selfobject concept needs to be significantly broadened in order to describe adequately the specific unfolding developmental needs of a particular child and how these are assimilated by the psychological world of each caretaker [p. 68].
>
> We are contending that *every* phase in a child's development is best conceptualized in terms of the unique, continuously changing psychological field constituted by the intersection of the child's evolving subjective universe with those of caretakers [p. 69].

Intersecting Universes

Atwood and Stolorow's idea of the "intersubjective field," which evolved from their psychobiological studies on the theoretical systems of Freud, Jung, Reich, and Rank (Stolorow and Atwood, 1979), is similar to the position of Schwaber (1980), who wrote:

> Bringing together as it does the self and the object, the selfobject concept suggests a system—something I have called a "contextual unit"—between patient and analyst (Schwaber, 1979). It is therefore not to be viewed as a construct pertaining exclusively to failures of differentiation between self and object or to a failed recognition of the autonomy of each, but more fundamentally as one which recognizes the immediacy of the surround as intrinsic to the organization and perception of intrapsychic experience [p. 215].

Stolorow and his colleagues' use of the broader concept of the intersubjective field supplemented rather than supplanted the idea of a selfobject function. Curtis (1986), in his criticism of the selfobject construct, asserts that the term has been used too broadly. Stolorow (1986a) agrees that this has sometimes been so. He sees integration of affects (see chapter 21, this volume) as a criterion for a selfobject function. The implication is that if such an integration is not fostered, the claim of a selfobject function is not appropriate. Another criterion applicable to a selfobject function is whether it appears as a manifestation of transference. Anyone can spin off theoretical labels for functions, but to be clinically useful, a selfobject construct has to emerge in a transference consistently and with a certain type of patient once a therapeutic bond develops. Even so, Stolorow's more universal notion of an intersubjective context may help stem the conceptual litter of a plethora of newly manufactured selfobject constructs.

Stolorow (1986b) is also careful to view the selfobject experience from a broader perspective. For example, he makes it clear that the selfobject dimension is only one part of a relationship: "A multiplicity of dimensions co-exist in any complex object relationship, with certain meanings and functions occupying the experiential foreground and others occupying the background, depending on the subject's motivational priorities at any given moment" (p.

275). Such a broad view allows for the possibility of background selfobjects and objects as other dimensions of experience.

As we end this chapter, we note that all the preceding discussion of the selfobject experience would be irrelevant if it were not for the idea of a self, the central metapsychological assumption of Kohut's work. The self, as Kohut conceived it, is not a static thing, a reified entity. It is a complex system. In the next chapter we shall explore the complex issues involved in the idea of a self system.

Readings for Chapter 15: Kohut, 1977, chapter 4; Chessick, 1980a; Stern, 1985, chapters 3-8.

Parts of a person serve as a selfobject.
Whole self is too complex.

15

The Self System

In self psychology the concept of the self replaces Descartes's "mythological and inexplicable" (Basch, 1988a, p. 100) concept of the mind as a machine. It also discards Freud's version of the mind as a mental apparatus with structures (id, ego, superego) and defense mechanisms. And the self's eventual central position in self psychology goes well beyond Hartmann's concept of a self-representation as a complement to object representations, although initially Kohut (1971) saw the self as an agency of the mind. In its final form, Kohut's concept of the self as a supraordinate agency, an independent center of initiative, is "without doubt the most problematic one in the theory of self psychology" (Stolorow et al., 1987, p. 17).

We begin with the belief that Freud's drive metapsychology is so inadequate (see chapter 5, this volume) and his concept of the mind has been so heavily associated with mechanistic and deterministic ideas (see chapter 4, this volume) that they are best discarded as unsalvageable. This chapter replaces the idea of a mind with the concept of a self and then shifts from the idea of a self as an entity to that of a self-system. It explores the following: (a) Kant's view, (b) Kohut's concept, (c) Stern's invariants, (d) nuclear self, and (e) organization of experience.

KANT'S VIEW

The decision to replace the idea of a mind with the concept of a self is not new to self psychology. It was made by Kant in response to the problem of the mechanical mind posed by Descartes and to the issue of the mind as *tabula rasa*, the passive register of empirical experience, raised by Locke and Hume. Kant's initial solution was to conceive of the mind as the "phenomenal self," which is actively and constantly involved with "empirical apperception" and a succession of mental states across time. With Kant's phenomenal self "there is no permanent or abiding 'self'" (Chessick, 1980a, p. 458).

Kant himself was not satisfied with the phenomenal self as a solution to the mind problem. Eventually he postulated an enduring self behind the knowable phenomenal self. There is "an antecedent, unknowable, permanent, on-going 'I' [that] lies behind our experienced activity of the mind" (Chessick, 1980b, p. 458). Kant claimed that because of this cohesive sense of a continuous self, the noumenal self, one is able to discern self-boundaries, hence the external world, and thus the experiences coming from the external world that are perceived by the phenomenal self.

Kant did not posit the noumenal self as an expansion of the phenomenal self; on the contrary, the phenomenal self is an expression of the noumenal self. To Kant, this noumenal, generating-of-experience self is directly unknowable. All that can be said about it is that it exists. It is only derivatively knowable through the phenomenal self. This unknowable noumenal self is the noumenal self in a negative sense.

In his later work, Kant, going against his earlier position of the noumenal self being unknowable, moved beyond the negative noumenal self. He moved to the noumenal self in the positive sense and suggested that we proceed as if the self were a simple concrete entity endowed with personal identity. At the same time, he believed that there remained an unknowable core that profoundly influenced the conscious flow of inner and outer experiences.

KOHUT'S CONCEPT

Chessick (1980a) sees a remarkable similarity between the way the concept of self developed in Kant and in Kohut. Kohut began with a phenomenal self knowable not through empirical data but through the data of empathy, vicarious introspection. Yet, by 1977 Kohut had moved toward a noumenal kind of self as a generalization derived from data. He, like Kant, saw the need for the concept of the noumenal self in the positive sense, that is, as a self that is depleted or empty, or yearning for mirroring or merger. In a fashion similar to Kant's, Kohut's self is an "as if" concept using anthropomorphic language.

When critics accuse Kohut of anthropomorphizing, he and his colleague Wolf (Kohut and Wolf, 1978, pp. 415-416, n1) plead "guilty," indicating that they use such language for evocativeness and conciseness. Unapologetically, Kohut (1977) conceived of the self as a supraordinate concept, that is, one beyond knowing empirically, a configuration transcending the sum of its parts, which has cohesiveness in space and continuity in time (p. 177). As an independent center of initiative, Kohut's self is a central metapsychological concept. In support of Kohut's concept, Goldberg (1980a) argues that any science must be granted the use of some metaphors and hypothetical constructs (p. 7). Wolf (1988) more adamantly states:

> To infer the existence of a psychological structure, the self, as part of a presumed psychological system is roughly on the same theoretical level as the inference, from all kinds of observations, of the existence of electrons as part of a presumed system of electromagnetic phenomena [p. 23, n.1].

Tolpin (1980) reminds us that Kohut's stress on the concept of the self is more than a philosophical leap into an unsubstantiated metaphysical supraordinate world. It is an illusion created in the infant through parenting; when the illusion is not created, the infant experiences severe disturbances. She sees the importance of Kohut's "discovery of the psychic reality of a selfobject environment which normally acts almost automatically to preserve and promote the child's automatic illusion ("delusion") of independence and his nuclear initiative" (pp. 63-64). Stern (1985), making a similar point, notes that parents treat infants as the people they are about to become and thereby participate in creating the illusion in the infant of being an agent-self. As examples, parents impute intention when they say to the infant, "Oh, you want to see that." A mother sees motive when she says, "You're doing that so mommy will hurry up with the bottle." And parents see authorship when they say, "You threw that away on purpose, huh?"

When Heinz Kohut conceived of the self as an agent, he had another alternative to Freud's concept of instinctual drives and based his idea of the self

> on the Zeigarnik phenomenon which postulates some kind of inner motivation of undeveloped structures to resume their development when given an opportunity; the energy behind this motivation has nothing to do with Freud's instinctual drives, and the origin of it is not explained [Chessick, 1980b, p. 470].

Kohut saw in the development of selfobject transferences an opportunity for this Zeigarnik phenomenon to occur.

Kohut appears to have been as entranced by the explanatory power of the self as Freud was with the Oedipus complex. Even so, by seeing the self as agent, Kohut was able to address problems of faith, free will, and morality. To Kohut, psychotherapy alleviates the tragedy of man's suffocating in an increasingly inhuman environment that he himself continues to create.

At first Kohut (1971) saw the self as another structure of the mind, existing alongside the id, ego, and superego and similar to a self-representation:

> The self, however, emerges in the psychoanalytic situation and is conceptualized, in the mode of a comparatively low level, i.e., comparatively experience-near, psychoanalytic abstraction, as a content of the mental apparatus. While it is thus not an agency of the mind, it is a structure within the mind since (a) it is cathected

> with instinctual energy and (b) it has continuity in time, i.e., it is enduring [p. xv].

By 1977, however, Kohut had clearly moved beyond that position to a supraordinate view of the self.

Kohut used the supraordinate concept of the self as a replacement for Freud's structural theory (id, ego, and superego). In so doing, he raised the question of how the self was formed. Kohut's (1971) self did not evolve as a coalescence of parts (p. 97), but was present from the beginning in a rudimentary form. This idea, which blossomed into the supraordinate self (Kohut, 1977, p. 177), follows the position outlined by Fairbairn (1944) and is now supported by Stern's (1975) observational evidence of day-old infants. To Kohut, the embryonic self is not a result of development; it is innate. What happens during development into an adult is a change in organization from an extremely rudimentary self to a complex one.

Tolpin (1986), expressing a similar point of view, writes:

> From the beginning of life, the self is an amalgam of "givens" and "experience," and its vitality and intactness correspond to the degree to which these two dimensions of selfhood complement one another in growth-promoting ways [p. 115].

By experience Tolpin here means "experience of parental selfobject functions."

STERN'S INVARIANTS

Stern's (1985) studies of infants a few days old made him aware that they were born with a capacity to distinguish the invariants from the variants in their "surround." He concluded that "an invariant pattern of awareness is a form of organization. It is the organizing subjective experience of whatever it is that will later be verbally referenced as the 'self'" (p. 7).

Stern sees the self as emerging as a more complex entity through what he calls "domains of relatedness" rather than phases or stages. By avoiding the concept of stages, he is being careful not to reflect a mechanistic, deterministic drive theory. These domains

0-2mo emergent self 15-36mo verbal self
2-8mo core self
8-15 mo Subjective self 36→ narrative self
mo
The Self System 183

are the emergent self from birth to two months; the core self during the two-month to eight-month period; the subjective self from the eight-month to fifteen month period; the verbal self from fifteen months to about thirty-six months; and then the narrative self.

We shall not discuss in detail here these five domains of relatedness. However, the idea of a core self as conceived by Stern merits discussion because of its association to Kohut's nuclear self. These two concepts, core self and nuclear self, may sound interchangeable, but they are "shorthand" for different processes. According to Stern, the differentiation of the infant from the mother occurs during the period between two and seven months, not later, as classical analysts and Mahler believe. A core self experience and an experience of being separated from others are two facets of the same process. Merger experiences (see chapter 13, this volume) are secondary to and dependent on an already existing sense of self and other. Major invariants of the core self are (1) self as agency (control), (2) self as coherence, (3) self as affectivity, and (4) self as history (memory).

Self as Agency

Kohut — nuclear self
Stern — core self

Volition may be the most fundamental area in which an infant gains a sense of agency, especially with motor control. Movements of the voluntary muscles are preceded by an elaborate motor plan of which we are unaware. They make our actions as though they belong to us, for example, when the hand goes to the mouth, in gazing, and in sucking. Evidence of a motor plan comes from the fact that small-sized and large-sized signatures are written by different muscles, yet they are exact replicas.

Self as Coherence

Coherence is experienced when sound and sight come from the same place. There is coherence of motion, when, for example, the mother is seen moving against a stationary backdrop "because all her parts are moving relative to some background" (p. 83). There is coherence of temporal structure through a sense of time. There is also a coherence of form in which the infant knows the mother's face whether it shows fear or surprise.

Self as Affects

The capacity to experience affect does not significantly change over a lifetime. The affective core guarantees continuity of experience across development in spite of the many ways we change (Stern, 1985).

> Affects are excellent higher order self-invariants because of their relative fixity: the organization and manifestation of each emotion is well fixed by innate design and changes little over development [Izard, 1977, cited in Stern, 1985, p. 89].

Stern points out that the invariants of affect are (1) the proprioceptive feedback from particular motor outflow patterns, to the face, respiration, and vocal apparatus; (2) internally patterned sensations of arousal or activation; and (3) emotion-specific qualities of feeling. (Understanding the function of affects in human development is so important that we devote chapter 21 to the subject.)

Self as History

History reflects a continuity of experience, a continuity that Winnicott (1960) called "going on being." Memory is a form of history. "It is now clear that there are recall 'systems' in an infant that are not language-based and that operate very early . . . . Motor memory is one of them" (Stern, 1985, p. 91). For example, the infant remembers how to suck a thumb.

DeCasper and Fifer (1980) believe that memory is present in the womb. They asked mothers in the last trimester to read (Dr. Seuss) scripts repeatedly to their pregnant bellies. After birth the infants to whom the story had been read showed greater familiarity (based on a sucking response) with the script than with a control story.

The basic unit of memory is an episode, a small piece of lived experience. "There are never emotions without a perceptual context. There are never cognitions without some affect fluctuations, even if it is only interest" (Stern, 1985, p. 95). Memory, however, is failure-driven in that a specific episode is relevant and memorable as a piece of lived experience only to the extent that it violates the expectation of the generalized episode. That is, we remember things that fail to meet our expectations. It is for this reason one can "commute" to a workplace for an hour and recall very little of the trip.

Memory uses Generalized Event Structures (GERs)(Stern, 1985). In a GER, a birthday, for example, means a series of events such as decorate cake, greet guests, open presents, sing "happy birthday", blow out candles, cut cake, eat cake, and thank guests. Memory also uses Representation of Interactions Generalized (RIGs). For example, a ten-month-old can form a prototype from a variety of faces.

THE NUCLEAR SELF

In contrast to Stern's core self, in Kohut's nuclear self three major developments occur. These are (a) the consolidation of central grandiose-exhibitionistic fantasies as ambitions, (b) the internalization of the idealized parent as fundamental ideals, and (c) the development of skills and talents. Realization of these nuclear ambitions, ideals and skills leads to a feeling of triumph and a glow of joy, not pleasure from tension discharge. These developments form Kohut's tripartite self, (initially called bipolar) believed by White and Weiner (1986) to be the "capstone of the supraordinate self" (p. 104).

For Kohut (1977), the nuclear ambitions are acquired during the second, third, and fourth years of a child's development, whereas basic ideals are gained mainly in the fourth, fifth, and sixth years of life (p. 179). Skills and talents develop during the latency period. These ambitions, ideals, and skills are so important in motivating the self that they are conceived by Kohut as forming two poles of the nuclear self with an intermediate area, a "tension gradient," between. This tension gradient consists of talents and skills gained through twinship transferences. In this way, by stressing the importance of (1) ambitions, (2) ideals, and (3) skills, Kohut arrived at his model of the nuclear self.

Kohut's tripartite theory of the self has been criticized from within self psychology itself. Stolorow and his colleagues (1987) have openly stated that Kohut's idea of a bipolar self, with its ambitions and ideals, contains the danger of reification, while the concept of a tension arc appeals to mechanistic thinking. They accept the use of the self as a metaphor and the need for some metapsychology but contend that Kohut did not heed sufficiently the warnings of Schafer (1976) about reification. They also believe that even though Kohut's metapsychology is different from the classical position, his concept of the bipolar (later, tripartite) self is open to the criticism that like Freud's, it is too objectified, materialistic, and mechanized.

The problem of reification in self psychology goes beyond Kohut's idea of the bipolar or tripartite self. As long as adjectives are used in conjunction with the word self, the grandiose self for example, there is the danger of reification. What can be understood as a description of the state of the self at a given moment, that is, the self in a grandiose state, can also easily be viewed as a reified object, that is, a separate subunit of the self. Thus, the reified grandiose self takes on a life and agency of its own. Additionally, there is a propensity for theorists to manufacture self concepts when there is the need to explain something. But naming does not explain. Naming a concept creates a tool to facilitate description. It is the means to an end, the beginning of an explanatory process, but not a substitute for the process itself.

The danger of seeing parts of the self as agents is present in Kohut's concepts of a nuclear self and a peripheral self. Both refer to an area or location of the self. The temptation is to view the peripheral self and the nuclear self as interacting with each other as if they have agency. This kind of temptation increases when the list of the various "selves" increases. Reiser (1986), for example, delineates five selves: the endangered self, the enraged self, the vulnerable self, the grandiose self, and the mirroring self (p. 230). And what about such well-known concepts as the true self, the false self, the disavowed self, and so forth? They are often used as if they were entities rather than descriptions of an authentic but transient quality of the self.

The danger of reifying and anthropomorphizing is less with the concepts of the cohesive self and fragmenting self. These are more easily conceived of as states of the self, on a continuum, with cohesion at one end and fragmentation at the other. Perhaps more significantly, these concepts are supported by behavioral correlates. By 1971 Kohut was proposing that symptoms of hypochondria, homosexual behavior, and work inhibitions were indications of a person whose self was in some degree of fragmentation, even if stabilized. Other evidence of self-fragmentation comes from dreams, especially of small bugs; sexual perversion; alcohol and drug abuse; and somatic illness.

ORGANIZATION OF EXPERIENCE

To help curb the use of constructs of the self as subagents, Stolorow and his colleagues prefer a different word for the idea of self as agent. They suggest "person." "We have found it important to distinguish sharply between the concept of the self as a psychological structure and the concept of the *person* as an experiencing subject and agent who initiates action" (Atwood and Stolorow, 1984, p. 34). By psychological structure they mean "organization of experience" (Stolorow et al., 1987, p. 17). Thus, the idea of a "fragmented self striving to restore cohesion," in which the agent "I" is transformed into a reified "it," is better expressed as "the person whose self experience is becoming fragmented strives to restore his sense of self-cohesion" (p. 19).

By calling the self acting as an agent, a person, Stolorow paves the way for self to be seen as "a psychological structure through which self experience acquires cohesion and continuity, and by virtue of which self experience assumes its characteristic shape and enduring organization" (Atwood and Stolorow, 1984, p. 34). Stolorow and his colleagues (1987) add, "the distinction between person and self enables us to separate conceptually the various functional capacities acquired by the person from the corresponding reorganizations and structuralizations of his self-experience" (p. 19).

The concept of the self as the organization of experience has an appealing simplicity. Not only does reorganization of experience take place, it does so continually as new experiences occur. The idea of the self is not of a static self; it is a self always in transition, a changing self:

> The idea that the self, a product of earlier givens and previous selfobject experiences, continues to be shaped by emergent givens and new self–selfobject encounters, suggests that the self is, throughout the life cycle, a self in transition, a changing self [Tolpin, 1986, p. 116].

If the self, the organization of experience, is viewed as being in transition, it has the characteristics of an open system. A system as von Bertalanffy (1968) defines it, is an entity identified by its function, rather than its physical attributes; it is a stable, information-processing collective made up of a hierarchy of interacting feedback cycles. Basch (1988a) sees that "the affective and cognitive information-processing activities of the brain form such a system--here called the *self system* which governs adaptation to the environment" (p. 100).

Lichtenberg (1988) defines the self as both the organizer of experience and the independent center of initiative. He links the initiating function to the idea of motivation (Lichtenberg, 1988, p. 61). He asks, what motivates the supraordinate "I," the person who is the self as agent? If Kohut's thinking on the tripartite self is viewed as motivation, then ambitions, ideals, and the need for skill mastery motivate a person to take the initiative and act.

Lichtenberg (1989) proposes five subsystems that motivate the self as agent. These are (1) the need for psychic regulation of physiological requirements, (2) the need for attachment-affiliation, (3) the need for exploration and assertion, (4) the need to react aversively through antagonism or withdrawal, and (5) the need for sensual enjoyment and sexual excitement. These motivational systems, derived as they were from the study of infants, are different from those which Kohut found through clinical work with narcissistic patients. They encompass the idea that "psychoanalytic theory at its core is a theory of structured *motivation*, not a theory of structures" (p. 1).

In contrast to, and yet basically congruent with, self psychology, Mitchell (1988) offers a relational definition of the self. "Mind [self] has been redefined from a set of predetermined structures emerging from inside an individual organism to transactional patterns and internal structures derived from an interactive, interpersonal field" (p. 17).

To summarize, the self in self psychology replaces Descartes's concept of the mind and Freud's mental apparatus. It is conceived as having two major functions: that of a supraordinate agent and the organization of experience. To avoid confusion and awkward language, the self as agent is better referred to as "person." Kohut's concept of the tripartite self, with its danger of reification, is better conceived as motivating systems of the self system as a whole. Stern's concept of the core self and its correlates of agency, cohesion, affectivity and history show potential usefulness in the treatment of severely disturbed persons.

Whatever the process of development of the core self, access to it in psychotherapy is through exploration of its organizing principles. These organizing principles are uncovered through the intersubjective context of the psychotherapeutic relationship. In chapter 18, we explore how these organizing invariants emerge and how they can be changed.

With the examination of the self system in this chapter, we have completed the survey of Kohut's major constructs, which began with his emphasis on the empathic method. His new ideas evoked responses from the analytic community that ranged from appreciative acceptance to outright rejection. To some, Kohut was Franz Alexander reincarnated. Much of the reaction to the challenge of self psychology emerged over the issue of conflict verses deficit theory. This is the subject of our next chapter.

Readings for Chapter 16: Kuhn, 1962; Hanly and Masson, 1976; Stolorow, 1983; London, 1985; Curtis, 1986.

conflict between conscious.
unconscious
mind

conflict — *id-ego-superego*
internal *agency*

16

Conflict and Deficit Theories *conflict within ego itself (Hartman)*

S elf psychology's new theoretical constructs and its successes in treating narcissistic disorders posed a major problem for psychoanalysis. At first self psychology's ideas broadened the scope of psychoanalysis by adding new theory, but as this new theory grew, the ideas of self psychology became a major complement to drive theory. They became such a major complement that eventually self psychology was proposed as an entirely new paradigm, able to explain neurotic conflicts as well as narcissistic deficits.

Most psychoanalytic theorists were able to accept self psychology's broadening of psychoanalysis, and even saw its potential as a major addition to drive-conflict theory. In general, however, they rejected self psychology as a radically new paradigm. Psychoanalysis' acceptance or rejection of self psychology's ideas often focused on the contrast between conflicts or deficits in psychic structure. In what follows we examine the concept of structural deficit under (a) deficit theory, (b) critical responses, (c) complementarity, (d) new paradigm, and (e) scientific revolution.

DEFICIT THEORY

As discussed in chapter 5, Freud's drive-discharge theory was an evolving theory of conflict. First, conflict was between the conscious and unconscious mind (topographical model), then between agencies of the mind (structural model); and, under the influence of Hartmann, conflicts also took place within the ego or between the ego and the external world. According to this drive-discharge/conflict theory, narcissism was seen as a pathological regression to avoid the conflicts of the Oedipus complex and was to be interpreted as such to narcissistic patients, despite discouraging results. The idea that longings expressed by narcissistic patients reflected genuine needs because of developmental deficits was a radical departure from this classical position.

The concept of arrested development, first introduced by Ferenczi (1913), was revived by Glover (1943), made prominent by Anna Freud (1965), and introduced to self psychology by Gedo (1966, 1967).

Kohut (1971) used the theoretical contrast between structural conflict and arrested development (structural deficit) to explain self psychology's contributions to psychoanalytic theory:

> The patient's reactions to the disturbance of his relationship with a narcissistically experienced object . . . occupy a central position of strategic importance that corresponds to the place of the structural conflict in the psychoneuroses [p. 92].

Discussing this conflict/deficit contrast, Stolorow and Lachmann (1980) noted a "crucial distinction between psychopathology which is the product of defenses against intrapsychic conflict and psychopathology which is the remnant of a developmental arrest at prestages of defense" (p. 5). In Stolorow's early position, conflict and deficit theory both coexisted. At first he and Lachmann acknowledged both a pseudonarcissistic neurotic personality and a narcissistic personality disorder. They did not completely reject the classical position on narcissism, but by limiting classical theory to one kind of narcissistic patient, they created space for Kohut's theorizing to describe a deficit kind of narcissism. Later, however,

Stolorow (1988) rejected this view of the relative parity of the conflict and deficit theories.

Early in the development of self psychology, Kohut attempted to integrate his new insights on the treatment of narcissism into psychoanalysis by "pour[ing] new wine into old bottles" (Stolorow, 1988). This phrase signifies Kohut's effort to conceptualize his ideas on the "Procrustean bed of Freudian metapsychology" (Stolorow, 1988), with its language of mental apparatus and drive-discharge. Fixations along the object-instinctual line of development led to neurotic disorders, whereas fixations along the narcissistic pathway resulted in narcissistic disorders. Kohut envisaged different theoretical models for different classes of psychopathology, a task taken up by Gedo and Goldberg (1973) in *Models of the Mind*.

In this book, Gedo and Goldberg make a case for arranging various modes of psychic functioning into an hierarchical schema. Such modes employ Ferenczi's (1913) concept of "lines of development." Gedo and Goldberg arrange these lines of development according to five phases, each of which requires a different model of the mind: the topographical model (introspection) for phase five; the tripartite model (interpretation) for phase four; the self psychology model (disillusionment) for phase three; a modified self psychology model (unification) for phase two; and the reflex arc model (pacification) for phase one.

Their hierarchical view of the mind enables Gedo and Goldberg to define arrested development as taking place only "when the crucial lines of development are all arrested within the same phase" (p. 135). Examples of these lines of development are danger situations, narcissism, sense of reality, and mechanisms of defense. Gedo (1988) further clarifies the concept of arrested development: "The concept does not apply to the numerous syndromes wherein one nucleus of the self remains archaic while the rest of the personality undergoes expectable maturation" (p. 56).

It is tempting to embrace an approach where drive theory interpretations are made when treating neurotic patients and self psychology explanations are given to patients suffering from disorders of the self. Putting such an approach into practice, however, is difficult and may be impossible, because people do not generally fall into neat diagnostic categories. More important, different theoretical models are often needed for the same patient at different stages of treatment. Such a multiplicity of theories applicable for a stage of treatment on the same patient points to the need for an overarching theoretical frame for making decisions about the use of a specific model. The hierarchical model of Gedo and Goldberg is one way out of this quandary.

A hierarchical model of the mind that incorporated disparate theories within its overarching frame paved the way for Kohut to explore self psychology as a distinctive paradigm unencumbered by drive theory. In *The Restoration of the Self*, Kohut (1977) sharpened the distinction between structural conflict and structural deficit theories by dropping drive-discharge concepts to explain the treatment of narcissistic patients and by introducing the concepts of Guilty Man and Tragic Man.

> Man's functioning should be seen as aiming in two directions. I identify these by speaking of *Guilty Man* if the aims are directed toward the activity of his drives and of *Tragic Man* if the aims are toward fulfillment of the self. To amplify briefly: Guilty Man lives within the pleasure principle; he attempts to satisfy his pleasure-seeking drives, to lessen the tensions that arise in his erogenous zones . . . . Tragic Man, on the other hand, seeks to express the pattern of his nuclear self; his endeavors lie beyond the pleasure principle. Here, too, the undeniable fact that man's failures overshadow his successes prompted me to designate this aspect of man negatively as Tragic Man rather than "self expressive" or "creative man" [pp. 132-133].

Kohut also used deficit psychology to explain psychopathology that was previously thought amenable to conflict psychology explanation. Specifically, he indicated that structural deficits subtend the oedipal neuroses. This trend in his thinking blossomed in his later work, especially *How Does Analysis Cure?* (Kohut, 1984).

CRITICISM

Criticism of self psychology may be in direct proportion to its perceived deviation from psychoanalysis. When viewed as supplemental or additive, it received very little criticism. When seen as separate but equal, it attracted considerable criticism. But when it was thought of as a new paradigm that subsumed and replaced the old analytic model, it elicited outright rejection.

Rejection took many forms, one of them a distortion of self psychology's position. For example, self psychology is seen by some as "idealizing and romanticizing" empathy (London, 1985, p. 100). Such a criticism, appropriate for the function of empathy in some theories, fails to appreciate Kohut's efforts to avoid this very difficulty by defining carefully empathy as vicarious introspection, *a specific method of gathering data*. It also ignores Kohut's idea of attenuated empathy, which makes it clear that idealized empathy in the form of empathic perfection is not only unnecessary but undesirable.

Rejection also emerges as "this theory is too different for me to feel comfortable with it." For example, in a critique that Friedman (1980) calls "clinical moralizing," Hanly and Masson (1976) attack the idea of narcissism as a developmental deficit by disagreeing with Kohut's concept of narcissism as a separate line of development. They claim (without substantiation either theoretically or clinically) that narcissism is not a separate line of development and therefore is a manifestation of conflict pathology, not a deficit. Significantly, except for Kohut's reference to the "oceanic experience," they reject the idea of healthy narcissism by ignoring Kohut's (1966) paper on the subject of transformed narcissism. They present no arguments to support the idea that narcissism is unhealthy and simply appeal to the authority of Freud.

A dream reported by one of their patients, as well as her behavior in the analytic relationship, suggests that she was hungering for a mirror transference as described by Kohut, but this patient's hunger was understood by Hanly and Masson as resistance to a properly conducted analysis. One gains the impression that Hanly and Masson have not been able to understand empathically how Kohut successfully treated narcissistic patients. They reject Kohut's position apparently because it differs from the classical view of narcissism.

Self psychology is also criticized for not using the techniques of traditional psychoanalysis. Kernberg (1975) calls it essentially supportive psychotherapy (pp. 285-309). For London (1985) self psychology is not compatible with psychoanalysis because it avoids conflicts, is not conducted from a neutral stance, and, he thinks, relies exclusively on empathy to the exclusion of interpretation. The idea that self psychology excludes interpretation, called by Kohut "explanation," is inaccurate. London is really presenting another version of the argument that the unfamiliar is unacceptable, irrespective of its merits. Loewald (1973) thinks that self psychology leads to excessive gratification or indulgence and hence fosters more narcissistic behavior, a view based on drive theory not on clinical practice.

The rejection of self psychology as something "foreign" implies that self psychology is a new paradigm outside of analysis. Stein (1979), for example, sees self psychology as such a radical departure from psychoanalysis that it is "difficult to accept as a genuine addition to psychoanalytic theory and practice" (p. 680). When he doubts that self psychology "is a sound piece of work, a true advance, a paradigm in Thomas Kuhn's sense" (p. 680), he clearly rejects it as another psychoanalytic paradigm and ignores the larger question of a new healing paradigm.

Stein apparently can reject self psychology only by oversimplifying and distorting it. He thinks self psychology is "based ultimately on the simple principle that disorders of the self are the result of lack of parental empathy; cures are brought about by the (kindly) efforts of an empathic analyst" (p. 677). He ignores such major elements in the theory as empathic failures, which, when explained (interpreted), lead to microinternalizations and structure building. He also does not seem to understand that treatment of narcissistic personalities involves eventual interpretations of the transference after a long period of empathic immersion. Instead, Stein caricatures Kohut's work as "the product, not so much of painstaking exploration, of trial and error, and of attempts to test the truth, as of a more purely subjective and inspirational process, largely confined to the empathic-introspective method" (p. 680).

In response Markson and Thomson (1986) suggest that such criticisms are "simplistic" (p. 31). Basch's (1986) response is more pointed:

> Analysts whose patients have benefited from supervision based on Kohut's insights will know from personal experience that accusations that Kohut and his students do not deal with aggression, do

> not know how to or choose not to analyze psychosexual conflicts, remain on the surface and do not plumb the depths, do not understand or do not work with unconscious fantasies, advocate cures based on love and on unanalytic attempts to gratify patient's wishes, and so on, reflect the anxiety of the critic and not Kohut's ideas or practice [p. 19].

A different criticism comes from Mitchell (1988), who accepts the need for a new paradigm to replace the drive-conflict model but thinks—and we agree on the basis of the need for a theory of trauma—that the concept of developmental arrest is an inadequate basis for a new paradigm. He rejects the notion of "developmental tilt," which sees perseverating babies stuck in developmental time:

> The two major problems generated by developmental tilt [are]: psychopathology . . . characterized in terms of missing infantile experiences rather than constricted patterns of relatedness in general, and the missing needs . . . regarded as residing *in* the patient, pressing to emerge, rather than a function of the interactive relational field the analysand experiences herself as living in [p. 155].

Mitchell would rather see a more interactive option than drive theory. He regards:

> developmental continuity as a reflection of similarities in the kinds of problems human beings struggle with at all points in the life cycle. Being a self with others entails a constant dialectic between attachment and self-definition, between connection and differentiation, a continual negotiation between one's wishes and will of others, between one's own subjective reality and a consensual reality of others with whom one lives. In this view the interpersonal environment plays a continuous, crucial role in the creation of experience. The earliest experiences are meaningful not because they lay down structural residues which remain fixed, but because they are the earliest representation of patterns of family structure and interactions which will be repeated over and over in different forms at different developmental stages [p. 149].

In contrast to the drive-conflict and developmental arrest models, Mitchell describes his new paradigm as the relational-conflict model.

COMPLEMENTARITY

By 1977 Kohut presented self psychology as a new paradigm freed from the structures of Freudian metapsychology. He saw the relationship between the old and the new as complementary and wanted drive and deficit theories to coexist just as wave and particle theories of light do in physics.

> What I am suggesting is that one might employ here and elsewhere two different theoretical frameworks—that, in analogy to the principle of complementarity of modern physics, we might indeed speak of a psychological principle of complementarity and say that the depth-psychological explanation of psychological phenomena in health and disease requires two complementary approaches: that of conflict psychology and that of a psychology of the self. [pp. 77-78]

Friedman (1980), on the other hand, sees self psychology as supplementary, not complementary to psychoanalysis, because it is an "elaboration of an unstressed aspect of existing theory" (p. 409). In his view, it should not be given equal weight with drive theory because it is not as comprehensive.

Schwartz (1978) also rejects the idea of complementarity because it implies that these different frames of reference have equal validity. He does not think they are equally valid, for he sees self psychology as being without the explanatory power of drive theory. He also doubts self psychology's potential as a separate theory of the future on the grounds that its useful ideas will ultimately be integrated into the body of psychoanalytic literature.

Stolorow (1988), theorizing from within self psychology, also dislikes the complementary approach to deficit and conflict theories.

guilty man – wants gratifications
feels guilt – because of it

> Although these formulations of complementary or combined models are not without heuristic value, it is my view that they are theoretically unsound. This is because conceptualizations of self–selfobject experiences and constructions of drive-discharge apparatus exist on entirely different theoretical planes deriving from completely different universes of discourse [p. 65].

Curtis (1986), too, thinks that conflict and deficit are two different levels of conceptualization.

Gediman (1989), however, concerned about the polarization occurring in psychoanalysis over the issue of self psychology, supports the idea of a psychoanalytic theory broad enough to permit multiple points of view. Asserting that clinical material suggests that the two points of view are not mutually exclusive, she writes, "Both phenomena, the neurotic and the narcissistic, and their underlying intrapsychic, prestructural and preoedipal and oedipal conflicts may be seen as essential features of all patients, granted in varying degrees" (p. 296).

Chessick (1980b), however, cautions:

> It seems to me virtually certain that Freud would not have accepted Kohut's theory of the psychology of the self in the broad sense as "complementary," but rather as a rival theory which uses a different treatment procedure from that of Freud's classical analysis [p. 470].

NEW PARADIGM

Kohut's discarding drive-discharge metaphysics to explain narcissism opened the way for him to see self psychology as a new paradigm. His editor, Paul Ornstein (1978), describes self psychology as undergoing a gradual advance and raises the question, "What was it that led to the basic change in direction that may rightfully be designated as the acquisition of a new paradigm?" (p. 105).

Blum (1982), a critic of self psychology, recognizes self psychology as a new paradigm: "[Self psychology] offers itself in many ways not only as an addition, supplement, or complement, an extension of our present theories, but as a new paradigm and theoretical advance" (p. 964). He is, however, critical of the structural-conflict/structural-deficit dichotomy as an oversimplification.

Curtis (1983), who notes the "already tenuous ties between psychoanalysis and the theoretical system of self psychology" (p. 285), questions whether self psychology is a "new paradigm" within psychoanalysis or is actually a "new depth psychology," derived from but no longer part of psychoanalysis (p. 272). Noting in Kohut's later letters an increasing use of the phrase "depth psychology" where ordinarily one might expect the word "psychoanalysis," he writes:

> In the absence of an explanation for such a preference, one is bound to speculate that this reflects a compromise between the need to retain a place within psychoanalysis and the desire for differentiation as "an independent psychology of the self" [p. 281].

How Does Analysis Cure? (Kohut,1984) reveals Kohut well down the road toward viewing self psychology as a new paradigm:

> We have begun to consider even the psychoneuroses—Freud's "transference neuroses"—as specific variants of self disturbances, that is, as analyzable self disturbances in the wider sense [p. 80] .... I believe the oedipal neuroses, too, should be viewed as self-disorders in a wider sense [p. 218, n.5].

And Kohut (1984) further says:

> Self psychology is now attempting to demonstrate, for example, that all forms of psychopathology are based either on defects in the structure of the self, on distortions of the self, or on weakness of the self. It is trying to show, furthermore, that all these flaws in the self are due to disturbances in the self–selfobject relationships in childhood. Stated in the obverse, by way of highlighting the contrast between self psychological and traditional theory, self psychology holds that pathogenic conflicts in the object-instinctual realm—that is, pathogenic conflicts in the realm of object love and object hate and in particular the set of conflicts called the Oedipus complex—are not the *primary* cause of psychopathology but its result [p. 53].

In this later view, Kohut understands psychic conflict as one of the sequelae of structuralized selfobject failures.

Miller (1988) also sees Kohut as developing a new paradigm by subsuming the old theory within his new framework.

> As self psychology developed Kohut no longer viewed it primarily as an alternative explanation for clinical phenomena of equivalent importance. Rather, he increasingly saw self psychology as the central, fundamental position of analytic psychology and believed it subsumed the classical position. It did not eliminate the classical position, certainly not entirely, but contained it and treated classical concepts and findings, in essence, as "special cases" within self psychology. This is analogous to viewing Newton's laws of motion as useful special cases within the more valid, larger viewpoint of modern physics. For example, as posited by self psychology, a pathological Oedipus complex is seen as a frequently occurring special-case deterioration of the normal oedipal stage [p. 81].

Markson and Thomson (1986) "believe that there is no clear cut distinction between neurotic and nonneurotic disorders. Conflict, defective structure, and underlying deficit are present in *all* cases" (p. 35). They also

> believe that in all psychopathology, including psychoneurosis, structural conflicts have their origin in deficits in the supporting structures of the self. These deficits have arisen from the accumulative trauma of failures within the child-parent selfobject milieu" [p. 39].

Markson and Thompson's position is consistent with Kohut's (1984) final view:

> informed therapeutic approaches to the classical transference neuroses relate to their different conceptions of the basic pathogenesis. The classical position maintains that we have arrived at the deepest level when we have reached the patient's experience of his impulses, wishes, and drives, that is, when the patient has become aware of his archaic sexual lust and hostility. The self psychologically informed analyst, however, will be open to the fact that the pathogenic Oedipus complex is embedded in an

tragic man - seeks self-actualization (nuclear self) & fails & suffers.

> oedipal self–selfobject disturbance, that beneath lust and hostility there is a layer of depression and of diffuse narcissistic rage. The analytic process will, therefore, not only deal with the oedipal conflicts per se but also, in a subsequent phase or, more frequently, more or less simultaneously (though even then with gradually increasing emphasis), focus on the underlying depression and the recognition of the failures of the child's oedipal selfobjects [p. 5].

Efforts to integrate theories with self psychology are focused at a general level possibly because, as Stolorow (1988) points out,

> Kohut's (1980) third (and, I believe, final) position on this issue was that efforts to integrate self psychology with other theoretical viewpoints, including the classical one, shall be postponed until the self-psychological system has become more fully elaborated and consolidated [p. 65].

When such an integration proceeds, however, it needs to follow two principles: (1) keeping the discussions "experience near," and (2) creating new constructs that are more general and inclusive. For example, Stolorow's idea of an intersubjective field is an attempt at "synthesizing the clinical understandings of classical psychoanalysis and self psychology into a unified psychoanalytic framework" (p. 69). The idea of an intersubjective field is suitable as an inclusive construct because it can contain many dimensions of experience, including both the self–selfobject deficiencies and the conflictual.

When Stolorow (1985) refers to the conflictual dimension of experience, he means that it is

> viewed always and only as a subjective state of the individual person . . . . When conflict is freed from the encumbering image of an energy disposal apparatus . . . the supposed antithesis between conflict theory and self psychology vanishes. When conflict is liberated from the primacy of instinctual drive, then the specific meaning-contexts that give rise to subjective states of conflict becomes an empirical question to be explored psychoanalytically [p. 193].

By the end of the 80s the conflict-developmental issue had faded in importance not only because self psychology could explain both arrested development and conflict by its paradigm, but because arrested development pointed to the importance of an adequate theory of trauma. "[Max] Stern [regards] the phenomenology of arrested states of psychological development [as] secondary to early emotional trauma" (Levin, 1991, p. 122). Stern (1988), for example, believed that night terrors, *pavor nocturnus*, reflect arrested development. Hence, self psychology has given increased attention to the theory of trauma, the subject of chapter 22.

SCIENTIFIC REVOLUTION

Late in its development, self psychology began struggling with issues common to scientific revolutions. Kuhn (1962), adumbrating his idea of scientific revolution, rejected the notion that significant scientific changes come from piecemeal additions to an ever growing stockpile of knowledge. Rather, his research into previous scientific advances revealed long periods of "normal science" based on the prevailing paradigm, interspersed with relatively short periods of crisis, during which radical shifts to a new paradigm occur.

During normal science, scientists engage in mopping-up operations, apply the paradigm with increased precision, and find new applications for it. A revolutionary paradigm shift occurs when the prevailing paradigm cannot account for persistent anomalies, and an alternative paradigm presents itself that can explain what was covered by the old paradigm, as well as the former anomalies. For example, Roentgen "discovered" X-rays when he noticed the anomaly of a glowing barium platinocyanide screen after he had covered his cathode-ray tube with black paper. Whatever was making the screen glow was passing through the paper and the space between tube and screen. When he held his hand in this space he could see his bones in the dark shadow (Rhodes, 1986, p. 41).

Science's reorientation by paradigm change is analogous to "picking up of the other end of the stick." The process involves "handling the same bundle of data as before, but placing them in a new system of relations with one another by giving them a different framework" (Kuhn, 1962, p. 85).

Kuhn also saw that each paradigm attracts a community of professionals committed to the paradigm. Hence, struggles between competing paradigms during a period of revolutionary science become struggles for the loyalty of practitioners. Students, particularly, become a target group. For example,

> Max Planck, surveying his own career in his *Scientific Autobiography*, sadly remarked that "a new scientific truth does not triumph by convincing its opponents and making them see the light, but rather because its opponents eventually die, and a new generation grows up that is familiar with it" [p. 151].

In a similar vein, a frustrated Ernest Rutherford, the father of atomic theory, once commented tartly that science moves forward one funeral at a time.

Using Kuhn's constructs, we see many of the critics of self psychology approaching it from the standpoint of "normal science," whereas self psychology represents a revolutionary scientific change. Its proponents make the case that the traditional analytic paradigm is in a crisis, that narcissism is the major anomaly with which the old paradigm failed to help the practitioners and that the new paradigm can explain treatment of a broader range of clinical syndromes, including the neuroses. Still remaining is the question of the allegiances of therapeutic practitioners, whose major work is psychotherapy. We take up the question of the difference between psychoanalysis and psychotherapy in the next chapter.

Readings for Chapter 17: Gill, 1951, 1954, 1984; Bibring, 1954; Stone, 1954; Kohut, 1980; Wallerstein, 1986, chapters 37-39.

paradigm
classical – deeper level when we reach wishes, hopes, fears etc. lust, hostility

self-psychology – deeper level when we interpret the depressed & narcissistic rage fails in oedipal selfobjects: underneath the wishes, hopes, etc.

p. 200.

17

Psychoanalysis and Psychotherapy

The question of the differences between psychoanalysis and psychotherapy preceded the emergence of self psychology. With the acceptance of psychoanalysis in the United States during the post World War II boom and the concomitant emergence of new psychotherapies, the 1950s saw efforts to define more clearly and distinguish these two modes of healing. Out of this debate came the consensus that psychoanalysis was the superior therapeutic treatment modality if the patient could undergo it, because it alone produced permanent structural change. Research into the results of analytic work since the 50s has not confirmed this belief, nor has the success of the theory and practice of psychotherapy using a self psychology paradigm supported this view. In what follows we examine psychoanalysis and psychotherapy under the following topics: (a) distinctions of the fifties, (b) The Menninger Psychotherapy Research Project, and (c) self psychology, psychoanalysis, and psychotherapy.

DISTINCTIONS OF THE 50S

Until the 1950s, the word psychotherapy was used in two ways: "First as a broad term to include all types of therapy by psychological means, under which psychoanalysis is included, and second in a narrow sense to designate methods of psychological therapy which are not psychoanalysis" (Gill, 1954, p. 772). This usage followed the lead of Freud, who "at times used the term 'psychotherapy' in its historical inclusive sense, or for psychoanalysis, or—when referring to 'other' psychotherapies—for explicitly nonanalytic procedures" (Stone, 1954, pp. 572-573). Such usage implied a distinction between psychoanalysis and psychotherapy as specific treatment modalities but did little to clarify the differences.

By the 1950s the vagueness of the distinction between psychotherapy and psychoanalysis was a problem. In the aftermath of World War II, the field of psychotherapy, and especially psychoanalysis, gained widespread acceptance and status. With psychoanalysis' dominance in Departments of Psychiatry, its "task became to facilitate its growth while continuing to prevent its identity from being blurred" (Rangell, 1981, p. 665).

The threat of blurring came from several quarters. A major challenge came from Alexander and French (1946) who modified psychoanalysis to a "corrective emotional experience" at the expense of insight, and dropped what they considered to be an artificial distinction between psychoanalysis and psychotherapy. Alexander (1953) infuriated the psychoanalytic establishment with his claim that the distinction between these two therapeutic modes was maintained, not on theoretical grounds, but for professional prestige. Coming from the President of the Institute for Psychoanalysis, Chicago, his challenge could not be ignored.

Although Alexander and French posed a danger to established psychoanalysis from within, they were not the only challenge. Fromm-Reichmann (1950), from her work with borderlines and psychotics, also saw that the "widening scope" of psychoanalysis made it barely distinguishable from intensive psychotherapy. Furthermore, at the "weller" end of the nosological spectrum, Carl Rogers's success using short-term counseling of college students raised serious doubts about the supreme efficacy of the insight/structural model.

The analytic community responded to these new psychotherapies with papers by Bibring, Stone, and Gill, all published in 1954. Bibring's paper was of particular importance. He discussed a number of techniques used in psychotherapy and psychoanalysis along a hierarchy of effectiveness for achieving structural change: (1) suggestive, (2) abreactive, (3) manipulative, (4) clarifying, and (5) interpretive, with suggestive being on the bottom of the hierarchy and interpretive on the top.

Suggestive means the inducing of ideas, feelings and actions by an authority independent of the patient's critical thinking. Abreaction is the releasing of emotional tension, so that an emotionally strong idea is transformed into a weak one. Its curative value comes from its combination with manipulation or clarification.

Manipulation can take several forms, in one of which the therapist neutralizes the obstacles to treatment by assuring a patient who is afraid of being influenced that he should never accept any explanation unless he is fully convinced of its validity and of the evidence offered. Another is encouraging a phobic patient to confront his fears. A third example is through experiential manipulation in which the patient is exposed to a new experience, either because the opportunity did not arise earlier or because—more likely—the opportunity was not recognized owing to inhibition or distorted conceptions. This is influence through a "corrective emotional experience" (Alexander and French, 1946).

Clarification, a term used by Rogers, helps the patient "see much more clearly." Clarification must not transcend the descriptive or phenomenological level. It does not seek to explain, nor does it refer to unconscious processes. Insight through clarification has some limited curative value.

Interpretation, aimed at insight, refers exclusively to unconscious material. Interpretation seeks to explain, thereby lifting the unconscious into the conscious and resolving pathogenic infantile conflicts.

After defining these therapeutic techniques, Bibring (1954) described psychotherapy as different combinations of these techniques (p. 765). To him, psychoanalysis distinguishes itself from psychotherapy by using primarily clarification and interpretation, and especially interpretation (p. 763).

Stone (1954) also makes interpretation the distinguishing feature of psychoanalysis: "It is interpretation which is ultimately relied on for the distinctively psychoanalytic effect" (p. 571). He states that "the mobilization of the transference neurosis holds a central place" (p. 572). Gill (1954) adds the feature of the analyst's neutrality. In a more formal definition, often quoted in the literature, Gill summarizes as follows: "Psychoanalysis is that technique which, employed by a neutral analyst, results in the development of a regressive transference neurosis and the ultimate resolution of this neurosis by techniques of interpretation alone" (p. 775). Gill's definition builds on the work of Strachey (1934), who used the term "mutative interpretation" to describe the interpretation of some transference investment by the patient in his relationship with the analyst.

Macalpine (1950) had four years earlier, offered a definition of psychoanalysis very similar to Gill's:

> To make transference and its development the essential difference between psychoanalysis and all other psychotherapies, psychoanalytic technique may be defined as the only psychotherapeutic method in which one-sided, infantile regression—analytic transference—is induced in a patient (analysand) analyzed, worked through, and finally resolved [p. 536].

Thus three components—analyst neutrality, regressive transference neurosis, and resolution of the regression by interpretation alone—became the pivotal defenses of psychoanalysis against the inroads of "experience" psychotherapy.

For a generation of psychoanalysts, each of these components was considered a necessary but not sufficient condition for psychoanalysis. Therefore, without an analyst's strict adherence to neutrality, say, a regressive transference neurosis does not fully develop. And even though the analyst may make extensive use of interpretation, as can happen in intensive psychotherapy, interpretations not aimed at resolving a transference neurosis will not be mutative, and so the process is not psychoanalysis. Similarly, even with strict neutrality, a transference neurosis may not develop if the patient lacks the capacity for one, and so psychoanalysis does not occur.

Further, even properly conducted attempts at psychoanalysis with both neutrality and a developing transference neurosis may not be psychoanalysis for lack of interpretation of the transference.

The value of Gill's definition is that it focuses on the analytic process rather than on the "ritualistic details" of the "extrinsic criteria" such as, frequency of sessions or the use of a couch. The definition also clearly delineates psychoanalysis from psychotherapy—but at a price. One problem is that Gill's definition can be used to argue that none of Freud's cases was psychoanalysis. For example, Dora was not in psychoanalysis according to Gill's criteria, because, as Freud himself reported, he did not interpret the transference. As a further example, in the case of the Wolf Man (see chapter 20, this volume) the major problem was not so much Freud's technical parameter (Eissler, 1953) of forcing a termination, but that Serge Pankejeff's regressive transference was never resolved, as evidenced in his "negative therapeutic reaction" and his status as a virtual "therapeutic lifer" (Wallerstein, 1986) in the de facto care of the analytic community.

Another problem with Gill's definition is that it limits the range of potential psychoanalytic patients to those who can undergo a transference neurosis, such as neurotics and some with milder character disorders. Further, Gill's definition excludes psychotherapy, but at the expense of theoretical flexibility and generalizability.

Having defined psychoanalysis as the optimal therapeutic method for structural change, Bibring, Stone and Gill all concede that psychotherapy can produce some change in patients who are unable to undergo a transference regression. Agreeing, Ticho (1970) notes:

> When we read about psychoanalysis of very regressed patients, we often discover, by carefully studying the therapeutic procedures, that the author is really referring to supportive (suppressive) or expressive-supportive psychotherapy. The same thing could be said of the "widening scope of psychoanalysis." Many of the case reports sound like psychotherapy on the couch, and often the difference seems to be a semantic one [p. 128].

Freud clearly saw the necessity and value of psychotherapy. In his introduction to Aichhorn's *Wayward Youth*, Freud (1925) wrote:

> The possibility of analytic influence rests upon quite definite preconditions which can be summed up under the term "analytic situation"; it requires the development of certain psychical structures and a particular attitude to the analyst. Where these are lacking—as in the case of children, of juvenile delinquents, and, as a rule, of impulsive criminals—something other than analysis must be employed, though something which will be at one with analysis in its *purpose* [p. 274].

Gill (1951) is interested in more clearly defining psychotherapy. He thinks that even though psychotherapy does not attempt to induce a regressive transference neurosis, the psychotherapist has to make decisions whether to support or uncover the patient's defenses. He says, "The two poles of either strengthening the defenses or analyzing them as first steps towards integrating the damaged ego, stand as the gross opposites of two theoretical modes of approach" (p. 65).

Gill also thinks that these supportive and uncovering (expressive) types of psychotherapy need to be distinguished. He sees uncovering psychotherapy as effecting more permanent change than supportive psychotherapy does, because the uncovering approach, by using interpretation, is closer to psychoanalysis and hence is more able to effect structural change. Kernberg and his colleagues (1972) likewise think that "expressive psychotherapy is generally preferable to supportive psychotherapy" (p. 169) because "supportive approaches, since they do not analyze negative transference components, are doomed to fail, because the patients inevitably 'are prevented from accepting the supportive aspects of psychotherapy'" (Kernberg et al., 1972, cited in Wallerstein, 1986, p. 699).

Sporadic appearances of transference in psychotherapy, can be usefully interpreted in expressive psychotherapy to foster some structural change. Stone (1954) wrote, "*Pathological fragments* of the transference relationship . . . [may] be utilized to great and genuine interpretive advantage by a skillful therapist" (p. 578).

What are these supportive techniques? Gill (1951) sees anything that strengthens a patient's defenses as supportive, including encouraging or praising the patient; avoiding attacking the patient's defenses; and making inexact interpretations (Glover, 1931) that uncover fantasies that are related symbolically to the ones creating the conflict and thus enable partial abreactions of instincts. Chessick (1974) sees the "essence of supportive psychotherapy as the reduction of anxiety by various techniques" (p. 63). To Wallerstein (1986) the basic feature of supportive psychotherapy is the "transference cure" (p. 390).

In the transference cure, the patient willingly strives for certain goals and changes "for the therapist" in gratitude for the therapist's gratification of his needs. The basis of a transference cure is a therapeutic quid pro quo:

> This mechanism of the transference cure operates widely, if not totally persuasively, in the supportive psychotherapies, and to varying degrees in the expressive psychotherapies (even psychoanalysis) as well—in fact, wherever there are unanalyzed transference components in the context of therapeutic changes [Wallerstein, 1986, pp. 390-391].

Another idea associated with supportive psychotherapy is the Alexander and French (1946) concept of a "corrective emotional experience" In it, the therapist attempts

> to alter or resolve expectations and behaviors of the patient by a planned counteraction within the transference situation, in which the patient is directly confronted with attitudes and behaviors of the therapist that are deliberately contrary to the patient's transference expectations [Wallerstein, 1986, p. 451].

Chassel (1953), taking an even stronger position in support of psychotherapy, wrote:

> We keep assuming that psychotherapy is a watered down procedure or is bound to be pure psychoanalysis alloyed with the baser metals of suggestion, and so on. My present thesis is that really psychodynamic psychotherapy is an approach as strong as or stronger than classical psychoanalysis, has increasingly greater range of applicability than classical psychoanalysis; is more inclusive theoretically, and that classical psychoanalysis may turn out to be a special procedure of limited but significant usefulness in certain cases [pp. 550-551].

Gill (1954) does not go as far as Chassel, but having defined psychoanalysis to distinguish it from psychotherapy, he does not want psychotherapy devalued, especially the expressive, uncovering type:

> Discussion of therapeutic results in psychoanalysis and psychotherapy too often views them as qualitative polar opposites, with psychoanalysis regarded as producing structural changes, and psychotherapy as unable to produce any significant intrapsychic change, but only altering techniques of adjustment through transference effects or shifts in defensive techniques [p. 787].

Gill declines to view psychotherapy and psychoanalysis as polar opposites:

> I am not suggesting that psychotherapy can do what psychoanalysis can do; but I am suggesting that a description of the results of intensive psychotherapy may be not merely in terms of shifts of defense, but also in terms of other intra-ego alterations [p. 793].

Influenced by the phenomenological viewpoint, Gill (1984), 30 years later, modified his position about psychoanalysis but continued to see the need for psychoanalysis and psychotherapy to be distinguished. He sees how the setting and the analyst's behavior help codetermine the transference because of inadvertent suggestions. This means that neutrality, an effort to avoid suggestive effects on the transference, "cannot accomplish that aim because the patient inevitably interprets the analyst's behavior in ways other than those the analyst intended" (p. 168). Therefore, the analyst inevitably has to explore the meanings of his own behavior for the patient.

Gill now places great emphasis on analyzing the transference in the here-and-now rather than on neutrality. Further, he discards the idea of transference regression as a distinguishing feature of psychoanalysis, because he believes that the idea of a regression as a revival of an earlier infantile state is an illusion. He thinks that analysis may induce an unnecessary, if not iatrogenic, regression: "I consider that a well conducted analysis is marked by a transference, not necessarily by a regressive transference" (p. 170). But in deemphasizing two of the three intrinsic criteria of his 1954 position, by discounting the extrinsic criteria, and by emphasizing exploring the transference in the here and now, Gill has, it may be argued, made it more difficult to distinguish psychoanalysis from intensive, uncovering (expressive) psychotherapy, even though he still views the differences as analyzing the transference in psychoanalysis as opposed to utilizing it therapeutically in psychotherapy.

THE MENNINGER PSYCHOTHERAPY RESEARCH PROJECT (PRP)

From 1954 to 1958, 42 patients who presented for treatment at the Menninger Hospital in Topeka, Kansas, were subjects of a major psychotherapy study. Twenty-two of these patients deemed suitable for psychoanalysis were treated with this modality for an average of about 1,000 hours each; twenty were given psychotherapy for an average of about 300 hours each. The patients, who ranged in ages from 17 to 50 and had a mean IQ in the "superior range" (124), were balanced for gender.

The study used a naturalistic design. Patients were assigned to the treatment modalities solely on the basis of anticipated best treatment; no randomization or matching occurred to make the two groups equivalent and establish a definitive sample for comparing the efficacy of psychoanalysis with that of psychotherapy. Using an idea similar to Rogers's (1961) design, each patient served as his own "control." (Rogers used patients waiting for treatment as a control group against whom he compared the results of a group of patients being treated.) The Menninger study, however, used Allport's (1937) strategy of "control"; that is, it compared each patient's progress against an original prediction.

Wallerstein (1986) explains the value of such predictions as follows:

> It might have been felt that the major conflicts that constituted the particular neurotic illness of a patient could only be resolved through psychoanalysis, and that various desired and specified changes would otherwise not occur. If the patient, for reality reasons, were in only a once-a-week psychotherapy, and some of

> the changes that had been postulated to be dependent on psychoanalysis with the working through of the full-fledged regressive transference neurosis, nevertheless did take place in this far less intensive (and regressive) therapeutic effect, then the assumptive bases on which particular predictions had rested would be seriously shaken [p. 114].

At the beginning, the project used Gill's (1951) conceptual difference between supportive and expressive psychotherapy. Before long, however, it was obvious that this supportive-expressive distinction was not "a particularly clarifying or useful endeavor" (Wallerstein, 1986, p. 686) because there was a significant blurring between the two modes. Agreeing with this finding, Schlesinger (1969) argued that all therapies are supportive and expressive and that it is more useful to ask "expressive, how and when?" and "supportive, how and when?" rather than "supportive or expressive?"

The results of this study can be seen in the global improvement ratings (p. 515) of the 42 patients. As Table 1 shows, there was as much very good to moderate improvement in the psychotherapy patients as there was in the psychoanalysis patients.

Additionally, measurements using a Health Sickness Rating Scale (HSRS) support the findings of the global ratings (Wallerstein, 1986, p. 532). The HSRS, with a range of 0-100, represents excellent mental health with the score of 100. In Table 2, the psychotherapy and psychoanalysis patients show equal improvement in scores at

TABLE 1
Percentage of Global Improvement
by Treatment Mode

Category	*Psychotherapy*	*Psychoanalysis*
Very Good improvement	45%	36%
Moderate improvement	15%	23%
Equivocal improvement	15%	14%
Failure	25%	27%

TABLE 2
Mean Scores of the HSRS

Modality	*Before*	*After*	*Follow-up (2+ yrs.)*
Psychotherapy	43	56.5	58
Psychoanalysis	48	62	65

the termination of treatment and a slight improvement at the follow-up stage over two years later. The persistent lower scores for the psychotherapy patients, before, after, and at follow-up, reflect their sicker status at the beginning of treatment. The slightly greater gains by the analysis group is a common pattern in research where preexisting differences between groups tend to increase over time.

Other results indicate that there was a significant tendency to misdiagnose patients by underestimating their pathology. One reason for this miscalculation was the patients' frequent withholding of significant negative diagnostic material until well into the treatment. This underestimation of pathology was reflected in the fact that of the 22 who commenced classical analysis, six had their treatment modified by parameters (Eissler, 1953), such as taking three months to explore an impasse and terminate if there was no resolution, and six were shifted into psychotherapy.

On the basis of a battery of projective tests given to each patient, Applebaum (1977) concluded that 19 of the 42 patients achieved changes far in excess of their developing insights. Sixteen of these patients were in psychotherapy. Wallerstein (1986) reports, "For 19 patients . . . the changes were substantially in excess of insights, and were thus presumably based on other factors than the interpretation of unconscious conflict leading to conflict resolution and concomitant insight" (p. 717). Further study of the results indicates that 10 of 11 patients who showed conflict resolution on the tests also showed structural change, as seen in lasting improvements in feelings, attitudes and behavioral functioning. Also, 7 out of 16 revealed no conflict resolution, yet showed improved structural changes. Applebaum (1977) concludes: "Both points of view, that structural change is associated with resolution of conflict and that structural change can come about in the absence of conflict resolution, receive support" (p. 207).

These results suggest extremely important conclusions for the issue of the difference between psychotherapy and psychoanalysis. While supporting the efficacy of classically conducted psychoanalysis, they indicate that the ability of psychotherapy to produce significant permanent change has been greatly underestimated. What has been challenged by these results is the supremacy of psychoanalysis as a treatment modality and its claim that it alone, through neutrality, the transference neurosis, and interpretation of this transference, can produce structural change. To the contrary, "fundamental changes can be brought about in people even though they are unable to develop much insight" (p. 214), and "conflict resolution cannot be considered essential to structural change and may be independent of it in some instances" (Applebaum, 1977, p. 208).

Horwitz (1974), using the results of the prediction study, came to similar conclusions. He focused on the stability of the change from supportive treatment. Wallerstein (1986) discusses Horwitz's findings:

> Patients who improved with supportive psychotherapeutic modes could maintain and even consolidate their functioning through the period of the follow-up observation. Furthermore, they could do so just as often without significant continuing contact that had initially been presumed to be required, since such supportive based changes had been expected to be less stable, less able to weather the stresses of subsequent life. Horwitz (1974) feels that three major factors could be contributory to such relatively enduring treatment gains in supportive psychotherapies (pp. 229-230): (1) continuing supportive environmental factors, such as the more appropriate marriages that some of these patients had by now entered into (the therapeutic process has helped these patients to understand better the nature of their needs, and thus influenced them to make wiser choices); (2) the positive feedback reinforcement from new, more adaptive behaviors, into which the therapists had implicitly or explicitly encouraged these patients; and (3) a continuing and durable positive feeling toward the therapists, seen as the conscious manifestation of significant shifts

> in the patient's inner world of object relationships and self and object representations [pp. 719-720].

Another finding came from investigating the question of transference cure among the study's patients. In 21 of the patients (50%), ten of the analytic cases and eleven of the therapy cases,

> clear-cut evidence was adduced of the important operation of this mechanism of transference gratification and transference cure in the result achieved, admixed with whatever other supportive and/or expressive mechanisms also characterized (or predominated) in their treatment courses [Wallerstein, 1986, p. 391].

Even more important was evidence during the follow-up studies of a "surprising (to us) durability of such changes" (p. 391).

The durability of the changes induced by a "transference cure" is of considerable significance. It cuts across the prevailing position in psychoanalysis and supports self psychology's theoretical position of the centrality of selfobject functions in psychoanalysis and psychotherapy. The research is all the more trustworthy because the results were obtained by professionals without any theoretical commitment to self psychology. In fact, the project was well under way before the emergence of Kohut's ideas. Indeed, the unexpected support for long-term changes based on a transference cure begs for a theoretical explanation. The traditional view of the impermanence of a transference cure may be wrong, but why?

One explanation, based on self psychology theory, is that selfobject functions are central to any form of psychotherapy, including psychoanalysis. Thus, the Menninger findings about the transference cure and the central place of selfobject functions in self psychology support each other. At a minimum, the Menninger findings help refute the critics of self psychology, such as Rothstein (1980), who see self psychology as nothing more than "a corrective emotional experience," that is, a transference cure and, by implication, not productive of lasting change and by further implication, not "true analysis."

In summary: (1) Classical analysis is efficacious in producing structural change with a carefully selected group of patients who seek long term psychotherapeutic treatment; (2) supportive-expressive psychotherapy is much more effective in producing structural change than the theoretical model underlying classical analysis predicts; (3) neutrality, regressive transference neurosis, interpretation and insight form a limited general theory of structural change; and (4) Bibring's hierarchy of techniques for structural change is an inadequate way of conceiving the psychoanalysis and psychotherapy issue.

SELF PSYCHOLOGY, PSYCHOANALYSIS, AND PSYCHOTHERAPY

Kohut (1980) thought there was value in differentiating psychoanalysis from psychotherapy. Psychoanalysis is aimed at a person with disorders of the self who need changes in a "sector" of the self, whereas self-psychologically informed, intensive uncovering psychotherapy is aimed at persons who need changes in a "segment" of the self (p. 532). Precisely what Kohut meant by these terms is not defined, but it is clear that "sector" involves a more major change than "segment." It is also obvious that both psychoanalysis and self-psychologically informed psychotherapy create new structures in the self through transmuting microinternalizations.

Even though Kohut believed that psychoanalysis and psychotherapy have different aims, he rejected the notion that they are polar opposites. They have more in common than they have differences. In both modes a selfobject transference emerges as the analyst/therapist becomes empathically immersed in the patient's narrative. In both modes, significant gross identifications may occur. The difference between the two lies in the working through process, whereby the patient gradually relinquishes the need for an archaic selfobject. Kohut (1980) wrote:

> In psychotherapy the working through process will play a less significant role and will, in particular, not be carried out as systematically in the transference as in psychoanalysis proper but will be activated—by transference interpretations—only to that minimal extent necessary to reach the psychotherapeutic goal. A minimum of transference interpretations may thus be necessary to enable the patient to make the shift from the selfobject analyst

> to other selfobject figures and to diminish his sensitivities sufficiently to enable him to make use of the selfobject support that he can obtain from appropriate people in the surroundings without immediate withdrawal from them when they disappoint him . . . . Our aim in psychotherapy is primarily the improvement of functioning and well-being and only secondarily the attainment of maximal structural change . . . . The goal of psychotherapy . . . is the replacement of the deficits in the patient's self structure by appropriate self-selfobject relationships . . . support that can be obtained from the patient's family, or friends, or from various social institutions (such as religious organizations).
>
> Having attempted . . . to delineate the borders between psychoanalysis proper and psychoanalytically informed psychotherapy, it behooves me to admit at the end that, in practice, these differentiating lines cannot always be drawn sharply [p. 535].

Kohut (1984) cites as an example of what he means by a psychotherapeutic result compared with a psychoanalytic one, the curative work of Dr. Schweninger, Otto Von Bismark's physician. Bismark suffered from a sleep disturbance:

> Schweninger . . . came to Bismark's house at bedtime one evening and sat next to the statesman's bed until he had fallen asleep. When Bismark awakened the next morning, after a full night's sleep, Schweninger was still sitting at his bedside, welcoming him, as it were, into the new day. I believe it would be difficult to find a more striking clinical instance demonstrating how, via a transference enactment, the fulfillment of a patient's need for an empathically responsive selfobject can restore the patient's ability to fall sleep [pp. 19-20].

Kohut continues, "Schweninger's responsiveness to Bismark's need for a soothing idealized selfobject lead to psychotherapeutic but not psychoanalytic results unless the transference is interpreted and analytically worked through" (p. 20).

Kohut also saw that structuralization itself does not distinguish between psychoanalysis and psychotherapy, because some structuralization occurs during the "understanding phase" in psychoanalysis and psychotherapy. He (1984) raises the question:

> Specifically should we characterize the acquisition of the minute amounts of new psychic structures that are provided via the understanding phase alone—even when the analyst is unable to supplement his accurate understanding with a correct interpretation (e.g., because he is informed by a nonfitting theory or because he has explained too soon)—a psychoanalytic success or should we subsume it under the heading of "psychotherapy" [p. 103]?

Such thinking led Kohut to conclude that the essential difference between psychoanalysis and psychotherapy consisted of the extent to which explanations were a part of an extensive working-through process.

In psychoanalysis, where gross identification plays a larger role, there is a more extended and systematic working-through process; the archaic selfobject is gradually relinquished; and there is a strengthening of the goals and ideals of the nuclear self. The new, firmly consolidated inner structures enable appropriate selfobject needs to be met through interactions in the present-day surroundings (Kohut, 1980, p. 534).

In the Menninger Research Project, although the analysts did not use self psychology theory, the extensive working through process meant an additional 700 hours of sessions, on the average, for each client (300 for psychotherapy and 1,000 for psychoanalysis). Perhaps with a less "difficult to treat" population than was treated at the Menninger Foundation, the amount of time for each mode of healing might have been less, but the ratio might well have remained the same. The issue of psychoanalysis verses psychotherapy may eventually come down to a choice of how extensive and permanent the patient needs the new structures to be and whether the patient is willing to endure approximately three times the cost and effort.

Goldberg (1980b), in basic agreement with Kohut, states the matter a little differently. He too sees the difference as less in the method and more on the goals of treatment. He views psychotherapy as a repair of the self and psychoanalysis as a reorganization of the self. By using the terms repair and reorganization, Goldberg avoids Kohut's use of the spatial metaphors of sector and segment.

The distinction between repair and reorganization, however, may not always be easy to discern.

Muslin and Val (1987) apply Kohut's ideas to the three therapeutic modalities of the 50s: supportive psychotherapy, intensive psychotherapy and psychoanalysis. From a self psychology perspective, they see the link between these three treatment modalities as the use of selfobject functions. Distinctive to these three modalities is their use of these selfobjects functions to achieve different treatment aims. To Muslin and Val, supportive psychotherapy seeks to restore a patient's equilibrium by using the selfobject tie as an uninterpreted transference cure. Intensive psychotherapy aims to solve specific problems in the patient's life by using the selfobject tie to focus interpretations on major figures in the environment. Psychoanalysis tries to change major defects in the self, relived in the self–selfobject encounter, through interpretation and through the microinternalizations of the working through phase.

Self psychology certainly recognizes that psychoanalysis and psychotherapy have different treatment goals. Yet the very idea that disorders of the self can be substantially engaged—and significant therapeutic gains made—through either psychoanalysis or intensive psychotherapy informed by self-psychological principles, flies in the face of the traditional belief that narcissistic disorders need to be treated with support, manipulation or by use of parameters. Paul Ornstein (1974) summarizes this old position under two categories: (1) "analysis," for those patients more severely disturbed and for whom various degrees of manipulative measures are instituted when it is anticipated that an analyzable transference neurosis cannot develop. This approach can be successful, but it leaves unclear what has been useful; (2) "analysis with parameters," for the less severely disturbed for whom some form of active intervention prepares a defective ego and eventually leads to a transference neurosis. These parameters do not engage the central pathology and are interpretively resolved prior to termination (pp. 129-130).

Ornstein emphasizes that Kohut's new theoretical understanding of narcissism built on clinical experience, "leads to an expansion of the psychoanalytic method without evoking the use of parameters" (p. 147). Nor did Kohut need to use the manipulative techniques of Franz Alexander. Of course, Kohut's method applies to the more

Kohut – bridged psychoanalysis and self-psychology.

functional, higher level, narcissistic patients he saw in private practice but is not necessarily applicable to the sicker end of the narcissistic spectrum, such as borderlines and other severe character disorders, where various types of parameters and supportive techniques may need to be employed.

Rothstein (1980), a critic of self psychology, does not accept the position taken by Kohut and other self psychology authors; he thinks it is impossible to conduct psychoanalysis using a self psychology paradigm. For Rothstein, treatment offered by self psychology is neither psychoanalysis nor uncovering psychotherapy. It is merely the supportive kind (p. 445) because "Kohut's 'cure' occurs through nonverbal reparative internalizations" (p. 442) and not through interpretation and insight. He sees it as another version of Alexander and French's (1946) "corrective emotional experience" with its manipulative techniques, In the context of the distinctions introduced in the 50s, this is strong condemnation. The difficulty with Rothstein's position is that this distinction has not held up after 40 years of practice. Nor has he grasped the fact that self psychology, whether as intensive psychotherapy or psychoanalysis, does eventually "explain" (interpret) the selfobject transferences.

The difficulty seen by Rothstein and other critics seems to come from their commitment to a specific form of psychoanalysis, narrowly defined to treat neurotic patients. Kohut's new ideas feel foreign unless a more general understanding of Freud and psychoanalysis is taken. Basch (1983c) says of Kohut, for example:

> His method of conducting an analysis had not changed; it remained based on the fundamental premises laid down by Freud, namely, that cure was effected through promoting the patient's understanding of his pathology. This understanding was made possible by the interpretation and working through of the patient's transference to the analyst. What had changed was Kohut's grasp of the scope of transference [p. 234].

Basch, who has written two books about psychotherapy, *Doing Psychotherapy* (1980), and *Understanding Psychotherapy* (1988a) grounded in self psychology theory, says, "Kohut's work finally makes the method of psychoanalysis applicable to the various psychotherapies" (Basch, 1983c, p. 237).

Stolorow, who defines psychoanalysis as the science of the intersubjective (Atwood and Stolorow, 1984, p. 64), states that self psychology from an intersubjective perspective applies to psychoanalysis and psychoanalytic psychotherapy interchangeably (Atwood, Stolorow, and Trop, 1989).

In summary, Kohut and self psychology theory have made it possible for competent, well-trained helping professionals to practice self-psychologically informed psychotherapy without feeling what they do is "second class." As every new paradigm ultimately stands or falls on the practitioners who find a paradigm useful, self psychology has the potential to cut across the traditional barriers that have long been a source of tension in the healing professions and form a new base of mutual influence between psychoanalysis and the broader therapeutic community. Like any successful revolutionary paradigm, self psychology needs to become concretized in a new community of scholars and practitioners, a community that may be in the process of being born.

Even though Kohut's self psychology paved the way for a new healing paradigm for a broad group of professionals and for a new approach to both psychoanalysis and psychotherapy, it still remained incomplete in many ways when Kohut died. For the remainder of this book we touch on the work of the post-Kohutians, former colleagues, students, and others who have continued to develop the self psychology paradigm. In the next chapter we take a look at the concept of transference and the idea that it represents an unconscious organizing principle. This leads us to the position of the intersubjectivists and their stress on a phenomenological approach to psychotherapy.

Kohut

Readings for Chapter 18: Stolorow et al., 1987, chapter 3.

- goals of psychotherapy -

empathy - to understand selfobject experience and longings of the patient

- analysis therapy - repair structural defects in nuclear self to enable development to occur.

Stolorow - intersubjectivists

empathy - to learn of organizing principles of patient. the way someone thinks, feels, their meaning.

"You are feel bad about yourself – it's a state of mind not necessarily true or fact."

– ex: new organizing principle in the grip of an old idea ...

18

Transference as Organizing Principle

Self psychology has significantly changed the concept of transference. These changes started when Kohut insisted that narcissistic transferences (see chapters 11, 12 and 13, this volume) were different from the transferences observed in the neuroses. The traditional view of transference, the "false connection" idea of Freud, was used by him "to describe both a process of exchange between the unconscious and the preconscious across the repression barrier, and the consequences of that process for dreaming and the analytic relationship" (Basch, 1986, p. 27).

In a general definition, Bacal (1988) states that transference is "the patient's experience of his relationship with the analyst as determined by infantile experience" (p. 129). If viewed broadly, such a definition covers both the traditional idea of transference and Kohut's narcissistic transference. The crucial issue is the nature of the infant experience. In the traditional view, it is an actual experience during childhood that affects the therapeutic relationship. In Kohut's concept of the narcissistic transference, it is the absence of a needed experience, or mismatches of caretaker and child, that create a deficit in structure and transference longings. Kohut did not deny that the traditional transference occurs with neurotic patients. He thought, however, that the idea of transference needed to be broadened to include the narcissistic kind. Opposed to Kohut's view are those who believe that a narcissistic transference is not a "true" transference. Classical analysis defines transference narrowly, as a projection of the analysand's prior experience with significant objects onto the blank screen of the analyst.

While a struggle was taking place over whether the narcissistic transferences should be included within an expanded understanding of transference, the idea of a narcissistic transference broadened into the concept of a selfobject experience (see chapter 14, this volume). The longings based on deficits, as seen in the narcissistic transferences, were generalized into the seeking of formerly unavailable selfobject experiences. In conceptualizing selfobject experiences, Kohut opened up the possibility of primitive deficits besides those that were a part of the narcissistic disorders. Further, as a central construct of self psychology theory, the selfobject experience had the advantage of no longer having the name transference attached to it. Consequently, as the term selfobject experience began to replace the term narcissistic transference, debates over what was a true transference declined. Concomitantly, the significance of the classical view of transference decreased within self psychology.

There are good theoretical reasons why the traditional view of transference imposes a severe limitation in clinical work with nonneurotic patients. As initially described by Breuer and Freud (1893-1895), transference was a "false connection" made by the patient and later conceived as a "distortion" of the analyst's "real" qualities (Stolorow et al., 1988, p. 106). Schwaber (1983b) and others have shown that such a view is based on a "hierarchically ordered two-reality view" (p. 383), one reality experienced by the patient and the other, known to be more objectively true, by the analyst. This view of reality and classical analysis is firmly rejected by Schwaber, and by Stolorow and his colleagues. They believe that a hierarchically ordered, two-reality view is the reason analysis has not been of therapeutic benefit to more disturbed patients, that is, those with narcissistic disorders or psychoses.

Stolorow et al. (1987) are also critical of the classical view of transference. They represent an intersubjective position in self psychology that, following Kohut's emphasis on empathy as a methodology, conceives of psychoanalysis as the science of the subjective. They represent one important position in the post-Kohutian era of self psychology. From their point of view, they critique four major views of transference: (a) regression, (b) displacement, (c) projection, and (d) distortion. They then present (e), transference as organizing principle, (f) the intersubjective field, and (g) concretization.

TRANSFERENCE AS REGRESSION

Waelder (1956) stated:

> Transference may be said to be an attempt of the patient to revive and re-enact, in the analytic situation and in relation to the analyst, situations and phantasies of his childhood. Hence, transference is a regressive process [p. 367].

Stolorow et al. (1987) have difficulty with the idea of transference as regression. A clinical regression model assumes an isomorphic reenactment of traumatic relationships from the early history. It is very doubtful that this is possible. For example, it has been believed, based on Freud's ideas, that serious disturbances such as schizophrenia involve a regression to the earliest months of infancy. Yet evidence from observations of infants strongly indicates that adult autism and schizophrenia have no counterpart in infancy. Even in the first few months of life, there is significant interaction between mother and child. This is seen during the three-to-five month period of infancy, when mothers give the infant control—or rather the infant takes control—over the initiations and terminations of direct visual engagement in social activities (Stern, 1985).

Evidence of significant interaction between mother and infant in the first few months of life also means that there is no undifferentiated symbiotic stage in infancy to which to regress. Mahler (1979) argued for such a symbiotic stage to describe the state of fusion with the mother in which the "I" is not yet differentiated from the "not I" (p. 78). But Stern's (1985) infant research does not support Mahler's concept. Already in early infancy there is an emergent sense of self in the infant, differentiated from the self of the mother. Nor can it be said that a person regresses to an infant state, because a prolonged or continuous period of symbiosis is neither typical nor normative for an infant. Stern (1983) says that the infant alternates between periods of oneness, as inferred from synchronous patterns, and periods of disengagement.

Behind the assumption of the classical view of transference, that persons regress to an oral, anal or phallic stage, is the idea of regression as failure of renunciation. Having failed to renounce the cravings associated with the id drives, a person's ego becomes weakened and a regression occurs. So the basic assumption behind regression is drive theory. Once drive theory is discarded (see chapter 5, this volume), the idea of regression loses its theoretical underpinnings and its usefulness as a clinical explanation.

In contrast to conceiving of a patient as regressing, Stolorow and his colleagues advocate understanding regression as movement to another level of organization, an archaic level that had been prematurely aborted, precluded, or disavowed. In psychotherapy, the task is to integrate this archaic form of organization into more mature modes. Rather than saying that the patient has regressed to an infantile period, we can only say that a "patient's experiences are shaped by archaic organizing principles" (Stolorow et al., 1987, p. 32).

TRANSFERENCE AS DISPLACEMENT

The concept of displacement, also based on drive theory, was initially used to describe one of the mechanisms of dream work. Nunberg (1951), on the other hand, sees transference as displacement: "[the patient] displaces emotions belonging to an unconscious representation of a repressed object to a mental representation of an object of the external world" (p. 1).

Stolorow et. al. (1987), reject the view that transference is displacement because materialistic notions lie behind it:

> In our view of transference, there is nothing removed from the past and attached to the current situation. It is true that the organization of the transference gives the analyst a glimpse of what a childhood relationship was like or what the patient wished or feared it could have been like. However, this insight into the patient's early history is possible not because an idea from the past has been displaced to the present, but because the structures that were organized in the past either continue to be functionally effective or remain available for periodic mobilization [p. 33].

Stolorow and his colleagues are concerned that the concept of transference as displacement has perpetuated the view that the patient's experience of the analytic relationship is solely a product of the past and not determined by the analyst's behavior. With such a view, a therapist's interpretation of transference is often followed by a severe depression in the patient and an extreme feeling of hopelessness.

TRANSFERENCE AS PROJECTION

This idea draws heavily on the ideas of Melanie Klein. Racker (1954), for example, using Klein's concepts, viewed transference as the projection of rejecting internal objects onto the analyst whereby internal conflicts become converted into external ones. The neo-Kleinian Kernberg (1975) sees archaic transferences as arising from the operation of projective identification, a primitive mechanism to externalize all bad and aggressive self- and object images.

For Stolorow and his colleagues (1987) the idea of transference as projection is too limiting. It obscures the developmental dimension of transference from the more archaic to the less archaic. Moreover, how can projection be a primitive defense if projection can take place only after a self–object differentiation has occurred?

Instead of viewing splitting and projective identification as ways of explaining archaic transference states, Stolorow et al. hold that such transferences are best understood as developmental arrests at early modes of experience in which self and object are incompletely distinguished. It is more plausible to believe that such difficulty with distinguishing self and object is the result of psychic trauma—the inability to integrate powerful affects by an immature nervous system—than the result of elaborate mental processes such as splitting and projective identification. Klein's formulations "grant the child perceptual and cognitive qualities that would not be compatible with the immature state of his central nervous system" (Giovacchini, 1979, p. 23; see also Glover, 1945, and Zetzel, 1956).

TRANSFERENCE AS DISTORTION

Sullivan (1953) used distortion as generalized regression, displacement, and projection. His view assumes that the goal of treatment is to correct the distortions of what the analyst knows to be objectively real. This approach leaves judgments about "truth" to the therapist and was abandoned for the same reasons mentioned earlier by both Schwaber (1983a, 1983b) and Stolorow et al. (1987).

Stolorow and his colleagues (1987) think that "therapists often invoke the concept of distortion when the patient's feelings, whether denigrating or admiring, contradict self-perceptions and expectations that the therapist requires for his own well-being" (p. 35). Gill (1982), in accord with Stolorow and colleagues on this point, suggests that rather than conceiving of transference as distortion, it is better to say the experience is subject to other interpretations. For Winnicott (1951), whose position was that transference is contrary to the idea of distortion, transference is a sampling of the psychic reality of a person. It belongs to the realm of illusion, an "intermediate area" of experience, unchallenged in respect of its belonging to inner or external reality (p. 239), a statement that also is revelatory of Winnicott's respect for illusion.

TRANSFERENCE AS ORGANIZING PRINCIPLE

What analysts experience as transference is the patient's revealing his organizing principles. "Transference is conceived . . . as the expression of a universal psychological striving to organize experience and construct meanings" (Stolorow et al., 1987, p. 37) Out of that striving, "organizing principles and imagery that crystallized out of the patient's early formative experiences" (p. 36) continue to influence a person's relationships. The concept of transference refers to

> all the ways in which the patient's experience of the analytic relationship is shaped by his own psychological structures—by the distinctive, archaically rooted configurations of self and object that unconsciously organize his subjective universe [p. 36].

Freud had two views of transference. One was as resistance to remembering; the other as reexperiencing. The "resistance to remembering" concept has to be abandoned, according to Stolorow and his colleagues, because it is an archaeological metaphor. They believe the view of transference as re-experiencing is much more useful because it provides access to the patient's psychic world, that is, to the patient's organizing principles. They also reject Gill's position on the resolution of the transference, because, in practice, resolution becomes a synonym for renouncement.

Freud's focus on the emergence of transference as reexperiencing is clinically useful. Kohut (1977), going further, realized that patients often resisted transference reexperiencing out of fear of retraumatization and a fear of loss of self in merger. Writing about the "dread to repeat" as a major impediment to the unfolding of the patient's organizing principles, Anna Ornstein (1974) made a similar point.

In a significant theoretical move, Stolorow and his colleagues define the ubiquitous countertransference as the analyst's organizing activity. Such a definition accepts countertransference as an inevitable fact in itself neither good nor bad. It does not view countertransference as a dangerous computer virus that has to be eradicated as quickly as possible to make the mental apparatus, the computer, function without error. Both transference and countertransference are necessary components of the configurations of self and object, or self and selfobject, that take place within the therapeutic milieu, which Stolorow and his colleagues have termed the intersubjective context.

The idea that the transference constitutes the distortion of reality by the patient leads to the corollary that the therapist avoids contaminating the therapy so that the patient can see his or her own distortion more clearly. Such a view of transference places the whole burden of change on the patient, lowers the chances that a therapeutic milieu can foster growth and development, and turns the therapeutic relationship into a hostile one. All this implies that the therapist's organizing principles play no role in the therapy whatsoever. This view is based on the illusion that the therapist can invariably be objective and neutral, and abstain from instinctual gratification in order to be a truly blank screen. Such a stance is as undesirable to maintain as it is impossible to achieve. Brandchaft (1989) writes:

> [Kohut] came to see the role of the analyst and the stance he adopts, which determines what he does and does not, what he says or what he refrains from saying, as an immanent force *in principle* and not simply as a factor of occasional and intrusive countertransference [p. 240].

Further, if transference is viewed as emanating entirely from the patient, it requires that the patient relinquish his organizing principles and psychic reality in favor of the therapist's. Such a process, if pursued relentlessly, may invite a psychotic collapse, force a masochistic surrender, or encourage the development, through conformity, of a new false self. From self psychology's point of view, the patient's resistance to relinquishing his own organizing principles under such a condition is an indication of health rather than a sign of pathology.

"Transference cure" has traditionally been applied pejoratively to patients who have "recovered" because of the unanalyzed influence of an unconscious instinctual tie to the analyst. The implication of a transference cure is that because the tie to the therapist remains unanalyzed, the cure is not permanent. By contrast, self psychology sees the exploration of the transference/countertransference dyad, the intersubjective field, as permanently changing the organization of the patient's self, hence alleviating the necessity for a continuing tie to the therapist. The results of the Menninger Psychotherapy Research Project (see chapter 17, this volume) support self psychology's position: changes that occurred from transference cures were surprisingly stable when investigated in the follow-up evaluation.

Traditional transference analysis requires that the patient renounce his infantile wishes toward the analyst. A better view of these wishes is to include them in an expanded self-organization. Self psychology holds that only as these transference longings are responded to by the therapist, functioning as a needed selfobject, is the patient able to transform his archaic wishes into mature selfobject needs. These needs are expressed through the establishment of a network of healthy adult relationships that provide an ongoing "empathic matrix" for the patient after psychotherapy.

THE INTERSUBJECTIVE FIELD

Taking the position that transference is an expression of a self's organizing principles, Stolorow and his colleagues (1987) see psychotherapy as an exploration and understanding of the interaction between the organizing principles of two subjective selves. In view of a self's need for selfobjects (see chapter 14, this volume), however, the idea of two selves interacting is an oversimplification. More accurately, the patient, using the therapist as a selfobject (one self/selfobject unit), interacts with the therapist, who uses the patient as a selfobject (another self/selfobject unit).

Combining this idea of a self/selfobject unit with the concept of organizing principles, we see that psychotherapy entails a very complex, special relationship. This relationship consists of the patient's organizing principles, including the self/selfobject unit, interacting with the therapist's organizing principles, including a self/selfobject unit. As can be readily understood, the description of a psychotherapeutic relationship using these terms becomes cumbersome indeed! Stolorow offers an alternative through the concept of analysis as the science of the intersubjective.

Although the idea of intersubjectivity comes from philosophy and has been familiar to infant developmentalists for some time (Newson, 1977; Trevarthan, 1977), Stolorow has approached it through Henry Murray's ideas of personology. Nurtured in this subjective tradition, Stolorow and Atwood eventually saw the need for the concept of intersubjectivity because of their psychobiological studies of the personal origins of the theoretical systems of Sigmund Freud, Carl Jung, Wilhelm Reich, and Otto Rank, which they collected in the book, *Faces in a Cloud* (Stolorow and Atwood, 1979). After the publication of this book, Stolorow and his colleagues made the intersubjective context their central explanatory concept for understanding psychotherapy. Stolorow sees the intersubjective field as comprising the interaction of two subjectivities—of the patient and of the analyst. Because the observational stance is always from within, there are often gross disparities between the therapist's and the patient's respective worlds of experience.

Stolorow uses the example of the borderline personality to illustrate what he means. One view, Kernberg's (1975), is that the borderline personality has a discrete, stable, pathological character structure rooted in instinctual conflicts and primitive defenses. Stolorow et al. (1987) view the borderline syndrome much differently. They see the clinical material believed to be indicative of instinctual conflicts and defenses as evidence of (1) the need for specific archaic selfobject ties and (2) the disturbances of such ties. When a shift in psychotherapy occurs whereby the needed understanding is felt to be present, the borderline features tend to recede and even disappear, only to return when the selfobject bond is again significantly disrupted.

The idea of an intersubjective field challenges the assumption of an "objective reality" that can be known by the analyst and eventually by the patient, an assumption that lies at the heart of the traditional view of analysis. Schwaber (1988b) argues against the notion of transference as distortion because of its embeddedness in "a hierarchically ordered two-reality view" (p. 383), "one reality experienced by the patient and the other 'known' by the analyst to be more objectively true" (Stolorow et al., 1987, p. 35). This concept of "objective reality" is an example of concretization of subjective truth (Stolorow et al., 1987, p. 134).

An early clinical issue surrounding the question of objective reality was whether childhood seductions or infantile fantasies accounted for the genesis of hysteria (Masson, 1984). Transcending both these views is the idea that the images of seduction, regardless of whether they derive from memories of actual events or from fantasy reconstructions, contain symbolic encapsulations of critical, pathogenic features of the patient's early subjective reality.

Intersubjective reality is not "discovered" or "recovered" or "created" or "constructed," but *crystallizes* during treatment. Though influenced by the analyst's organizing activity, intersubjective reality is articulated through a process of empathic resonance, that is, through attunement.

Atwood and Stolorow (1984) claim that the importance of the intersubjective field is evident in the variability of results of analysis, depending on the analyst conducting it. The actual conduct of a case consists of a series of empathic inferences about the nature of a person's life, inferences that alternate and interact with the analyst's acts of reflection on the involvement of his own reality in the ongoing investigation.

"tangibalization" goes on intrapsychically

CONCRETIZATION

manifestation —

Stolorow and his colleagues (1987) also see the idea of concretization as an important construct for a psychoanalytic science of human experience. They define concretization as the "encapsulation of organizations of experience by concrete sensorimotor symbols" (p. 132). Concretization explains a variety of psychological phenomena,

> including neurotic symptoms, symbolic objects, sexual and other enactments, and dreams A broad range of psychopathological symptoms are thereby recognized as concrete symbols of the psychological catastrophes and dilemmas that emerge in specific intersubjective fields [p. 132].

Neurotic Symptoms

The first major demonstration of the use of concretization in the development of psychopathological symptoms came from Breuer and Freud (1893-1895), who discovered that hysterical conversion symptoms and other neurotic inhibitions could be relieved by uncovering their unconscious meaning. Unfortunately drive theory, mired in drive-energy formulations that resorted to cryptophysiological energy transformations for explanation, led therapists away from the idea that the use of concrete sensorimotor symbolism was at the core of symptom formation.

Atwood and Stolorow (1984) give a clinical example of concretization. A 33-year-old woman in the midst of a four-year treatment reported a new symptom—a tightening of her throat and a difficulty with swallowing—that coincided with recent successes she had in comparison with some other women. Investigation uncovered childhood feelings of guilt whenever she presented her chronically depressed mother with a success. The patient reported, "Whenever I brought home an 'A' from school . . . it was like shoving my success down my mother's throat" (p. 86). As Atwood and Stolorow point out, "the sensorimotor symbolism of the throat encapsulated her sense of guilt over the injury her success might inflict on her mother, and the concretization served the purposes of atonement and self-punishment" (p. 87).

Symbolic Objects

Winnicott's (1951) "transitional object" is a ubiquitous example of concretization. He noticed that small children use something soft and cuddly to temper the anxiety and depression evoked by separations—both physical and psychological—from the mother. The transitional object makes concrete the illusion of a maternal presence. In Atwood and Stolorow's terms (1984), "The material object symbolically encapsulates the soothing, comforting, calming qualities of the maternal selfobject, and the concretization serves a restitutive function in mending or replacing the broken merger" (p. 88).

Clinical examples of transitional objects abound. A patient of one of the authors carried his business card with raised lettering in her pocket. When she needed soothing, she rubbed her fingers across the raised lettering of the card. Another patient called the office when she knew her therapist was not there just to hear his voice on the answering machine; there was seldom a need to leave a message. Other patients audiotaped portions of sessions for listening over weekends and vacations. As Atwood and Stolorow (1984) explain,

> Winnicott's conceptualization of the transitional object can . . . be seen as a particular instance of a more general psychological process whereby needed configurations of experience are symbolically materialized by means of concrete physical objects" [1984, p. 89].

Hence, they restore self-cohesion and defend against the experience of self fragmentation.

Enactments

Enactments, although referring to the same behavioral observation or clinical experience as acting out, are in no way understood as the same thing. Acting out is a concept based on classical analysis and drive theory; erotic and aggressive drives are acted out as a result of the failure of sublimation, repression, and ultimately renunciation. The importance of enactments in concretizing and maintaining organizations of experience cannot be overstated. A self-psychological view of character rests on the assumption that

> recurrent patterns of conduct serve to actualize (Sandler and Sandler, 1978) the nuclear configurations of self and object that constitute a person's character. Such patterns of conduct may include inducing others to act in predetermined ways, so that a thematic isomorphism is created between the ordering of the subjective and the interpersonal fields [Atwood and Stolorow, 1984, p. 91].

Thus, enactments perform a vital function requiring concrete courses of action to maintain the structural integrity of a subjective world. Atwood and Stolorow (pp. 92-97) provide an excellent analysis of the reasons so many people use sexual enactments to restore and maintain precarious structures of subjectivity.

Dreams

Freud (1900) held two theories of dreams, one metapsychological, the other clinical. The metapsychological theory, thoroughly discredited by Klein (1976), received far more of Freud's attention than did the clinical theory. In it he conceptualized dreams as mechanical consequences of energic charge "striving to find an outlet." In his clinical theory, he asserted that dreams are deliberate and serve both defensive and wish-fulfilling purposes.

In stark contrast, Atwood and Stolorow (1984) contend that dreams serve a vital psychological function:

> By reviving during sleep the most basic and emotionally compelling form of knowing—through sensory perception —the dream affirms and solidifies the nuclear organizing structures of the dreamer's subjective life. Dreams . . . are the *guardians of psychological structure*, and they fulfill this vital purpose by means of concrete symbolization [p. 103].

Understanding the concept of concretization is important for clinical practice, because concretization mediates the relationship of experience and action. Concretization is the basis of neurotic symptoms, symbolic objects, enactments, and dreams. All are used for the concrete symbolization that crystallizes and preserves the organization of the subjective world.

In summary, self psychology as understood by those stressing intersubjectivity has changed the idea of transference as distortion to one of transference as an organizing activity. When the organizing activities of therapist and patient interact, they set up an intersubjective field. Therapeutic change occurs as a result of exploring and understanding this intersubjective context and the concretizations that express the patient's subjective experience. How to make such change more lasting involves the process of structuralization, the focus of discussion in the next chapter.

Readings for Chapter 19: Kohut, 1984, chapter 6; Mitchell, 1988, pp. 46-52; Terman, 1988.

19

Structuralization

During the last hundred years, psychotherapy has amply demonstrated its ability to help persons to change their thoughts, feelings and behavior. Lasting personality changes, however, have been more difficult to achieve. Issues of lasting changes raise questions about structuralization. How does psychotherapy cure? Can personality deficits be corrected through the building up of new, permanent patterns of responding, traditionally called psychic structures?

This chapter makes two points about structuralization. First, the term better describes the process underlying lasting personality change than do the terms internalization or introjection. Second, structuralization best takes place under conditions of both optimal empathy and repairs to empathic failures. We emphasize these points during exploration of the following subjects: (a) definition, (b) internalization, (c) optimal frustration, (d) selfobject failures, (e) structuralization during empathy, and (f) resistances to structuralization.

structuralization —
reorganizing principle—

DEFINITION

Structuralization is the process of acquiring "structures of experience" (Atwood and Stolorow, 1984, p. 33). It is the opposite of self-fragmentation (Stolorow, 1980, p. 164). A structure is defined as an "enduring reorganization of the subjective field" (Atwood and Stolorow, 1984, p. 39). By enduring organization or structure Rapaport (1959) meant configurations with a slow rate of change. Such structures are also called systems of ordering, organizing principles (Piaget, 1970), cognitive-affective schemata (Klein, 1976), and patterns (Goldberg, 1988). Terman (1988) defines structure formation as the "acquisition of pattern and meaning" (p. 114).

INTERNALIZATION

Mitchell (1988, pp. 46-51) clearly describes Freud's development of the concept of internalization. He shows how Freud developed the idea in searching for an explanation for pathological mourning. In "Mourning and Melancholia" Freud (1917) argued that the self accusations of the psychotically depressed patient who has lost a loved one are but castigations directed to the internalized deceased person. This explanation left Freud questioning the reason for the internalization. His solution was to link internalization to a gross identification with the lost object so as to preserve a channel for drive regulation. The lost object is clung to in its internalized form, a more pleasant experience than renouncing the lost object and searching for new objects.

Freud (1921) expanded his concept of internalization in "Group Psychology and the Analysis of the Ego". He developed the idea that identification is "the earliest expression of an emotional tie with another person" (p. 105). Freud thus broadened the concept of identification to a more general theory of child development and seemed almost seemed ready to abandon drive theory for a relational model. Then Freud (1923) solved the problem by resorting to the concept of the superego in his "The Ego and the Id". The superego derives from the internalization process that is compensation for the child's renouncing of oedipal wishes. Thus, the superego is "the heir to the Oedipus complex" (p. 36). By postulating the superego, Freud was able to retain drive theory and yet hold a view of identification associated with what he believed was the pivotal loss/wound of childhood—the oedipal defeat. To Freud, then, internalization accompanies the identification that occurs from a significant object loss.

Goldberg (1990) is critical of Freud's view of internalization because of its "storehouse" theory of mental representations. Such a theory involves the storing and retrieving of perceptions about the world. Representations are meant to be an accurate record of everything that takes place, gradually filling the empty mind of the child. As Goldberg notes, "The infant has no ideas until they are given, no words until they are taught: the infant has no sense until instructed" (p. 95). The purpose of such representations is to avoid the inconvenience of literally carrying around the objects of the world to use as a comparison, but they serve the same function. A representation, as a substitute or stand-in, is an inner "picture" of an outer phenomenon.

Freud's concept of the mind as internalized representations is considered by modern theorists as too simplistic and too limiting. Only some parts of language, speech, and thought are connected to internal pictures. According to Friedman (1980), internalization involves high-level abstractions that have been heavily influenced by theory. "Thus, representations are not records of raw experience as much as they are inferences from a person's experience" (Goldberg, 1990, p. 100). They are not the same as memory.

Representations involve unconscious organizing of experience. Hence, searching for repressed representations in a classically conducted psychoanalysis must inevitably lead to frustration. In contrast to this storehouse theory of representation is connection theory. As Goldberg states, "Connection theories are, in contrast, not corrective; they do not assume that the world is initially copied and periodically compared, but rather that it is continuously formed" (p. 112). If a theory of internalization is to be retained, it needs to be different from Freud's theory of representations.

Hartmann (1939) had a different view from Freud's. As he conceived it, internalization is a process through which autonomous self-regulation replaces regulation from the external environment. Kohut (1971) utilized Hartmann's idea to conceptualize internalization as the process by which the selfobject functions needed by narcissistic personalities are transmuted into psychic structure. Kohut used the phrase "transmuting internalization" (p. 49), for which there are three necessary prior conditions: (1) maturational readiness, (2) frustration by a cathected object, and (3) a shift from the whole object of cathexis to some of the object's functions. Transmuting internalization may have been the major, perhaps only, way Kohut envisaged structuralization. Nevertheless, we take the view that internalization is only one form of structuralization.

Schafer (1976) criticized Hartmann's notion of internalization because it used physicalistic and spatial reifications. Schafer thought it could be too easily viewed as Melanie Klein's introjective identification, which uses the analogy of a person taking in an object as if eating it. So Schafer attempted to do away with the construct of internalization altogether and develop the idea of self-regulatory capacities conceptualized in nonspatial terms. As Schafer (1968) defines it, "Internalization refers to all those processes by which the subject transforms real or imaginary regulatory interactions with his environment, and real or imagined characteristics of his environment, into inner regulations and characteristics" (p. 9).

Goldberg (1983) also thinks that the concept of internalization creates problems because it is linked to the idea "that continuing growth and structuralization lead to adult positions of independence and autonomy" (p. 298). He agrees with Schafer that we need an alternative to the concept of internalization, but until we find one, Goldberg finds some useful clinical advantage in shifting the focus to ideas of ownership, privacy, and representability (p. 300). These are subjective states that clients experience as being important.

Stolorow, however, retains the concept of internalization but interprets it in the nonintrojective sense as "an enduring reorganization of the subjective field in which experienced qualities of a selfobject are translocated and assimilated into the child's own self-structure" (Atwood and Stolorow, 1984, p. 39). Wolf (1983b) too, wants to redefine internalization as "a reorganization and reintegration of perceptions and their associated ideas, and not any location in a space-occupying mind" (p. 314).

Grotstein (1983), taking a position similar to Stolorow's and Wolf's, asks:

> Does the infant (child) take in aspects of the selfobject and internalize these as its own self-regulating function, as Kohut

transmuting internalization —
change idea of self

optimal frustration —
not exclusive —

indicates? Or is this self-regulating function always there potentially from the beginning, and is it more maturation and development that takes place under the auspices of the interpersonal other? Perhaps what one internalizes is not so much the object and its functions, as one's *experience* with the object. If we take Fairbairn's and Bion's point of view, we might rephrase Kohut's idea of transmuting internalizations as transmuting *realizations* or *transformations* of undeveloped functions that exist in the infant from the very beginning. The selfobject experience then "shepherds" the development of these rudimentary functions [pp. 176-177].

OPTIMAL FRUSTRATION

Most of the debate around Kohut's ideas of structuralization in narcissistic personalities centers on his belief in the necessity of "optimal frustration" by a bonded selfobject. Some self psychologists are uncomfortable with Kohut's theory of transmuting internalization through optimal frustration. They are not satisfied with his use of internalization as a special form of introjection, even though Kohut differentiated himself from Klein by describing internalization as a whole series of minor introjections (microinternalizations) over a period of time. To make sure that internalization does not mean Klein's macrointrojection, for example, Wolf (1988) refers to internalization as structure formation. "Transmuting internalization is Kohut's term for a process of structure formation in which aspects of the function of the self-selfobject transaction are internalized under the pressure generated by optimal frustration" (p. 187).

Other self psychologists are dissatisfied with the idea that structuralization takes place only through optimal frustration. Stolorow, for example, is especially critical of Kohut's use of the term "optimal frustration." He and colleagues (1987) remind us that optimal frustration was formulated by Freud under the mechanical assumptions of drive theory (p. 22). To Freud (1923), "the ego is that part of the id which has been modified by the direct (frustrating) influence of the external world" (p. 25). Kohut (1984) thought that the repeated interpretation of the patient's experiences of optimal frustration by the narcissistically invested selfobject would result in a process of fractionalized withdrawal of narcissistic cathexis from the object and a concomitant redeployment of these cathexes in the gradual formation of particles of psychic structure, which then exercised the functions that had been performed by the object. According to Stolorow et al. (1987), this classical interpretation of internalization is incompatible with self psychology.

Kohut, however, is not without some support for his position that frustration can foster structuralization. For example, infant researchers Stechler and Kaplan (1980) view self development as a series of syntheses, active resolutions of crisis that occur when expectancies about a relationship are violated. The child tries to repair the "violations" by taking on aspects of the caretaker's functions and in so doing, develops self-regulating functions. This form of support for Kohut's position does not imply that optimal frustration is the only means of structuralization, nor the most effective.

SELFOBJECT FAILURES

By 1984 Kohut had shifted his thinking slightly from "optimal frustration" to "temporary, and thus nontraumatic, empathy failures—that is, his 'optimal failures'" (p. 66). Kohut sees "the acquisition of self-esteem-regulating psychological structure in the analysand" (p. 67) as taking place through empathic lapses on the part of the therapist. He still maintains that "psychological structure is laid down (a) via optimal frustrations and (b) in consequence of optimal frustration, via transmuting internalization" (pp. 98-99). Supporting Kohut in his position is the observation of infant specialists that "psychic structure is created when disruptions occur and the infant is able momentarily to take over functions of the parents" (Beebe and Lachmann, 1988, p. 20). Terman (1988) responds that "Kohut put his concepts directly in line with classical theory and carefully divorced his theories and techniques from the onus of providing gratification" (p. 113). Even so, with usage, Kohut's optimal frustration became to mean "empathic failure."

Clinical experience with narcissistic patients generally supports the importance of monitoring a patient's behavior for symptoms that indicate an experience of "empathic failure." Stolorow (1986a) stresses that empathic failure refers "not to things that the analyst

→ one internalizes The experience of being with another person in a positive transference.

does or fails to do, but to psychic reality—that is, to developmentally predetermined subjective experiences of the patient, revived and analyzed in the transference" (p. 44).

When a therapist learns to recognize a patient's way of signaling an empathic lapse and is able to discuss this openly with the patient, this discussion is usually enough to repair the bond between the patient and the therapist. In fact, the therapist's acknowledgment of an empathic lapse may considerably strengthen the bond and lead to the surfacing and exploration of deeper material. Without interpretation of a patient's experience of an empathic lapse, the treatment of narcissistic disorders would be difficult, if not impossible. This approach is now followed by many self psychologists, not because they believe in the necessity of optimal frustration, but because the recognition and repair of empathic failure strengthens the therapeutic bond and is an opportunity for structuralization to take place.

In chapter 9 it was posited that the major purpose of the empathic method is to understand the selfobject functions the therapist fulfills. If this is so, then the idea of a selfobject failure is a more useful way of viewing the need for a repair of the therapeutic bond than is the idea of an empathic lapse. Supporting this selfobject failure position is the fact that there are many areas of a patient's life where a therapist's lack of empathy does not produce the experience of a "temporary and nontraumatic failure" in the patient. On the other hand, where there is selfobject failure, explaining what has happened, as a means of repairing the therapeutic bond, is essential. Stolorow and his colleagues (1987) prefer to use the term selfobject failure rather than empathic failure because selfobject failure "more clearly designates a subjective experience of the patient in the transference" (p. 17, n.1).

A vignette from the senior coauthor's case of Mr. B illustrates a selfobject failure and its repair. Presenting as a depressed person, Mr. B began twice-a-week psychotherapy that extended over an 18 month period and led to a bond that shifted between idealized, mirror, and twinship transferences. Mr. B then sought disability insurance requiring his therapist to fill in a short form. The insurance company's posted form to the therapist was returned because of a wrong address and then sent to the patient. After a brief discussion in which he expressed aversion to this intrusion into his privacy and a reluctance to have the information sent, the patient acceded to the therapist's answering the insurance company's questions.

Two sessions afterward, the patient arrived 15 minutes late. He was clearly depressed. He had been rejected for the disability policy, and his insurance agent blamed the therapist. When the patient suspiciously asked about the diagnosis, the therapist said "It was 'dysthymic disorder' as we had discussed."

Exploration confirmed that Mr. B was angry because he was experiencing the therapist as not supporting him. He also experienced painful, resurrected feelings of anger with a father who had never supported him against the irrational control of his mother. The therapist did not defend his own behavior or apologize. He said that the patient was experiencing him (the therapist) as failing him. After the patient had confirmed these feelings, the therapist indicated a willingness to write a detailed letter to the insurance company, supporting the liability insurance request and stating that the patient was a low disability risk because he had sought psychotherapy and had a good prognosis. This offer was accepted and a letter sent. Two sessions later the patient's spontaneous flow of material indicated that the bond had been repaired.

Even though the concept of structuralization, when viewed as internalization or introjection, has dangers of spatial and physicalistic reification, the subjective experience of having a nourishing, sustaining presence "inside" seems to have brought great comfort and been of immeasurable help to countless human beings throughout history. Khan (1974) for example, wrote that the famous "Montaigne established a private space in his library at Chateau de Montaigne for himself, and in this space he lived through an extremely devout relationship to an inner presence" of his dead friend La Boetie (p. 102).

Before Montaigne, everything in human self-experience had found its authenticity through an experience of God. This secularization of self-experience was "Montaigne's unique contribution towards the epistemology of self-experience" (p. 103). It was a revolutionary step, and it reminds us that "in the medieval ages, it was not unknown for persons of sensibility and imagination to retreat into monastic orders and concentrate on their self-experience in the presence of God" (p. 103). Such a phrase as the "presence of God," often seen as pious posing and not easily understood by persons in a secular age, seems to have been a religious way of expressing the valuable experience of structuralization.

STRUCTURALIZATION DURING EMPATHY

Structuralization is also fostered by empathy. Empathy, especially in conjunction with affective states, is experienced as a facilitating medium reinstating developmental processes of self-articulation and self-demarcation that were aborted and arrested during formative years. Structure formation occurs primarily when the bond is intact or is in the process of being restored is optimal empathy (Stolorow et al., 1987). Most who support this view of optimal empathy accept the idea that empathic failure may foster structuralization; they see it as a minor means, but certainly not the only means of structuralization

Terman (1988) is another who takes the position that structuralization takes place under conditions of empathy and that changes in his patients occur from experiences in the analysis that have nothing to do with frustration. He supports his clinical experience with the developmental studies of Vygotsky (1978), who stressed the interpersonal genesis of the acquisition of language. He also saw all higher cognitive functions as originating in actual relations between people, for to him, "an interpersonal process is transformed into an intrapersonal one" (p. 57). For Vygotsky "the structuralization of the mind grew out of human relationships and could not be understood apart from them" (Terman, 1988, p. 115).

Terman sees the work of Kaye (1982) as supporting the idea that structuralization arises from other than frustration and internalization. Vygotsky stresses the "outside in" process; on the other hand, Freud and Piaget saw development as "inside out," that is, as the unfolding of innate, internally determined patterns. Like Vygotsky, Kaye sees the infant as an apprentice who is induced into a societal system by the goals and techniques of the parent. "Those structures which appeared to Piaget to evolve autonomously seem, for Kaye, to arise from the matrix *parental* goals and expectations" (Terman, 1988, p. 115). According to Kaye, at two months sharing begins as a unilateral responsibility of the parent. Parents guess the intentions underlying an infant's activity, speak to their child through many modes, and integrate the child into their already existing social system. By eight months or so, the sharing of intentions has become a two-way process. The development has been from apprenticeship to full partnership.

Kaye describes seven ways that parents "frame" a child's behavior, that is provide essential regularities for the child. These are nurturant, protective, instrumental, feedback, modeling, discourse, and memory functions. Around these functions the dialogue with the child takes place, with the child gradually taking them over. Through these functions the mother creates the structure of the dialogue with the infant.

This structuring changes the schemas, the patterns, with which the child organizes the world. As Terman (1988) states:

> The changing and growth of patterns occur in the context of intense interaction. The *interaction*, not the spaces between the interactions, changes the structures. It is not the *loss* of the transaction, but rather its *presence* that structures . . . . It stretches credulity to maintain that the *withholding*, or *delay*, of such transactions is *the* essential step in development of the structures that accrue from them. Further, to concentrate on a hypothetical delay to the neglect of the transaction misses the central areas of experience without which there can be nothing [p. 117].

Beebe and Lachmann (1988) emphasize the role of interactional patterns in organizing an infant's experience: "The model of psychic structure formation underlying this discussion is that characteristic patterns of interactive regulation organize experience" (p. 20). They concede that structure is formed when a child resolves "breaches" by taking on aspects of caretaking functions; they conclude that "a combination of the two models yields a fuller picture of the complexity of the early organization of experience" (p. 21).

Flexnor's (1967) account of George Washington and political structural change involving the 13 states during the American revolutionary war, relates a process analogous to that of structural change in an individual. Initially, the revolt was by 13 independent colonies who formed an alliance to battle the forces of the British king, George III. If the military forces of the 13 colonies had been successful in the initial campaigns—Breed's Hill and Long Island—the result would have been 13 independent countries that had temporarily united for a common task. The sovereignty of each state would have remained unchanged.

As it was, the protracted eight-year struggle led to a permanent army (Continental), whose formation became the first executive function of a new corporate entity, the federal government. The states resisted the symbolic representation of the emerging nation—the army—by refusing to pay into the common treasury from their taxes. They used the "power of the purse" to resist giving up some state sovereignty. The army's development forced structural change over an eight year period that was difficult, indeed impossible, for the states to reverse.

Structuralization becomes an issue in the corporate world under the concept of "vertical integration" (Schonberger, 1982, p. 173). With vertical integration, a major manufacturing corporation, for instance, takes over the production of a part that was previously made by one of its vendors. Options involved in this process illustrate the differences between internalization as incorporation and structuralization. Sometimes the manufacturer buys the vendor company and manufacturers the part using the ex-vendor employees in a move similar to incorporation. The manufacturer is then in a position to control more closely the production of the part. Often such vertical integration is precipitated by serious, repeated failures by the vendor to supply a quality part on time and in accurate quantities.

Even when a frustrated manufacturer seeks vertical integration, the vendor firm, or another suitable vendor firm with a capacity to produce the part, may not be for sale. The manufacturer may then set up a department to manufacture the part. That is, influenced by the experience with and knowledge of the vendor's operations, the manufacturer organizes (structures) the production of the part within its own manufacturing plant. Thus, the business world conceives of corporate structuralization as taking place both with and outside the process of incorporation of the vendor into a larger organization. More often than not, the structuralization involved in vertical integration takes over the functions previously performed the vendor, without incorporating the vendor as a total unit (buildings, machinery, and personnel). That is, only the way (pattern) the part was made by the vendor is structured into the manufacturing process.

RESISTANCE TO STRUCTURALIZATION

Resistances that occur in the middle phase of psychotherapy often interfere with structuralization. One form of resistance is the wish to leave treatment as soon as the patient begins to feel better. Another occurs when the patient experiences a boring stalemate after months of meaningful sessions and a deep therapeutic bond has developed. This growing bond may have awakened fears of an unbreakable dependency and the loss of individuation and is a sign that the patient recognizes value in the therapist's functioning. If these needs went unrecognized, there would be no conscious fear of a life-long dependency on the therapist. Ironically, the success of the initial phases of therapy is usually a precondition for resistances to the processes of structuralization.

Such a resistance to structuralization is resolved by exploring with the patient the reason for the stalemate, looking carefully for evidence of dependency fears that the successful movement through the initial stages has enabled to emerge. This exploration leads to an explanation that a gradual, unconscious structuralizing of the therapeutic functions the patient finds useful takes place over time in psychotherapy. Once the structuralizing purpose of the last phase of the therapy is accepted by the patient, resistance to structuralization fades, if not disappears.

Another sign of resistance to structuralization is the patient's regular sharing of a "blow by blow" description of the therapy to a spouse, parent, or close friend. Structuralization is fostered by keeping what passes in the treatment as secret or private (Goldberg, 1983). The converse is that those who find it hard to keep secrets lack many of the functions that make for a cohesive sense of self. Not keeping secrets seems to serve as a form of triangulation, that is, a three-person relationship (Bowen, 1978) that defends against the dangers inherent in an overdependent two-person relationship and is a special variation of the resistance to structuralization just discussed.

Yet another type of resistance to structuralization may be taking place when patients want to stay in therapy forever. Such a "therapeutic lifer" (Wallerstein, 1986) may have a strong need for a merger transference in which the therapist is used as a transitional selfobject. This patient feels secure by experiencing control over the therapist as if the therapist were an intimate part of the patient. Once the merger experience has continued long enough to satisfy the patient's need for cohesion, the patient gradually experiences the therapist as more individuated and becomes motivated to structuralize the functions that the therapist performs. As the need for the therapist as a transitional selfobject recedes and the illusion of control disappears, so the resistance to structuralization diminishes.

In summary, self psychology now views structuralization as a broader process than was covered by Kohut's construct of transmuting internalization. Hartmann's notion of internalization, as used by Kohut, can be discarded because it too easily conveys the idea of introjection. Drive notions of gratification can also be discarded to allow for structuralization under conditions of empathy, as can Kohut's notion of structuralization as following the repairing of empathic failures. Even Kohut's idea of empathic failure is better viewed as selfobject failure. Even so, Kohut's emphasis on the importance of structuralization in psychoanalysis and psychotherapy is retained within self psychology. The amount of structuralization attempted is seen as the major difference between psychoanalysis and psychotherapy. Successful therapeutic work demands major attention to the resistances to structuralization, especially the fears of perpetual dependency.

Resistances to structuralization are not the only source of stalemates in psychotherapy. Termed originally by Freud as "negative therapeutic reactions," such impasses not only may threaten to derail or undermine therapeutic gains, they may also present powerful opportunities for therapeutic growth. We examine this important subject in the next chapter.

Readings for Chapter 20: Balint, 1936; Brandchaft, 1983; Schwaber, 1983a; Atwood, Stolorow and Trop, 1989.

20

Negative Therapeutic Reactions

Toward the end of Freud's life, growing reports of negative therapeutic reactions in cases of even competent analysts, along with Freud's growing doubts about the long-term effectiveness of psychoanalysis, suggested that something was seriously wrong with the analytic paradigm. As Brandchaft (1982) says "Psychoanalytic literature . . . abounds with descriptions of patients who react negatively and relentlessly refuse to yield to analytic interpretation" (p. 328). We examine the concept of negative therapeutic reaction under the following topics: (a) definition, (b) the Wolf Man, (c) narcissistic resistances, (d) intersubjectivity and impasses, and (e) intersubjective conjunctions and disjunctions.

DEFINITION

A negative therapeutic reaction in psychotherapy is an exacerbation of patient symptoms in response to a "correct" interpretation.

> There are certain people who behave in a quite peculiar fashion during the work of analysis. When one speaks hopefully to them or expresses satisfaction with the progress of the treatment, they show signs of discontent and their condition invariably becomes worse. One begins by regarding this as defiance and as an attempt to prove their superiority to the physician, but later one comes to take a deeper and juster view. One becomes convinced, not only that such people cannot endure any praise or appreciation, but that they react inversely to the progress of the treatment. Every partial solution that ought to result, and in other people does result, in an improvement or a temporary suspension of symptoms produces in them for the time being an exacerbation of their illness; they get worse during the treatment instead of better. They exhibit what is known as a "negative therapeutic reaction" [Freud, 1923, p. 49].

One would expect that if the interpretation is correct and well-timed, then a negative reaction should not result. Theoretically a correct, well-timed interpretation should lead to an amelioration, not exacerbation of symptoms. This anomaly, first discovered by Freud, has been a challenge to psychotherapy aimed at permanent personality change, irrespective of theoretical orientation. Nor can this negative reaction be attributed to idiosyncratic interpretations of individual therapists, especially as the psychotherapy is sometimes conducted under close individual or group supervision. What then accounts for such a negative reaction?

If the interpretation is "correct," then the reaction can arise only from some malignancy entirely within the patient's psyche. This is exactly the position taken by Kernberg (1975) and Masterson (1981), who interpret the negative therapeutic reaction as an expression of a self-destructive aggressive drive. Ironically, an interpretation of this intrapsychic understanding of the negative reaction generally results in its exacerbation. With circular logic, further exacerbation of symptoms is then cited as evidence that the interpretation of a self-destructive aggressive drive is itself correct.

THE WOLF MAN

Freud (1918) first described the negative therapeutic reaction in "From the History of an Infantile Neurosis," in which he related the case of the Wolf Man. The Wolf Man "never gave way to fresh ideas without one last attempt at clinging to what had lost value for him" (p. 68). The Wolf Man

> showed a habit of producing transitory "negative reactions"; every time something had been conclusively cleaned up, he attempted symptoms which had been cleared up [p. 69].

The Wolf Man case illustrates the problem of negative therapeutic reactions. This case, more than any other, established that psychoanalysis was capable of treating seriously disturbed persons. The Wolf Man, a wealthy Russian aristocrat named Dr. Serge Pankejeff, had seen a succession of therapists before Freud, and he saw another analyst (Ruth Mack Brunswick) after seeing Freud. He also enjoyed the friendship of the analyst Muriel Gardiner for 30 years. Further, as Anna Freud indicates in the foreword to Gardiner's (1971) book, "The Wolf Man stands out among his fellow figures by virtue of the fact that he is the only one able and willing to cooperate actively in the construction and follow-up of his own case" (p. xi). The Wolf Man also gave a valuable description of how he subjectively experienced his four years of treatment with Freud from 1910 to 1914.

The Wolf Man had an animal phobia, which was reflected in his wolf dream at the age of four.

> I dreamt that it was night and that I was lying in my bed. (My bed stood with its foot towards the window; in front of the window there was a row of old walnut trees. I know it was winter when I had the dream, and night-time). Suddenly the window opened of its own accord, and I was terrified to see that some white wolves were sitting on the big walnut tree in front of the window. There were six or seven of them. The wolves were quite white, and looked more like foxes or sheep-dogs, for they had big tails like foxes and they had their ears pricked like dogs when they pay attention to something. In great terror, evidently of being eaten up by the wolves, I screamed and woke up [Freud, 1918, p. 29].

Freud, through elaborate associations, linked this dream to the primal scene of parental intercourse and to the Wolf Man's fears of castration.

The Wolf Man was very disturbed when, aged 23, he commenced his first session with Freud. The Wolf Man began by saying, "This man is a Jewish swindler; he wants to use me from behind and shit on my head" (Fish, 1989, p. 526). Years later, he said of Freud, "I had the feeling of encountering a great personality," something that we would now identify as a powerful idealizing transference (Blum, 1974, p. 737). He also said that Freud would "occasionally let fall some remark which bore witness to his complete understanding of everything I had experienced" (Gardiner, 1971, p. 138). Freud intuitively kept the idealizing transference alive by making the Wolf Man feel less like a patient and more like a co-worker. The Wolf Man experienced Freud's behavior as empathic. Freud also mentioned that a period of "long education" was needed to facilitate the analysis of the Wolf Man.

For four months in 1919, Freud had further analytic sessions with a demoralized Wolf Man, now a penniless refugee from the Russian revolution, and helped him attain a relatively adequate level of adult functioning. Remarkably, Freud also took up a collection every spring for six years so that the Wolf Man could pay his wife's hospital bills and take a vacation. Clearly, Freud's special treatment encouraged Pankejeff's perception of being "Professor Freud's famous patient."

In 1923, upon learning of Freud's operation for a malignancy, the Wolf Man became hypochondriacal and showed other signs of self-fragmentation. This decompensation lasted until 1926, when the Wolf Man was referred to Ruth Mack Brunswick. Brunswick forced the patient to confront his rage about having been abandoned by Freud, not only through Freud's referral to her, but as a consequence of the destruction, by Freud's illness, of the illusion of omnipotence required of an idealized parental imago (Gardiner, 1971).

Blum (1974) claims that the Wolf Man had a borderline personality:

> The paranoid states that subsequently erupted occasionally, the hypochondriasis and life-long depressions, the tendency to act out his fantasies, the lack of ego synthesis and cohesive personality organization, recurrent crises requiring supportive intervention—all point toward a borderline personality [pp. 724-725].

Chessick (1980a) also speculates about the personality structure of the Wolf Man. He mentions the uncanny capacity of the Wolf Man to encourage the continuing interest of a vital segment of the early analytic community.

> Such a capacity for stirring up the interest of others is usually absent in schizophrenic people, but it is not rare in a polished and intelligent narcissistic personality. It seems clear that we are dealing with a borderline personality disorder or at best a narcissistic personality disorder in a man who never was really capable of forming a mature, loving relationship with anybody, but whose survival throughout a long life rested on an uncanny capacity to keep more successful individuals interested in him [p. 95].

For example, when his wife committed suicide by turning on gas as the Nazis occupied Vienna, the Wolf Man reacted narcissistically, saying, "The question kept hammering away in my mind: how could Therese do this to me? And as she was the only stable structure in my changeable life, how could I, suddenly deprived of her, live on?" (p. 122).

The possibility that the Wolf Man suffered a borderline syndrome is supported by Mahony's (1984) description of Pankejeff's parents. His mother was a "jealous, intensely hypochondriacal, obsessively pious" woman who was "distant with her children . . . . The restless father, diagnosed by Kraepelin as a manic-depressive psychotic, had especially severe attacks every several years that necessitated rehabilitation in a sanatorium" (p. 4). An anecdote illustrates the mother's lack of empathy:

> She told her children she was taking them to town to see something pleasant; but there the innocently expectant children were taken aback to observe their father, absent for several months, now pitiful looking and recuperating in a sanatorium [p. 4].

Magid (in press) has reexamined the Wolf Man from a self psychology perspective. He sees a narcissistic person forever "at the mercy of those who could promise some enlivening mixture of excitement, idealization, attention, and maintenance." Like Mahony,

Magid thinks the primal scene-based story is nonsense and that it evolved out of Freud's need to impose his theoretical expectations. The terrifying stare of the wolves may represent a "malignant transformation of the mirroring he wished to receive" from his father, who had just humiliated him in front of guests for being unable to play the accordion on command and whose image in young Serge's eyes was then undergoing a traumatic deidealization. Magid then makes a crucial theoretical point: "The fact that there *could* be an alternative, equally cogent explanatory scheme eliminates the very basis of Freud's argument, that the primal scene is necessary to make sense of the case."

Geha (1988), who has studied Freud's style as a fictionalist, agrees with Mahony and Magid that the primal scene is a figment of Freud's imagination:

> Once Freud arranges the stage of the primal scene, the entire drama unfolds within a psychic reality from which there is no egress. Freud constructs this passionate play. He *creates* it. Out of what? Primarily out of dream material allegedly fashioned by a four-year-old child and remembered twenty years later. Yet, to say that from his patient's recollection of a dream Freud builds a primal scene misleads us somewhat. The dream text, of course, did not manifestly reveal such an episode. No, Freud's interpretation reveals, or, rather, creates, this *mise en scène*. And how is this interpretation confirmed? Never directly; historical interpretation can never be confirmed. And the reality that would confirm it by correspondence is simply non-existent [p. 110].

To Magid (in press), the Wolf Man's solution to his narcissistic vulnerabilities was to employ a "masochistic" strategy. He constantly accommodated his "subjective reality to the powerful influence of Freud's vision in order to maintain the desperately needed selfobject tie." This pattern was unrecognized and left unresolved by Freud and also by Ruth Mack Brunswick.

Brandchaft (1983), who thinks Freud's analysis of the Wolf Man achieved a great deal, especially when viewed from a self psychology perspective, says of the Wolf Man case:

> Freud provided the Wolf Man with a potent source of self-esteem, which enabled the patient to integrate himself. From a position of

> obscurity, a nonentity lost in a welter of symptoms designed to frantically maintain a tenuous and primitive psychological organization at whatever cost—to keep the wolves from his door—the Wolf Man acquired, with Freud's active assistance, a healing sense of his own importance and uniqueness, a feeling of being cared about, listened to, and understood [pp. 333-334].

NARCISSISTIC RESISTANCES

Freud's experience of the negative therapeutic reactions of patients led to three key theoretical concepts. The negative therapeutic reaction was the basis of his concept of the superego (Freud, 1923). It also forced an explication of his metapsychology, including structural theory (Freud, 1933). Above all, the issue of negative therapeutic reaction focused his mind on narcissism. It is significant that Freud (1914) wrote the narcissism paper toward the end of the Wolf Man's four-year treatment.

While it is evident that Freud understood the importance of narcissism for clinical theory, it was Abraham's (1919) "A Particular Form of Neurotic Resistance" that clearly identified narcissistic resistances as the primary source of the negative therapeutic reaction. Abraham noted several features of this narcissistic resistance: an unusual degree of defiance, evidenced by a refusal to free associate; an unusual sensitivity to injuring self-esteem, including being humiliated by the findings of the analysis; an attempt to convert the analysis from its objective of self-understanding to one of narcissistic enhancement; and an inability to form a "true" transference. Such patients begrudge the analyst the role of father and are easily disappointed. Because these patients wish to be loved and admired, and since the analyst cannot satisfy these narcissistic needs, a true positive transference does not take place. In its place, Abraham advocated focusing on their resistance to a true transference by tracing it to its emergence as a drive. His technique, however, assumed that narcissism was a regression from or avoidance of an oedipal conflict rather than a developmental deficiency.

Balint (1936) raised the same issue as Abraham, but for a different reason. He had noticed that a narcissistic deficiency became evident at the end of a long and successful analysis, at the termination phase, when the wish for gratification emerged. When he explored this wish, he concluded that it derived from childhood failures. Such patients were in need of a "new beginning."

Balint also suggested that sadism and masochism were not normal stages of psychosexual development but were the products of faulty environmental responses, especially empathic failure. He therefore disagreed with those, including Freud, who viewed sadism as an endopsychic cause of the negative therapeutic reaction.

Balint anticipated self psychology's view of the negative therapeutic reaction. He put forth the concepts of "primary love" and "basic fault" in an attempt to explain transference-countertransference impasses with certain kinds of difficult patients (Mitchell, 1988). Such "patients become stuck in analysis, demanding a responsiveness from the analyst without which they seem unable to progress. Balint characterizes these longings and the patient's efforts to gratify them as a need for 'primary love'" (p. 141).

Riviere (1936) explained that narcissistic resistances come from a highly organized system of defenses against a depressive condition in the patient and operate as a disguise to conceal this. Narcissistic resistances are also a defense against admitting dependence on objects. Consequently, contempt and depreciation are marked features of narcissistic resistances, as are attempts at tyrannical control and mastery of the objects of dependency.

For Riviere, typical refractory patients were those who tried to exercise omnipotent control (frequently masked) over the analyst; refused to associate freely; denied anything that discredited themselves; refused to accept any alternative point of view or interpretation; were defiant and obstinate; lacked generosity; accepted help from the analyst while refusing to help the analyst or acknowledge his value; and, above all, were deceptive. According to Riviere, narcissistic resistance arises from the imperative need to avoid dependence at all costs and thus guard against depression. Change is a profound threat to the precarious psychic organization of patients.

INTERSUBJECTIVITY AND IMPASSES

Self psychology understands the negative therapeutic reaction to be a result of the analyst's insisting on the correctness of well-intended interpretations and self psychology claims that the negative reaction is exacerbated by the explanation that such reactions arise solely from within the patient's mental apparatus. The result of the negative therapeutic reaction is to repeat severe, narcissistically traumatic developmental failures.

Reading the case of the Wolf Man after becoming acquainted with Kohut's ideas, one discerns a link between Freud's description of negative therapeutic reactions and Kohut's idea of empathic failure. The aggravation of symptoms may have been a sign that the Wolf Man was experiencing Freud's interpretations, however correct, as unempathic.

When Brandchaft's (1983) client shows signs of a negative therapeutic reaction, the patient is experiencing and communicating about a traumatic event. What is called for is an intensified effort to identify and recognize the kernel of truth within the patient's complaint. From five cases with therapeutic impasses, Brandchaft came to accept that his goals in each case were incompatible with the goals the patient was pursuing: "I had to conclude that I must abandon my goals when they were incongruous with those of my patients and stop insisting that in their opposition they were defeating both themselves and me" (pp. 347-348).

Brandchaft's experiences with these cases led him to concentrate more on the "primary factor," which is the emergence of archaic, intensified, distorted longings in the therapy sessions following the therapist's prolonged, empathic immersion in the subjective experience of the patient. As one patient said, "The first thing I had to get across to you . . . was how important what you thought of me was" (p. 348).

In evaluating each of these cases where negative therapeutic reactions occurred, Brandchaft found that "the patient had sustained a significant injury to the self immediately prior to the reaction" (p. 349) and that, as the therapist, he had failed to recognize the significance to the patient of the injury. Further, when the impasse occurred, Brandchaft was initially inclined to interpret it as the patient's attempt to deny dependence or hostile envy; or as the need to triumph over him; or as unconscious guilt that stood in the way of patient's getting well. He eventually realized that, whatever his intention, these interpretations were experienced as blaming the patient for the stalemate. Brandchaft had inadvertently turned the patient into a selfobject of blame.

Brandchaft further describes wounding and the negative therapeutic reaction:

> Behind the precipitating injury, an old and decisive one had been exacerbated. The intense drama reenacted before me [with the negative therapeutic reaction] was a condensed, encapsulated, and updated version of a host of earlier nuclear experiences in which these patients, as children, had desperately attempted to get a parent to see things from their point of view. These were efforts to salvage and restore a needed and cherished part of a sinking self and to keep open a developmental channel. The parents, however, had insisted that these children see things from the parents' more "objective" view, always for the children's own ultimate good [p. 351].

It can be seen, then, that the philosophical assumption of "objective reality," long pervasive in classical analysis, can be a major contributor to the formation of negative therapeutic reactions. As Stolorow, Atwood, and Brandchaft (1988) indicate:

> This assumption [of "objective reality"] lies at the heart of the traditional view of transference, initially described by Breuer and Freud (1893-95) as a "false connection" made by the patient and later conceived as a "distortion" of the analyst's "real" qualities that analysis seeks to correct [pp. 106-107].

It seems now that this "objective" view of transference helped create an iatrogenic effect. The classical view of transference as a distortion can hinder psychotherapy because it reflects a "hierarchically ordered, two-reality view" (Schwaber, 1983b, p. 383)—one reality experienced by the patient and the other "known" by the analysts to be more objectively true.

Once the superiority/inferiority assumptions of reality implied by classical analysis are rejected, we are left with two different views of reality, the therapist's and the client's. Discounting the automatic assumption that the therapist's view of reality is superior, however, may not be sufficient to lessen iatrogenic effects. Iatrogenic effects may occur because the two-different-views-of-reality simply set off a competitive struggle to see which one is superior—with obviously nontherapeutic results. This second position still actually assumes there is a superior view of reality but accepts that it is not automatically the therapist's view. In a third position, the two different views of reality are accepted as an opportunity to explore each view of reality mutually without either necessarily being superior to the other. Where such mutual explorations take place through empathy, feelings of being understood occur, and symptoms abate.

As Brandchaft (1989) states:

> The understanding of development and the psychoanalytic situation as profoundly intersubjective in nature, namely, the product of the intersection of differently organized subjective worlds, led to an interest in the further exploration of the patient's subjective reality from a *stance within* rather than outside that perspective [p. 239].

Schwaber (1983a) writes:

> Rather than being viewed as a distortion to be modified, it (the transference) is seen as a perception to be recognized and articulated, in the hope that it will facilitate a deeper entry into the patient's inner world . . . . We will, to be sure, still need to check the patient's perception and view of reality against our own, but this is primarily to maintain vigilance against the superimposition of our view, which may be conveniently rationalized as our theoretical stance [pp. 274-275].

Support for Schwaber's idea that the two-tiered, hierarchical view of reality creates iatrogenic affects comes from the negative therapeutic reactions that occur in treatments conducted according to a wide variety of theoretical perspectives, including nonanalytic intensive psychotherapies. Nor are those who practice psychotherapy from a self psychology perspective immune to the experience, especially if subtle nuances of a self-psychological theoretical superiority pervade the intersubjective context. Thus, while self psychology may have emphasized a greater awareness of, and a newer understanding of, a negative therapeutic reaction, eradicating this iatrogenic problem is another matter. Self psychology seemed, at first, just as bedeviled by the negative therapeutic problem as was any other treatment.

A promising approach to negative therapeutic reactions emerged once impasses were recognized as ubiquitous to psychoanalysis and to intensive psychotherapy aimed at structural change. The ubiquity, even inevitability, of impasses stems from the conflict between two different views of reality, the patient's and the therapist's. If these impasses are not given analytic attention, they eventually become entrenched as negative therapeutic reactions. Once self psychologists, such as Stolorow and his colleagues, recognized the ubiquitous nature of impasses, they realized that these impasses "provide a unique pathway—a 'royal road'—to the attainment of psychoanalytic understanding" (Atwood, Stolorow, and Trop, 1989, p. 554).

INTERSUBJECTIVE CONJUNCTIONS AND DISJUNCTIONS

The impasses that repeatedly occur in the interplay between the subjective worlds of patient and therapist are of two major kinds: intersubjective conjunctions and intersubjective disjunctions.

An intersubjective conjunction occurs when the organizing principles structuring the patient's experiences give rise to expressions that are assimilated into closely similar configurations in the psychological life of the therapist. Intersubjective disjunction, by comparison, arises when the therapist assimilates the patient's material into a configuration that differs significantly from the patient's configuration. Atwood and his colleagues (1989) see repetitive occurrences of intersubjective conjunctions and disjunctions inevitably accompanying the therapeutic process.

So what if there are intersubjective conjunctions and disjunctions? To such a query Atwood and his colleagues reply, "Whether these intersubjective situations facilitate or obstruct the progress of therapy depends in large part on the extent of the therapist's capacity to become reflectively aware of the organizing principles of his own subjective world" (p. 555). For example, in a conjunctive experience, if the therapist is aware of it, he may use the analogs of his own experience as an invaluable supplementary source of information regarding the possible background meanings of the patient's material. Unrecognized for what they are, though, intersubjective conjunctions can impede exploration of the meanings of important issues. The intersubjective approach in self psychology does not assume that similarities in experience guarantee greater empathy, as tends to be assumed by many who make empathy the central construct in their theory.

Atwood and his colleagues offer the case of Peter as an example of an impasse resulting from an unrecognized intersubjective conjunction. Peter repeatedly complained about the mechanization and depersonalization of the American way of life. His therapist, who shared this view of society, never explored with the patient the subjective meaning of these beliefs, because he assumed they represented good reality testing. This assumption led to an unwitting silent collusion between therapist and patient that prevented painful confrontations from occurring around issues of intimacy and attachment and limited the patient's potential to incorporate this disavowed material into an expanded, more adaptive sense of self.

Intersubjective disjunctions can interfere with treatment. The overt disparity between the subjective worlds of patient and therapist may lead to dramatic confrontations and countertherapeutic spirals and replace empathy with misunderstanding. What Freud called a "negative therapeutic reaction" in his analysis of the Wolf man may be a description of an extreme impasse of a prolonged and unrecognized form of intersubjective disjunction. Freud's negative therapeutic reaction explained the situation in which interpretations assumed to be correct actually made patients worse rather than better. Freud attributed these negative reactions exclusively to intrapsychic mechanisms in the patient.

By contrast, Atwood and colleagues think that such therapeutic impasses cannot be understood apart from the intersubjective context. They illustrate an intersubjective disjunction with the case of Robyn, a woman who traced her difficulties back to the lack of confirming and validating responsiveness by her family. The only exception to this pattern was her father's sexual interest in her, which led to her coy, seductive style and ultimately to a pattern of compulsive promiscuity with father surrogates in a desperate effort to stave off feelings of depletion.

Robyn's analyst followed the precepts of classical analysis, including an overly literal interpretation of the role of abstinence.

This abstinence meant responding to the patient's urgent requests for affirming and mirroring responses with silence or, at most, a brief interpretation. Robyn experienced this neutrality and seeming aloofness as a retraumatizing deprivation, to which she responded either by sexualizing the relationship or with deep rage.

The central configuration of the therapist's subjective world concerned control. In his relationship with his mother, he had resisted submitting to what he felt was her tyrannizing and oppressive will. Hence the patient's urgent demands for responsiveness were assimilated into the therapist's themes of power, evoking a stubborn resistance and an entrenching of his unresponsive style. Unaware of this countertransference reaction, the therapist saw the increasing demands of the patient as a malignant need for domination. "A vicious spiral was thereby created, in which the disjunctive perceptions, needs and reactions of patient and therapist strengthened one another in a reciprocally destructive way" (Atwood et al., 1989, p. 559).

In summary, Atwood, Stolorow and Trop claim that when the therapist explores with a view to understanding the unconscious organizing principles of both himself and his patient, psychotherapy becomes far more effective. It also becomes more effective if attention is given to a patient's affects, a subject we examine in the next chapter.

Readings for Chapter 21: Basch, 1983a; Stolorow et al., 1987, chapter 5; Demos, 1988.

21

Affects

Affects play an important role in structuralizing the self. Stern (1985), for instance, conceives of affectivity as a self-invariant that enables the infant to experience a core sense of self. According to Demos and Kaplan (1987), an infant's sense of self develops from an inner experience of recurrent affective states that are responded to by a caregiver. Stolorow et al. (1987) also see affects as the prime organizers of self-experience. This chapter covers affects under the following headings: (a) definition, (b) theory of specific affects, (c) infant studies and affect theory, and (d) affect integration and psychotherapy.

DEFINITION

Basch (1983a) defines affect as "the reaction of the subcortical brain to sensory stimulation" (p. 692). In doing so, he distinguishes affect from feeling. A feeling is a cognition, a cortical association just like any other thought. Feeling is the awareness of an affect, that is, the

surprise interest anger shame fear — affects
(motivational qualities)

affects motivate us —

cortical consciousness of an affective subcortical reaction. Technically, emotion is not a synonym for affect or feeling but has a complex state, such as depression, that involves a mixture of primary feelings. Basch (1988c), then, sees affect as having its own "line of development" with a "normal progression from affect, to feeling, to emotion, and finally to the capacity for empathy with others" (p. 147).

SPECIFIC AFFECTS

Self psychologists such as Michael Basch have appropriated the work of Silvan Tomkins, a pioneer in affect theory, in theorizing about the function of affects in therapeutic change. For instance, Basch (1983a) writes:

> Discussions of psychoanalytic technique have been hampered in the past by our acknowledged lack of an acceptable theory of affect that could serve as a base and a reference point for such deliberations . . . . [Previously,] I sought to show that this deficit has been practically resolved by the work of the psychologist Silvan Tomkins [p. 692].

Tomkins (1962-63) believes that affects are present in infants from the first moments of birth. He conceptualized affects as biologically inherited programs controlling facial muscles, the autonomic nervous system, bloodflow, respiration, and vocal responses. On the basis of a study of the facial muscles, he presents evidence for nine primary affects: surprise, interest, enjoyment, distress, contempt, disgust, anger, fear, and shame. Because the facial muscles in humans are more finely articulated and can change more rapidly than can the correlated autonomic responses (three-tenths of a second verses one to two seconds), the face is the primary sight of affect and takes the lead in establishing and creating an awareness of an affective state, with other correlated responses coming in more slowly.

Tomkins also asserts that the affect system is the primary motivational system in the personality. He postulates that affects function as abstract and general amplifiers of variants in the density of neural

Sander, Kaplan, Demos →

pattern of invariant affect = temperament
tendency of affect = temperament

stimulation. There are three classes of such variants, in which (1) stimulation increases to activate surprise, fear, or interest depending on the suddenness of the increase; (2) stimulation levels remain nonoptimally high to trigger distress or anger depending on the level; (3) and stimulation decreases to activate enjoyment. Affects evoked in this way act as amplifiers, generating, by means of the correlated sets of facial muscle, autonomic, blood-flow, respiratory, and vocal responses, an analog of the gradient or intensity characteristics of the stimulus. They also add a special analogic quality that is intensely punishing or rewarding. Thus affects make either good things better or bad things worse.

To Tomkins, affects motivate the organism to act. There are no innate responses to affect; there are, instead, an infinite variety of learned behavioral patterns. Discrete affects are present at birth, and development consists of the gradual construction of affect complexes or ideoaffective organizations. That is, Tomkins sees affects as having a line of development.

Contrary to Tomkin's idea that specific affects are present at birth is one that cognitive theorists follow: James-Lange's (1890) theory of a global visceral response, which, when given a cognitive label, is experienced as an affective state. But this cognitive view invites the question of how the labeling takes place. Tomkin's model suggests that it is through a selfobject experience of a parent's recognizing and responding to affective clues that the infant becomes cognitively aware of affect.

INFANT STUDIES AND AFFECT THEORY

Tomkin's theory of the specific nature of affects at birth has received support from neurological studies reported by Pribrim (1980). Evidence from Pribrim's laboratory indicates that the autonomic nervous system is involved in stabilizing emotional states already set in motion at birth.

Ekman (1971, 1977) and Izard (1977b) independently explored the validity of the facial expression patterns described by Tomkins. Their work demonstrated that these expressions were produced, recognized, and given similar meanings in a wide range of Western and non-Western cultures. This cross-cultural consensus supports

Daniel Stern – baby watches –

genetic predisposition → possible –

the proposition that affects are biologically inherited responses, shared by all humans. Other infant researchers (see chapter 23, this volume) have demonstrated that infant facial expressions are not random, but occur in the organized patterns isolated by Tomkins.

Tomkin's premise, following Darwin's, is that the face is a valid indicator of an internal state. Ekman, Levenson, and Friesen (1983) have reported evidence to confirm this part of Tomkin's theory. By instructing experimental subjects to contract their facial muscles in specific ways that replicated the universal emotion patterns, they produced emotion-specific autonomic activity, as measured by changes in heart rate, in right-hand and left-hand skin temperatures and in skin resistance. Four negative emotions—disgust, anger, fear, and sadness—showed distinct autonomic patterns that were different from the patterns of the positive emotions of joy and surprise.

Darwin (1872) argued that the expressive forms of emotion in humans and animals were selected for evolutionary survival because of their function as preparations for action. Thus, for example, the baring of teeth in primates evolved as an expression of anger because it prepared the animal to bite. It came secondarily to serve a communicative function as a warning signal to an approaching animal. The facial expression of anger in humans is characterized by lowered and knitted brows, creating vertical lines between them; by tensed upper and lower eyelids, so that the eyes have a hard stare and may take on a bulging appearance; and by open, tensed lips in a squarish shape, which bares the teeth, or by lips pressed tightly together with the corners straight down, (Ekman and Friesen, 1975). This expression suggests preparation for biting or shouting. Also, when anger is on the face, the heart rate increases and the skin temperature rises. This correlated set of responses does, indeed, seem to prepare the organism to act in a specific way.

Sroufe (1979) and Emde (1980; Emde, Gaensbauer and Harmon 1976), differ from Tomkins in that they view the physiological responses of early infancy as precursors to affects; only when the infant develops cognitions can we speak of psychophysiologic tensions and affects. Brenner (1974, 1982) and Arlow (1977) argue for global pleasure and unpleasure in the beginning. Tomkins is alone in asserting that affect and cognition can vary independently of each other and that cognition need not be involved in activating or prolonging an affective state.

Modern views of infant perception support Tomkin's position. From these views, a young infant is seen as a highly competent perceiver, able to operate across sensory modalities and to abstract from stimulus events their general properties.

> We must, then, begin to accept the possibility that the young infant is capable of experiencing the full range of primary affects, and that this experience is real and meaningful, in the sense that the discrete affective quality of each negative affect will be experienced as uniquely punishing, and the distinctive qualities of each positive affect will be experienced as uniquely rewarding [Demos, 1988, p. 34].

Summarizing support for the idea of discrete affects, Demos writes:

> The interested baby will focus its eyes intently on a stimulus, holding its limbs relatively quiet, and will tend to scan the stimulus for novelty (Wolff, 1965; Stechler and Carpenter, 1967). The joyful baby will smile and tend to produce relaxed, relatively smooth movements of its limbs, savoring the familiar, (Tomkins, 1962; Brazelton et al., 1974). The angry baby will square its mouth, lower and pull its brows together, cry intensely, holding the cry for a long time, then pause for a long inspiration, and will tend to kick and thrash its limbs forcefully, perhaps even struggling against a caregiver, (Tomkins, 1962; Demos, 1986). By contrast, a distressed infant will produce a more rhythmical cry, with the corners of the mouth pulled down and the inner corners of the brows drawn up, and will tend to move its head and limbs around restlessly (Tomkins, 1962; Wolff, 1969). Thus the discrete characteristics of each affect are important aspects of the infant's early experience because they create discrete motivational dispositions in the infant and therefore become occasions for learning . . . .
>
> In a model such as Tomkin's, where affect is seen as an adaptive biological system, it is assumed that the occurrence of negative affect is inevitable and unavoidable. The task for the organism then becomes one of learning how to modulate, endure, and tolerate such experiences in order to benefit from

> the adaptive function of affect. This, in the case of negative affect, is to create a punishing, urgent state that will focus the organism to do something about the situation. Thus, the organism must learn how to keep negative affects within some optimal range of density that still contains sufficient information but allows the organism to remain in the situation and to develop or produce adaptive responses. Neonates possess some capacity to modulate their negative affective states at a low level of intensity, but as the intensity level rises they tend to continue to escalate, in a positive feedback loop that can lead from distress, to intense distress, to anger. Infants are therefore dependent on caregivers to modulate, soothe, and maintain them at more moderate or optimal density levels [pp. 34-36].

Sander's work links in with Tomkin's theory. Interested in an infant's state of organizational coherence, Sander (1970) makes three propositions. The first is that the ego begins as a state ego and not a body ego. "The organization of state governs the quality of the inner experience" (Sander, 1982, p. 16). To Sander, this organization comes from the sleep-wake cycles; Demos thinks that the awake states are affective states.

Sander's (1982) second proposition is "that the infant's own states, where coherent, recurrent, desired, or essential to key regulatory coordinations that become established with the caregiver, become the primary target or *goals* for behavior" (p. 16). Demos (1988) illustrates Sander's second proposition as follows:

> Kaplan and I (1987) have reported elsewhere on two infant girls whom we videotaped in their family settings every two weeks during the first year. At roughly five and a half weeks of age, each baby when left alone briefly was observed to regulate her gazing behavior in order to modulate mild fussiness. The following sequence occurred. As fussy vocalizations began and as arms and legs began to cycle, each baby began to move her head from side to side and started to scan the environment. They each found an object, visually focused on it, became motorically and vocally quiet, and continued to gaze for several minutes. Then they would look away, the fussiness would begin to build up again, and they would return their gaze to the object, once again becoming focused and quiet. This cycle was repeated several times before the mothers returned and intervened.

An elaborate explanation of the obvious

> We are assuming that although the initial scanning may have been unmotivated and part of the fussy movements and thus the first encounter with the object may have been accidental, the subsequent refocusing on the same object looked like an active attempt by each infant to repeat a successful organizing experience. In other words, the infants were motivated to recapture the affective experience of interest with its organizing potential, which felt more rewarding than the unfocused fussy state [p. 43].

Sander's third proposition is that infant competence in initiating and organizing self-regulatory behaviors to achieved desired states as goals represents a systems competence. The emergence of infant-as-agent must be granted by the system because this emergence means a reorganization of the system to admit the newcomer. If the system is such that it can permit the entrance of a new agent within it, it provides conditions that not only establish the capacity for self-awareness, but insure the use of such inner awareness by the infant as a frame of reference in organizing his own adaptive behavior, for example, being in a position that permits him to appreciate which behaviors lead to which states. The valence of this inner experience under these conditions of self-initiated goal realization is felt as the infant's "own" (Sander, 1982, p. 17).

Demos (1988, p. 44) illustrates with the example of Cathy. At three and a half weeks, whenever Cathy gazed intently at her mother's face, without smiling, the mother would interpret this quiet, focused interest as boredom. The mother would then pull her own face back, out of Cathy's visual range, and jiggle a toy in front of Cathy's eyes. Also, whenever Cathy's older brother was around, the mother would turn away from Cathy and focus her attention on him, even though this attention to her son often meant interrupting or foreshortening an exchange with Cathy. Cathy's response was to diminish facial animation or look away with a somewhat blank expression. From this interaction, Cathy learned (1) that her states of interest and enjoyment did not last long; (2) that she had no control over initiating, prolonging, or ending such experiences and thus did not experience herself as an active agent; and (3) that she was not a source of interesting events.

mirror Kohut affirm accept
ideal selfobject function

differentiate
affect states

intersubjective
tolerate affect —
mature

neg-
affect
=
signal
by
monition
by
change.

AFFECT INTEGRATION
AND PSYCHOTHERAPY

Affects function as organizers throughout development if they are responded to by an affirming, accepting, differentiating, synthesizing, and containing selfobject (Stolorow et al., 1987). If they are not empathically responded to, affect integration is undermined, affects are disavowed, and they then disrupt precarious structuralizations. Affect integration occurs when "contradictory affect states [are experienced] as issuing from a unitary continuous self" (p. 71). The role of selfobjects is crucial to this process of affect integration: "Selfobject functions pertain fundamentally to the affective dimension of self experience, and the need for selfobject ties pertains to the need for specific, requisite responsiveness to varying affect states throughout development" (p. 67).

Stolorow's view of affects as organizers of the self is supported by Levin (1991), who, following the work of Maclean (1962), claims that the use of affects as organizers goes back 200 million years to the evolution of the therapsid, a mammal-like reptile. In mammals, it is conjectured, memories are stored in the limbic system according to the affects that have been experienced. The limbic system developed in conjunction with the use of affects as organizers of a memory system, the mechanisms of the middle ear for hearing in the air, the capacity for vocalization, and an increased bonding between mother and child. A case can be made that all these systems developed as a part of an evolving strategy of survival in which mammals depend more on learning than did reptiles, who respond to situations primarily from genetic inheritance. As Levin (1991) says, "Reptiles communicate by means other than sounds, and their affects, which are not an organizing principle of experience, are not apparent vocally" (p. 212).

Levin's extensive exploration of the neurosciences from an analytic perspective, suggests that affect integration may become problematic when the three information-processing systems in the brain—the vestibulocerebellar, the corticostriatal, and the cortico-limbic—encounter interference with their "uploading" and "downloading" of memories stored in an intermediate area (p. 136). When affects are disavowed, memories filed under specific "affects" in the limbic system (p. 56) are not available for this complex interchange of perspectives among the three systems. It may be that information exchange occurs during periods of sleep, when there is no rapid eye movement (NREM)(p. 125). Through disavowal, affects are not experienced as feelings.

Stolorow and his colleagues see Kohut's conceptualization of the mirroring and idealized selfobjects as special instances of the way selfobject functions integrate affects. Kohut discussed the importance of mirroring grandiose or exhibitionistic experiences so that healthy pride, expansiveness, efficacy and pleasurable excitement are seen as being a part of the self.

Discussing affectionate and assertive affect states characteristic of the oedipal phase, Kohut (1977) referred to selfobjects as integrators:

Kohut vs. oedipal stage

paradigm shift ...

> The affectionate desire and the assertive-competitive rivalry of the oedipal child will be responded to by normally empathic parents in two ways. The parents will react to the sexual desires and competitive rivalry of the child by becoming sexually stimulated and counteraggressive, and, at the same time, they will react with joy and pride to the child's developmental achievement, to his vigor and assertiveness [p. 230].

Basch (1985) expands the concept of the mirror function to encompass broad areas of "affective mirroring":

> Through affective attunement the mother is serving as the quintessential selfobject for her baby, sharing the infant's experience, confirming it in its activity, and building a sensorimotor model for what will become its self concept. Affect attunement leads to a shared world; without affect attunement one's activities are solitary, private, and idiosyncratic. . . . [If] affect attunement is not present or is ineffective during those early years, the lack of shared experience may well create a sense of isolation and a belief that one's affective needs generally are somehow unacceptable and shameful [p. 35].

AFFECT INTEGRATION DURING PSYCHOTHERAPY

Case Illustration #1

Stolorow et al. (1987) illustrate the process of affect integration with the case of Steven, a 26-year-old, single, male, computer programmer. Steven presented for treatment with an obsessive dread of his feelings. This dread had arisen from

> terrifying emotional reactions to countless disturbing childhood experiences (especially his parents' divorce and his mother's hospitalizations) that were dissociated and repressed, solidifying his obsessional, cerebral character style. A state of pure, affectless intellectuality became his self-ideal of perfection, embodied in his intense idealization of the Star Trek character Mr. Spock, whose life seemed completely free of the "imperfections of emotions." His struggle to attain this affectless ideal became poignantly clear as the treatment began to bring forth hitherto disavowed aspects of his emotional life [pp. 82-83].

Steven feared the experience of depression. Whenever possible, his female therapist

> clarified his fears that she, like his mother, would find his feelings intolerable and unacceptable and would thus respond to them with spreading panic or angry belittlement, or become emotionally disturbed herself. Through this repeated analysis in the transference of Steven's resistances to depressive affect and the anticipated, extreme dangers that made them necessary, the therapist gradually became established for him as a person who would comprehend, accept, tolerate, and aid him in integrating these feelings [p. 84].

This experience of the therapist's empathy led Steven to recover many painful memories of the past; to explore formerly dissociated feelings of suicidal despair; to crystallize a conviction that his dynamic feelings were a threat to others; and to become able to immerse himself in intensely pleasurable experiences.

The defensively formed affectless state of Steven is similar to the analysis of the malaise that Soren Kierkegaard called "leveling." In this process of leveling, there is a replacement of "passion," or commitment, by detached intellectual reflection. Such commitment is the means whereby a person defines his world and thereby himself. Without such a commitment there is a despair, which is "sickness unto death" (Rubin, 1989).

Case Illustration #2

Brandchaft also illustrates the process of affect integration. Mr. N, a gifted musical composer, was treated over a 15-year span for an "intractable depression" that became severe and disabling after any success. During these depressions, Mr. N experienced a feeling of despair, believed that his fate had already been determined, and thought that he had an incurable and global defect. Such a depression, a complex of emotions, is made up of a mixture of negative primary affects, cognitive awareness of these affects (feelings), and cognitions (beliefs) connected to these feelings.

Mr. N's treatment was made difficult by his belief that the analyst was critical of him for continuing to feel depressed and that the analyst felt burdened by this depression. Brandchaft slowly developed a strategy to hold Mr. N's despair in check while sustaining his own hopeful attitude. He did so by working hard to understand Mr. N's experience and his own response to it and not trying actively to alter Mr. N's mood. By way of demonstrating his understanding of Mr. N's experience, Brandchaft (1988) experienced depression (attenuated) with Mr. N:

> Repeated experiences of shared affect, though without confirmation of his perspective, had the ultimate effect of establishing for Mr. N the necessary conditions for a feeling of safety and harmony that subsequently carried over into other affect states and made the understandings I could convey assimilable [p. 138].

Exposed to Brandchaft's consistent stance of sharing Mr. N's depression with him, gradually Mr. N began to believe that he could overcome his depression. He soon came to acknowledge that it was his analyst's hope that had sustained him. Whenever Brandchaft was disappointed with Mr. N or lost confidence in himself, Mr. N experienced this disappointment as loss of the bond and saw himself as a victim, unable to work. Only by persistent reinstatement of the therapeutic bond through the analyst's renewed feelings of hope could Mr. N regain a sense of buoyancy. Because of this therapeutic experience with Mr. N, Brandchaft is convinced that

> the deepest source of depression in Mr. N . . . was the underlying belief that no tie could be formed and no pathway sustained in which the central strivings to give meaning to a life of his own and the disheartening internal obstacles he encountered could find empathic resonance and understanding so that he might ultimately prevail [pp. 149-150].

As can be seen from these two illustrations, a lack of needed selfobject relationships leads not only to a failure in the process of affect integration, but to the establishment of defenses against experiencing the affects. Such defenses, according to Stolorow et al. (1987) "become necessary to preserve the integrity of a brittle self-structure" (p. 67).

Defenses against affect frequently emerge during treatment when patients reveal a need to disavow, disassociate, or defensively encapsulate affect. Such defensiveness seems to be rooted in the patient's expectation that his emerging feeling states will meet with the same faulty responsiveness of the original caregiver. Once these defenses against the "dread to repeat" are interpreted (A. Ornstein, 1974), the patient's arrested developmental needs will be reawakened in the transference with the therapist. As Stolorow (1987) says:

> The analyst's ability to comprehend and interpret the feeling states and corresponding selfobject functions as they enter the transference will be critical in facilitating the analytic process and the patient's growth toward an analytically expanded and enriched affective life [p. 74].

As mentioned in chapter 14, a patient's ability to integrate previously disavowed affects is a test of a therapist's functioning as a needed selfobject. Hence, the emergence of previously disavowed feelings is a sign of therapeutic progress. Attention to the previously disavowed feeling is a valuable safeguard against the therapist's being lulled into believing that the patient is using him as a selfobject function, when, in fact, this is not the case. Just as the theory of selfobject functions limits an overinclusive use of empathy as an explanatory principle, so the theory of affects restricts the overinclusiveness of a theory of selfobject functions.

In summary, self psychology views affects as important in the organization of experience and in the structuralization of the self. Affects are understood as biologically based in the subcortical brain, with specific patterns of response as shown by Tomkins (1962-63). When the affective systems, particularly the negative systems, are extremely aroused, trauma occurs, and a person struggles to maintain self-cohesion amid signs of fragmentation. In the next chapter, we explore the extreme arousal of the affective systems in a self-psychological theory of trauma.

Readings for Chapter 22: Freud, 1917e; Balint, 1969; Krystal, 1978; Ulman and Brothers, 1988, chap. 1.

contradictory affect states
need to be seen as from one self
integrated.

22

Trauma

One of self psychology's theoretical shifts has been from drive/conflict theory to trauma theory. Kohut's trauma theory differs from Freud's (1917) theory, according to which trauma is determined by both "environmental circumstances" (stressor events) and the "disposition" of the person experiencing the event. Kohut's emphasis, on the other hand, is on the function of the self and selfobjects in any traumatic experience. To understand the significance of Kohut's contribution and the increased role of trauma theory for the conduct of psychotherapy, we cover the following: (a) definition, (b) traumatogenic objects, (c) trauma and the self, (d) trauma and selfobjects, and (e) trauma and psychotherapy.

DEFINITION

The word trauma comes from the Greek word meaning "wound" (Figley, 1985). Freud initially defined psychic trauma as "any experience which calls up distressing affects—such as those of fright, anxiety, shame or physical pain" (Breuer and Freud, 1893-95,

Freud
unbearable affect state = trauma

p. 6). However, as Krystal (1978) indicates, "Alongside the ('unbearable affects') model of psychic trauma, Breuer and Freud developed another one: that of the dynamics of unacceptable impulses" (p. 83). Freud held both models in his mind for many years. Thus the discrediting of Freud's drive theory and the idea of unacceptable impulses still leaves Freud's unbearable affects theory of trauma intact.

With the advances in affect theory by Tomkins and others (discussed in the previous chapter), trauma theory promises significant advances in understanding the processes involved in psychotherapy. Consistent with Freud's affect theory of trauma and self psychology's emphasis on the self system, one way of defining trauma is as the self's experience of its affect systems in an excessive or prolonged state of excitation (Selye, 1950) In this view, trauma occurs when "extensive regions of the body deviate from [a] normal resting state" (p. 9). Physiologically, trauma is an "alarm reaction" in which an organism's defenses are overwhelmed, and the organism goes into a full-blown shock, creating profound weakness, flaccidity of muscles, pallor, perspiration, a weak pulse, and a low arterial blood pressure. If the condition progresses, coma ensues and finally death.

Such excessive stimulation of the affective system occurs in conjunction with the shattering of "central organizing fantasies of self in relation to selfobject" (Ulman and Brothers, 1988, p. 295). Trauma can be defined psychologically, therefore, as the shattering (Kohut's fragmenting) of these fantasies.

The definition of trauma as a process involving overstimulation of the affective system and the shattering of self-fantasies contrasts with a more "objective" view of trauma as a sudden, catastrophic, stressor event, such as rape. Undoubtedly many events that are violent, destructive, brutal, and tragic have a high probability of producing a traumatic response in those who are made victims by the event. But whether or not a trauma occurs depends on the internal state of the person experiencing the event.

TRAUMATOGENIC OBJECTS — Balint

What Freud called environmental circumstances and social scientists call stressor events Balint (1969) called traumatogenic objects.

environmental circumstans
— events leading to trauma

Self psychology — intersubjective to each individual

Historically, a sudden bereavement (Lindemann, 1944) has been the model traumatogenic loss. In recent years this model has been expanded to include such life events as death of a loved one, divorce, loss of a job, children going to college, and change of residence, a list that Holmes and Rahe (1967) incorporated into a Social Readjustment Scale to measure the cumulative effect of stressor events over a short period of time. Among the items in the scale, and the stress points attached to them were death of a spouse, 100 stress points (maximum); divorce, 73; marriage, 50; pregnancy, 40; and beginning or ending school, 26. Holmes and Rahe showed that the higher the stress score over a 12-month period, the higher the probability of developing a medical illness in the following two years. Their attempt to objectify and quantify trauma, useful though it may have been in demonstrating one of the possible consequences of trauma, so focused on the stressor event that it helped promote a reified view of trauma.

Catastrophic events also have a high probability of inducing trauma. Parson (1985) lists a wide range of such events and cites studies associated with them:

> Many traumatic symptoms and reactions ranging from mild to severe, from normal to pathological, and from acute to chronic states, can be found in those who have experienced the horrors of the Holocaust (Furst, 1967; Krystal, 1968); the Hiroshima Blast (Lifton, 1968); severe head injuries (Adler [sic], 1945); rape trauma (McDonald, 1979); industrial accidents (Bloch and Bloch, 1976); and other personal injuries (Horowitz, Wilner, Kaltreider, and Alvarez, 1980). Additionally, stress symptomatology is observed in women with miscarriages (Friedman and Cohen, 1980); in hostages taken in prison (Wolk, 1981); in repatriated prisoners of war (Corcoran, 1982; Ursano, 1981; Ursano, Boydstun, and Wheatley, 1981); in survivors of combat in the Yom Kippur War (Moses, Bargel, Falk, HaLevi et al., 1976); in veterans of World War II and Korea (Archibald and Tuddenham, 1965); and in veterans of the Vietnam War (Figley, 1978; Parson, 1984b) [pp. 316-317].

Catastrophic natural disasters, such as tornadoes (Bloch, Silber, and Perry, 1956), earthquakes, dam collapses (Tichener and Kapp, 1976), floods or blizzards (Burke et al., 1982), need to be added to Parson's list. Other events include witnessing a homicide (Bergen,

1958; Schetky, 1978; Pruett, 1979), child abuse (Green, 1983), kidnaping (Senior, Gladstone, and Nurcombe, 1982), and incest (Donaldson and Gardiner, 1985), the last being the original stressor event used by Freud to develop his theory of trauma. Undoubtedly the list of stressor events, can be expanded.

Enough research has been done to establish that dramatic, catastrophic events and the stress symptoms they induce have attracted widespread interest and fostered the erroneous notion that trauma is solely an objective event. Self psychology, like traditional psychoanalysis, sees trauma as more than an objective stressor event. But unlike traditional psychoanalysis, self psychology cannot conceive of trauma without the presence of some kind of external stressor event to trigger the internal processes. Where self psychologists disagree with social theorists is in the area of the objectification of such stressor events as rape, so that all rape by definition is traumatic to every person who goes through the experience. An experience of rape is traumatic to most, but not all, who are forced into the experience (see Kilpatrick et al., 1985). The external event, therefore, by itself is not trauma, even though it is a very important component. subjective experience

TRAUMA AND THE SELF

Freud (1917) gave personality disposition a place in his theory of trauma. His ideas about trauma associated with a death consisted of the actual event itself and the premorbid personality of the person experiencing the loss: "In some people the same influences produce melancholia instead of mourning and we consequently suspect them of a pathological disposition" (p. 243). Implied in this theory is an explanation why two persons, each faced with a painful loss, undergo completely different processes: one may go through "normal" grieving, while the other may respond "pathologically" and never recover because of a loss of "ego" (self-cohesion). Generalized, Freud's theory of trauma contains the idea of an external stressor event and the personality structure (constitutional and developmental) of the person experiencing this event.

Some current literature on trauma supports Freud's theory of trauma. Green et al. (1985), for example, acknowledge that in

Stolorow
trauma:
failure of affect attunement

response to a catastrophic event "not all people develop a formal stress disorder" (p. 57). These authors have developed a model that takes "into account characteristics of a particular individual (survivor) and characteristics of the environment in which that individual experiences and attempts to recover from the trauma" (p. 57). Thus "different people who are present at the *same event* will have different outcomes because, not only will their experiences differ, but the individual characteristics they bring to bear upon the psychological processing are different" (p. 59). Green and colleagues also think that most who study disasters now take an "interactional approach, assuming that neither individual characteristics nor aspects of the stressful event solely determine the outcome" (p. 60).

In a study of rape victims, Kilpatrick et al. (1985) found that the victim's personality was a key factor in the intensity of affect stimulation experienced: "It is not unreasonable to assume that the psychological distress produced by a rape might vary as a function of the victim's characteristics and the nature of the rape itself" (p. 120). The authors cite several studies to support their contention:

> Frank, Turner, Stewart, Jacob, and West (1981) found that victims with histories of psychiatric treatment had poorer initial adjustment than those without such histories. Atkeson et al. (1982) reported similar findings in that pre-rape history of anxiety, depression, or physical health problems was modestly predictive of post-rape depression, while the amount of [apparent] trauma that occurred during the rape itself was not predictive of subsequent depression. The McCahill et al. (1979) study also found that victims with pre-rape history of adjustment problems had more severe post-rape problems [p. 121].

The concept of the self is critical for a theory of trauma. Some theorists accept that personality structure codetermines the symptoms of trauma without the self's playing a crucial part in the subjective experience of trauma itself. A person's self-organization may be prone to a subjective experience of trauma when confronted with a stressful event, or it may interpret the meaning of a stressor event so that the impact of the event on the self's affective and cognitive systems is modified and a subjective experience of trauma does not occur. For example, of a sample of 65 U.S. Air

Force prisoners of war in Vietnam, 15 showed no evidence of the Concentration Camp syndrome, the normal way that stress was manifest after a long, constricted confinement (Corcoran, 1982). This finding supports the idea that persons with different self-organizations have different levels of psychological immunity to external stressors.

Ulman and Brothers (1988) place the self's organization at the center of trauma theory and reject the idea that trauma is a fantasy event. They argue that real events shatter the narcissistic fantasies that are central to the organization of the self. Thus they emphasize the cognitive rather than the affective dimension of a traumatic experience. They write: "in this shattering and subsequent faulty (defensive and/or compensatory) attempts to restore these fantasies lies the unconscious meaning of the traumatic event" (p. xii). Consequently, "there is a severe 'developmental arrest' (Stolorow and Lachmann, 1980) in the psychic structuralization of the incest survivor's self-experience because these central organizing fantasies are repeatedly shattered and faultily restored with each incestuous assault" (p. xiii).

At the heart of their theory is the idea that the subjective experience of trauma is the shattering of a persons's beliefs about self. The self has core archaic narcissistic fantasies that are representations of the self in relation to a selfobject. Ulman and Brothers see their construct of the self as fantasy as an experience-near level of theorizing, and not as the supraordinate, experience-distance self of Kohut: "Kohut originally thought of archaic forms of narcissism (that is, fantasies of self in relation to selfobject) as an ultimate 'psychic reality' or subjective frame of reference" (p. 19). Piaget (1970) might have termed these fantasies "unconscious meaning structures."

Ulman and Brothers claim no originality for their idea of trauma as the shattering of archaic narcissistic fantasies. They borrowed the concept of organizing fantasy from the work of Nunberg and Shapiro (1983), who suggest that each person develops an organized system of fantasy. They also see their concept of trauma as similar to the notion of shattering a person's assumptive world. Janoff-Bulman (1985), for example, sees three basic assumptions, which if shattered, will constitute a trauma. "These three assumptions include: (1) the belief in personal invulnerability; (2) the

Ullman brothers —
sense of self shattered =
traumatic experience
— subjective —

perception of the world as meaningful and comprehensible; and (3) the view of oneself in a positive light" (p. 18).

To test their idea of trauma as a shattering of archaic narcissistic fantasies, Ulman and Brothers (1988) interviewed 150 survivors of stressor events (50 incest victims, 50 rape victims, and 50 combat survivors). Of these 88 (59%) had been diagnosed as having a posttraumatic stress disorder. Eventually 10 from each trauma group were selected for self-psychologically informed psychotherapy, where it was quickly obvious that many were suffering from a severe blow to their grandiosity or a sudden disillusionment of their idealized figures.

Ulman and Brothers's case of Fran illustrates the treatment of trauma informed by self-psychological theory:

> By the time Fran entered school, her trust, respect, and admiration for both parents had been repeatedly shaken. Again and again, her mother had rebuffed her efforts at closeness. Again and again, she had submitted to her father's bizarre sexual demands. They were, in other words, figures who constantly interfered with Fran's need to unconsciously enact a fantasy of idealized merger with omnipotent parental imagos. In addition, her parents were grossly unempathic to Fran's need for mirroring
>
> [Fran's] central organizing fantasies of grandiose exhibitionism, as well as those of idealized merger, were repeatedly shattered. As she grew up, Fran's self-experience was increasingly organized by these fantasies, which underwent ever greater defensive and compensatory elaboration. For instance, the exhibitionistic displays Fran staged during her school years, as well as her inflated estimation of her musical ability, may be understood as unconscious efforts at defensive restoration of her grandiose fantasies [p. 35].

Ulman and Brothers's concept of the self as fantasy diverges from that of Atwood and Stolorow (1984), who conceive of structures as subjective organizing principles. "Stolorow maintains that structures of subjectivity are primary whereas fantasy is secondary" (Ulman and Brothers, 1988, p. 20). Stolorow's belief in the primacy of structures is consistent with his understanding of concretizations: he sees subjective structures as being perceptually concretized as sensorimotor symbols, such as fantasy.

As a consequence of their self-psychologically informed treatment of trauma patients, Ulman and Brothers see a theory of trauma as the key element in a paradigm shift away from conflict theory. They note that Cohen (1980) has referred to the emergence of a "trauma paradigm" in psychoanalysis and views their work as supporting this position. It differs slightly from the thesis of the present volume, which recognizes a major paradigm shift as occurring, but one much larger than from conflict theory to trauma theory. The question of the size of the paradigm shift, and whether self psychology itself represents only one piece of a larger paradigm shift, is taken up in the final chapter.

TRAUMA AND SELFOBJECTS

Balint (1969) paved the way for understanding the function of selfobjects (before Kohut defined the term) for a theory of trauma. He conceived a new theory that moved beyond seeing trauma as "an external event causing a severe psychical upheaval with lasting consequences" (p. 429) and also beyond the idea of trauma as patient fantasies determined by the inner state of the self. This new theory came from recognizing the potential of the infant–mother relationship to act as a traumatogenic object. Conditions necessary for a parent to function as a traumatogenic agent are that (1) the child has a dependent, trusting relationship with a parent, (2) this parent does "something exciting, frightening or painful" (p. 432), and (3) when the child

> approaches his partner again with a wish and an offer to continue the exciting passionate game, or, still in pain and distress about the fact that in the previous phase his approach remained unrecognized, ignored or misunderstood, now tries again to get some understanding, recognition and comfort. What happens quite often in either case is a completely unexpected refusal [p. 432].

In other words, it is not so much the excitement or fright or pain that produces the trauma in an infant, but the faulty responding and outright rejection by the adult with whom the infant has a dependent relationship.

Balint illustrated his point by describing an incident (p. 433). A baby of around six months old was placed on a table and left for a moment unattended. Apparently he managed to wiggle over the edge and drop to the floor. He was obviously shocked. His mother picked him up and cuddled him, and when he calmed down completely, she fed him and changed his diapers. Then she kept him in her arms for a couple of hours although the boy was asleep. With this incident Balint pinpointed the importance of the mother as a calming selfobject, even though the actual term itself came later with Kohut. Balint then raised the question of what would happen if the "mother did not recognize the child's 'communications,' misinterpreted and misunderstood them, and in consequence her response was wrong or inadequate" (p. 434). The lack of an appropriate response, not the fall to the floor, is a traumatogenic object. In taking this position, Balint touched on the idea that a person's selfobject experience is central to the concept of trauma.

Kohut (1984) thought that an infant would be traumatized by the repeated absence of a developmentally needed selfobject experience. Referring to the unavailability of a therapist to his patient, Kohut noted that "the patient's self disintegrates temporarily because the withdrawal of the mirroring selfobject repeats the traumatic unavailability of self confirming responses in early life" (p. 102). In infancy, then, it is the unavailability of the necessary selfobject experience that is the major reason for the experience of trauma. Ferenczi (1933), similarly, thought that the major element in trauma was not the incestuous act per se, but the experience of the parent's betrayal of the child's trust and, therefore, of the needed selfobject function.

Some of the "objective" studies of the traumatic effects of catastrophic events touch on the selfobject factor in trauma theory. For example, Green et al. (1985) mention the importance of a "recovery environment": "We found that family and friends of survivors often formed a sort of membrane around the survivors which functioned to protect them from people and circumstances that threatened to be further traumatic" (p. 61). And Kilpatrick et al. (1985), in studying rape victims, write:

> The victim's post-rape interactions with significant others, family members, friends, law enforcement agencies, hospitals, and/or treatment providers can have either positive, negative, or mixed effects on subsequent psychological adjustment in that they can serve as additional sources of stress, enhancers of coping ability, or some combination of the two [p. 122].

While the idea of the potential role of a supportive recovery environment (and by implication, selfobject experience) is seen by social researchers as a useful addition to a theory of trauma, their view does not reflect the central function of selfobjects in maintaining the self's organization of experience. As "support," selfobjects are still viewed as auxiliary to an actual "traumatic event."

In comparison, a self-psychological theory of trauma, while acknowledging the catalytic role of traumatic events, understands the experience of trauma as the loss of a selfobject, with resulting affect overstimulation and self-fragmentation. Selfobject loss or absence is seen as the key to the psychology of traumatization, and the stressor event and the self-system as ancillary to such loss or absence. The memory of early trauma involving persistent absences of necessary selfobject experiences leaves the self vulnerable to further potentially traumatizing events. These psychological "allergies," the defenses against their activation, and the components of self-organization are involved in the experience of trauma. Later stressor events retraumatize, that is, reproduce an uncomfortable, overstimulated affective state without expectation of selfobject soothing. On the other hand, adults with internalized experiences of adequately responsive selfobjects when infants are more immune to a subjective experience of trauma despite the impact of a catastrophic event such as rape.

This new perspective on trauma based on selfobject experience makes possible a less pessimistic view of the consequences of catastrophic events. It leads to a disagreement with disaster specialists who assume that all victims of a catastrophic event are traumatized and who therefore believe that those showing no symptoms of stress are going through massive denial that will later manifest as psychopathology. A theory of trauma with the selfobject factor as the key does not hold that everyone will be traumatized by a catastrophic event. Many, of course, *will* be traumatized, and almost immediately show symptoms of trauma. Others exposed to the stressor event and traumatized by it, but who disavow what has happened, will have a delayed reaction to their traumatic experience. Some, however, may not be traumatized in any significant way as the following case illustrates:

Case Illustration

Mr. M, who suffered congestive heart failure, underwent successful open-heart surgery for an aortic valve replacement without experiencing trauma. His 800 hours of psychotherapy, which had ended 5 years before, resulted in the structuralized sense of the presence of his therapist.

While in hospital preparing for the surgery, Mr. M, as a way of coping with presurgery "jitters" and helping to evolve a strategy to enhance surgical results, recalled his experiences of his therapist as a calming selfobject in past situations. Under this strategy, he saw and handled the valve that was to be placed in his heart, obtained and read articles about the aortic valve in the medical literature for the preceding five years, and learned that the five-year survival rate for person's using this valve was 83%.

Another part of the strategy was to introduce humor to the surgical team. Mr. M had obtained an empty aortic valve box from a nurse friend and placed a plumber's valve in it. He handed it to the surgeon the night before the surgery and said, "Doc, I've changed my mind about that valve and want you to sew in this one." Mr. M's fantasy was of a Monday morning surgical team, slow to get going and still distracted by memories of their weekend, laughing and quickening their attention to the task at hand when the surgeon held up the plumber's valve to show them what this "crazy guy" had wanted them to do. Just imagining this scene helped Mr. M feel better.

Three days after surgery Mr. M had another session with his "internal therapist." The operation and the first two days had gone well, but on the third day, when Mr. M was transferred out of

introject

intensive care, he was exhausted from coping with the 42 persons with whom he had interacted that day. There were two new nurses each shift, a different physiotherapist every six hours; a resident doctor; many medical students listening, poking, and asking questions; student nurses; aides; a different blood technician every four hours; a dietitian; the cardiologist; two surgeons; and others. Every time he dozed off to sleep, someone soon awakened him for something. The task (thing), always more important than his needs, turned him into a selfobject to the schedules of others. In that night's imaginary therapy session, he told his therapist about the psychological battering and exhaustion he was experiencing and imagined his therapist saying, as he had done many times before, "Well, what are you going to do about it?" So, in the presence of his internalized therapist, he evolved a plan.

The next morning a nurse bounced into the room at 6 a.m. and opened the blinds with "Good morning." He deliberately greeted her with a grumpy, "What's good about it?" After she left the room quickly, Mr. M felt better. The next interaction was with a physiotherapist who was greeted with "None today thank you." The shocked "physio" said, "But your doctor ordered it!" Mr. M: "I'll deal with him when he comes in!" Counter: "But you need it." Counter reply: "Like a hole in my head." Then with a triumphant note of finality, Mr. M said, "I'm refusing treatment!"

Next came the students. They received a,"School's-out today, try tomorrow." By the time Mr. M's wife visited in the early afternoon, he was ready to sleep. While she sat "on guard" in the room's doorway and turned away numerous persons with the insistence that Mr. M be left undisturbed, he had five hours of the best sleep since coming into hospital. The cardiologist, who came later to a refreshed and prepared Mr. M, said, "I hear there has been a little trouble." Mr. M: "There was yesterday, but today's been wonderful!" Cardiologist: "I hear you are refusing treatment." Mr. M: "Yes, but just physiotherapy." Counter: "I'll reduce it by half." Reply: "No. I am prepared to sign something absolving you of the legal responsibility."

That night, as Mr. M recalled his day's work, he felt good about regaining his sense of agency. His recovery then was rapid; he left the hospital a day earlier than the norm and was back at work four weeks after the surgery, two weeks ahead of schedule. The internally structured presence of a calming, soothing selfobject had helped Mr. M become more adaptive and modify the traumatic effects of the open-heart surgery.

Critics of a self psychological theory of trauma may misinterpret aspects of this case. Dorpat (1990) for example, wrongly claims that self psychology is wedded to drive theory and fantasies activated by unconscious drives and is not interested in the "real occurrences in the social world of shared experience" (p. 456). Van der Kolk (1988) also thinks that self psychology undervalues "the interpersonal dimension of psychological agony" (p. 376). Both are wrong. The fantasies that Ulman and Brothers mention derive from experiences with selfobjects, not from id drives. And as we have previously stated, self psychology sees the stressor event as a necessary element in trauma theory. Self psychology does not deny that such events can be so horrible, so overwhelming in nature, as to warrant the descriptive appellation "traumatic." But self psychology makes the distinction between trauma as an *event* (perceived extrospectively) and trauma as a *process* (experienced introspectively).

The process of traumatization involves both a traumatic event and the psychological sequalae that follow in its wake. The strength of a self-psychological theory of trauma resides in its sensitivity to the whole process of traumatization, with an interest in minimizing the devastating repercussions of a traumatic event and preventing maladaptive structuralizations. Mr. M was subjected to a traumatic event, and yet, owing to structuralized selfobject experiences, he was largely successful in resisting the subjective *experience* of being traumatized.

TRAUMA AND PSYCHOTHERAPY

Trauma theory enlarges our understanding of the process of psychotherapy in three ways: (1) by helping explain the severe resistances of many patients to the development of an empathic bond in the beginning phase of treatment, (2) by illuminating psychotherapy as an immunizer against future trauma, and (3) by emphasizing the repair of selfobject failures as another means of lessening sensitivity to trauma.

Trauma Theory Helps Explain the Severe Resistances of Many Patients to the Development of an Empathic Bond in the Beginning Phase of Treatment.

Not everyone reacts in this way, of course. But for many, despite their hunger to be understood empathically and their need for cohesive selfobject experiences, the fear of being retraumatized is so great that they resist the very experience they most need. Anna Ornstein (1974) offered a similar idea with her concept of the "dread to repeat," specifically "the 'dread to repeat' archaic infantile defense patterns" (p. 232), because she sees these archaic defenses as being "in response to childhood narcissistic traumata" (p. 232). It is clear, however, that she views the dread as associated with both retraumatization and the archaic defenses that accompany it.

Trauma Theory Illuminates the Experience of Psychotherapy as Immunization Against Future Trauma.

When psychotherapy acts as such an agent, the therapist is intensively and consistently available, is empathically understanding, is a responsive selfobject, and is internally present.

Support for the idea that even brief psychotherapy can reduce the subjective experience of trauma comes from the research of Florell (1971). He studied 100 patients who received a psychotherapy session the evening before they underwent elective orthopedic surgery. Dependent measures of stress before and after the surgery were compared with those of 50 orthopedic patients not given the presurgery psychotherapy session. Significant differences were obtained on most of the dependent measures. The comparison group, who did not receive the treatment, stayed more than a day longer in hospital, needed more pain medication, had higher pulse and respiration rates for days after the surgery, had more lines of nursing notes, made more calls to the nursing station, and showed more anxiety on the Spielberger State Trait Anxiety Inventory several weeks after the operation. Other studies cited by Florell showed similar results for brief psychotherapy conducted in anticipation of a high-stress event.

To such experimentally designed studies of brief psychotherapy for reducing stress, case studies of effective, long term, intensive psychotherapy can be added. For example, the case of Mr M, described earlier, showed the value of a therapeutic relationship in modifying the subjective impact of a stressor event.

The Repair of Selfobject Failures During Psychotherapy is Another Means of Lessening Sensitivity to Stressor Events or "Triggers."

The recognition and repair of selfobject failures is a major task already discussed under transmuting internalization and structuralization (see chapter 19, this volume). The signs of such failures are often indirect because of the urgent need to maintain the therapeutic bond as a means of keeping the self cohesive. Problems with paying bills, lateness, dreams of bugs (Stolorow, 1975), or excessive drinking are examples of behavior suggesting the possibility of a selfobject failure needing exploration.

In summary, we have seen how the responsive selfobject functioning of the parent is crucial to a child's becoming able to function as an adult. The absence of a needed selfobject, on the other hand, helps produce pathologically structured ways of behaving. In the following chapter, we see the importance of the selfobject experience in the mother/infant dyad and the patterns that occur in the first few months of development.

Readings for Chapter 23: Beebe, 1985; Beebe and Lachmann, 1988.

23

Mutual Influence Theory

The clinical experience of patients needing a selfobject bond with the therapist raises questions about their early childhood. Specifically, what was their interactive pattern with mother in the early months of life? The mother/infant studies by Beebe and Lachmann (1988) offer some answers. This chapter uses their material extensively, but not exclusively, to discuss mutual influence under the following topics: (a) theory of early infancy, (b) multimodal evidence, (c) self- and object representations, (d) matching communication, (e) aversive interaction, (f) coactive and alternating matching, and (g) psychotherapy.

THEORY OF EARLY INFANCY

Beebe and Lachmann (1988) state that "the mother-infant interaction in the first six months of life can illuminate the development of psychic structure" (p. 3). These early interactive structures are made up of "patterns of mutual influence" that provide an important element in the organization of infant experience. They go on to say, "The dynamic interplay between infant and caretaker, each influencing the other to create a variety of patterns of mutual regulation, provide one basis for the representation of self and other" (p. 4).

These statements, and those of other infant researchers, for example, Stern (1985), are in sharp contrast to Freud's idea of an infant's autistic stage of development for the first two months of life. In this autistic stage "the infant is postulated as not only [being] unaware of his person, but also as essentially unaware of his environment" (Shane and Shane, 1980, p. 28). Infant researchers also see a baby as very different from the one hypothesized by Abraham, Klein, or Mahler, who conceived of it as

> endangered from within by its own libidinal and hostile-aggressive drives and their "early objects," by introjective, projective, and splitting mechanisms of defense against the dangers from drives and drive objects, and by resultant archaic psychic conflict [Shane and Shane, 1980, p. 51].

Nor do infant researchers see evidence that after the autistic phase the infant fuses with a hallucinated representation of an omnipotent maternal symbiotic object or part-object for the next five to six months as Mahler, Pine, and Bergman (1975) assert. What emerges from recent infant studies is a very active person from day one.

Mutual influence theory also stands in contrast to the one-way model, in which either the parent influences the child or the child the parent. It reflects a systems perspective in which experiences are perceived as the property of the infant-caretaker system, rather than the property of the individual (Sander, 1977, 1983). It also reflects Winnicott's (1960a) declaration that "there is no such thing as a baby" and that the "infant and mother together form an indivisible unit" (p. 39).

The interaction of the mother-infant dyad includes feeding, the management of tension states, social interaction, and play. From birth, the infant is innately structured to actively seek stimuli.

> Neonates show rooting, sucking, molding, and orienting behavior; the ability to scan visually, focus on, and track a moving object;

> and the capacity to respond to visual stimuli by widened and brightened eyes, changes in respiration, a decrease in random movements, and fine nuances of facial expressions (Als, 1977; Brazelton, 1974; Oster, 1978) . . . . Neonates not only seek and initiate social interaction (Als, 1977) but can also modulate or regulate social stimulation in the face of aversive conditions with self-quieting measures, inhibiting their responsiveness or habitation to a disturbing stimulus (Brazelton, 1974). These innately organized patterns of behavior equip the infant to engage in primary relatedness with the human partner [Beebe, 1985, p. 29].

MULTIMODAL EVIDENCE

Empirical literature on mother-infant interaction reinforces the existence of mutual influence in the formation of organizing structures in infants. Observations of mutual regulations have been made with respect to (1) vocalizations, (2) sleep–wake states, (3) gaze, (4) affective engagement, (5) shared rhythms (temporal organization), and (6) expectancies.

Vocalizations

Two studies document mutual influence in mother–infant vocalizations (Stern et al., 1975; Anderson, Vietze, and Dokecki, 1977). These studies show that if one partner in the dyad begins to vocalize, there is a greater than chance probability that the other partner will begin vocalizing. There is a tendency for the vocalization to occur almost simultaneously, that is, as a coaction.

verbal attunement

Sleep–Wake States

A mutual influence structure acts as a "basic regulatory core" that jells in the early weeks of life in relation to the caretaker environment (Sander, 1983). Sander formed this idea from the regularities in the sequence and duration of infant sleep-wake and feeding states. Such regularities are established over the course of the first days and weeks of life only as mother and infant mutually influence each other to establish predictable sequences. Chapell and Sander (1979) write:

> The infant's wakefulness determines the activities of the mother, the activities of the mother determine in some degree the course of infant state over the interaction period, and the modifiability of infant state by maternal manipulation determines the mother's further activities [p. 106].

An infant's "alert state" is greatly facilitated by the mother–infant mutually influencing interaction.

> Most healthy full-term infants have no difficulty achieving a robust, lusty crying state and can return to a sleep state relatively readily. The ability most neonates seem to establish in the first several weeks after birth is increasing stabilization of the alert state in their transition from sleep to aroused crying states and back down to sleep states. In the two-day-old full-term infant the alert periods are still much more difficult to achieve and are embedded in long stretches of sleep and episodes of crying. By two and three weeks, these periods of alertness have become increasingly reliable and solidified; by one month to six weeks, many infants easily spend an hour and more in an alert, socially and cognitively available state [Als, 1986, pp. 11-12].

Gaze

According to Beebe and Lachmann (1988):

> In studying the mutual regulation of gaze during face-to-face play at four months, Stern (1974) similarly documented that each partner influences the other . . . . The infant's initiation of gaze at mother increases the likelihood that mother will continue gazing. When mother and infant are gazing at each other, it is more likely that the infant will gaze away. In fact, it is the infant who makes and breaks mutual gazes, since the infant initiates and terminates 94 percent of all mutual gazes, while the mother tends to gaze steadily at the infant [p. 5].

Affective Engagement

To study affective engagement, Stern (1977) set up two video cameras for a split-screen view, one focused on the infant and the other on the mother. He asked mothers to play with their children.

Later analysis of 16mm films made from the tapes, pairs of frames at a time, and use of a scale of "affective engagement" revealed action patterns. These patterns showed an inexact matching of emotional engagement, but mother and infant matched each other's direction of engagement change, both increasing and decreasing. That is, they each tracked the process of change in the other. More than this, a statistical time series regression analysis showed that each partner influenced the other to follow his or her own direction of affective change.

Tronick, Als, and Brazleton (1980) also conducted a study on affect engagement and came to a similar conclusion. Viewing the split-second by split-second affective involvement between mother and infant in play at around three months, by noting positive or negative responding, they found that the changes in involvement tended to be simultaneous (coactive) rather than on an alternating (reactive) basis.

Affective communication is critical to the guidance of an infant in a social referencing situation. Researchers (for example, Emde et al., 1978) placed year-old infants in uncertain situations, such as at the brink of an apparent cliff. The infants were lured by an attractive toy to crawl across a "visual cliff" created by placing a thick piece of glass over a real drop off. Infants facing this uncertain situation look toward mother to read her face for its affective content to see how they should feel. When the mother follows the instructions to show facial fear, the infant turns back. When the mother's face shows encouragement, the infant crawls across to the toy.

Shared Rhythms (Temporal Organization)

Condon and Sander (1974) present evidence that infants move their bodies in precise unison with adult speech. Even though Dowd and Tronick (1983) failed to replicate this finding, other investigators have discovered movements where both partners are synchronized. Stern (1974), for instance, discovered simultaneous head movement in three-month-old twins interacting with their mother. Perry (1980) found coordination of the changes in the direction of head movement with no noticeable lagtime by either partner. Beebe (1985) reports that

> both Stern and Perry explain their results as reciprocal mutual regulation; where the behavior of each partner is influenced by the other, so that the intensity and quality of social contact is adjusted on a moment to moment basis [p. 31].

Studies indicate that mother–infant interaction patterns occur in half a second or less. This rapidity of engagement suggests a process that is either partially or fully out of conscious control. Adult conversations can also have matching patterns. "When adult strangers match rhythms, they like each other more and perceive each other as warmer and more similar than when their rhythms do not match" (Beebe and Lachmann, 1988, p. 13). If persons who walk together do not match each other's pace, one will soon be ahead of the other. Similarly, in any conversation, if one participant never pauses or waits too long before responding, the other may well tune out. Studies of mother–infant interactions when the infant is three months show that they match each other's pauses, each other's "turns," and the duration of such actions as orienting to look.

Expectancies

Mutual influence structures organize infant experience through expectancies. Decasper and Carstens (1980) used infants' capacity to time events to teach them that if they paused longer (or shorter) between sucking bursts, they could turn on music. When the infants' expectations were confirmed, that is, when their longer pauses between sucking produced music, the infants' affect was positive. In a second experiment, after the infants had learned to turn on music by pausing longer between sucking bursts, the experimenter turned on and off the music randomly. The infants' affects then became negative: the babies grimaced, whimpered, cried, and in some cases stopped sucking altogether. In a third experiment, a new group of infants was first randomly exposed to music before being subjected to the first experiment, in which music was turned on after longer pauses between sucking. The startling result was that the infants could not learn the contingency between their behavior and the music.

> The findings of their last experiment suggest that if the environment were completely noncontingent, which would be a very extreme condition, then the infant's very capacity to organize experience within a dyadic relationship would be interfered with [Beebe and Lachmann, 1988, pp. 6-7].

Decasper and Carstens's (1980) work points to a new view of infant memory. What the infant remembers is not simply an event, but a particular contingency relationship between behavior and environmental event. That is, the infant *remembers an interaction*! Infants learn, remember, and anticipate from birth; they can, thus, participate in many mutually regulated interactions from the beginning of life. Those interactions that repeatedly reoccur, and are thus characteristic of the infant, become generalized as structures that organize the infant's experience. Structures are understood in Rapaport's (1959) sense: as configurations or patterns with a slow rate of change.

SELF-REPRESENTATION AND OBJECT REPRESENTATIONS

Beebe and Lachmann (1988) point out that developmental theorists such as Werner, Piaget, Church, and Schilder conceptualize representation in a similar way. They all consider activity—that is, sensoriaffective-proprioceptive experience—as the primary factor. "Representation is defined as interiorized actions, so that children can now do with mental images what before they did with their own actions" (p. 7). Representational capacity can be seen after seven months but does not reach full capacity until the third year.

Beebe and Lachmann take the theory of representation a step further:

> [Representation is] interiorized *interaction*: not simply the infant's action, nor simply the environment's response, but the dynamic mutual influence between the two (see Beebe, 1985). Interiorized patterns include actions, perception, cognition, affect, and proprioceptive experience [p. 8].

Seeing representation as interiorized interaction led Beebe and Lachmann to a further conceptual step. They envisage a "transformational model of development where earlier structures are understood both to shape and to be shaped by subsequent experience" (p. 8). Such an interiorized interactive model of self-representation is in sharp contrast to the analytic view that self- and object representations grow out of the instinctual experiences of pleasure and unpleasure (Jacobson, 1964). It also shifts the focus from a representation clearly delineated from a "significant other" to one that is a "self with a significant other." Nor does the interactive model see representations built up piecemeal; the capacities to construct representations, memory, expectancies, and mutually regulated interactive patterns are present at birth.

MATCHING AS COMMUNICATION.

The experience of matching provides each person in the dyad with the means of entering the perceptual and affective world of the partner. As Beebe and Lachmann put it, "The implication is that similarity in behavior is associated with a congruence of feeling states; that there is a relationship between matching and empathy" (p. 14). That is, matching offers a way of seeing how the sharing of subjective states can occur.

In a very important experiment by Ekman (1983), professional actors were taught a series of facial muscle movements that reflected emotions. Then, when they were asked to relive various emotions, their recorded autonomic indices indicated that simply producing the facial-muscle action patterns resulted in more clear-cut autonomic changes than the attempt to relive emotions.

> The implication is that by contracting the same facial muscles as perceived on another's face, the onlooker can literally feel the same autonomic sensations as the other person. Reproducing the expression of another (for example, in mirroring) can produce in the onlooker a similar emotional state [Beebe and Lachmann, 1988, p. 15].

AVERSIVE INTERACTION

The importance of mutual influence is reflected in the filmed "chase and dodge" sequences of behavior between a four-month-old infant and his mother (Beebe and Lachmann, 1988). Instead of inhibiting the normal gazing pattern, this infant glanced only briefly at the mother during a six-minute period. The interaction reflected an intense struggle of wills in which the mother tried to engage the infant, but the infant was very determined not to be engaged.

> To every overture by the mother, the infant ducked, moved back, turned away, or pulled his hand out of her grasp. The infant appeared to exercise near "veto" power over his mother's efforts to engage him. He also systematically affected the mother's behavior: his avoidance maneuvers elicited further maternal "chase" movements, such as looming toward him, following the direction of his movement with her head and body, or pulling him toward her [p. 16].

During the chase and dodge behaviors of mother and infant, the mother demonstrated signs of negative affect: "She grimaced, frowned, bit her lip, and thrust her jaw out" (p. 16). When finally the infant went limp, so did the mother. Only in this way could the infant induce the mother to lower her level of stimulation. This pair was obviously "misattuned" even though they were still relating to each other. The infant's dodges and averting his head influenced the mother to increase her stimulation. "The infant comes to expect that he cannot benefit from his mother's participation in the management of his affect-arousal states" (p. 19). The infant was able to calm himself down only by moving away.

At a public lecture in Chicago using the "chase and dodge" film, Beebe remarked that the mother of the infant had been eager to please the researchers. We believe that whatever the reason for the mother's need to please the researcher, whether that Beebe was a displaced parental figure or that the play session reflect well on her, or some other reason, her need obviously took priority over the infant's needs, thus leading to prolonged unempathic pressure on the infant to perform. This pressure may have been experienced by the infant as an intrusive, persecutory pattern of interaction. The infant's dodge behavior may also have been a refusal by the infant to be a selfobject for the mother.

COACTIVE AND ALTERNATING TYPES OF MATCHING

The two mutual influence patterns of coactive and alternating invite speculation. Both types have been shown to occur in vocalization and facial modes. The coactive pattern appears to promote bonding and the feeling of "being with" the other person (Stern, 1985). The alternating, or turn-taking, pattern fosters a learning process, such as later speech development.

> The coactive pattern, where both partners "join in"—for example, cooing together at exactly the same moment, or both opening and widening their mouths to achieve a wide-open "gape smile" at the same split second—has a special evocative appeal. These coactive episodes seem to have a powerful effect on observers, who feel particularly empathic or "drawn into" the interaction at such moments. The subjective experience for the adult partner participating in these special coactive moments with the infant is a "high," an almost magical sharing [Beebe, 1985, p. 34].

With this pattern, "respect for the floor," where the interrupter backs off when challenged, is systematically violated. Instead, there is relative pressure for the continuation of coaction. The follower, whether mother or infant, joins in, presses on, and produces synchrony. An absence of this experience deprives both partners of sharing the same state, that is, the subjective experience of merging. Coactive mirroring is the ultimate example of this kind of sharing. Stern (1983) suggests that these coactive experiences play an important role in the development of the capacity for subjective intimacy and self esteem.

The alternating pattern is found in half-second cycles from the onset of one partner's behavior to the onset of the other partner's behavior (Beebe, 1985). Both partners contribute to the rhythmic matching, which can be seen as a precursor to adult dialogue. With this pattern, the "turn" of the leader is respected. An absence of this turn-taking experience may set back the development of speech and some related sequential cognitive functions. In this mode, neither partner "interrupts" the other, but, rather. each pauses and processes the information of the other before acting or responding.

It is important to note that both coactive and alternating patterns perform important functions in the dyad and that the infant is an active partner in both kinds of interactions.

PSYCHOTHERAPY

Infant studies, with their stress on mutual influence in the coactive and alternating rhythms of mother-infant interactions and upon affective engagement, suggest that rhythmic and affective empathy on a primitive level take place outside of conscious awareness. The empathic process, as described by Kohut in the treatment of narcissistic disorders as "vicarious introspection," uses a cognitive approach in conjunction with the patterns of interaction discovered in the study of early infancy. Some primitive empathy, necessary in the treatment of narcissistic disorders, may be critical for the treatment of more disturbed and heavily traumatized patients. This is a promising area of research.

The discovery of such primitive patterns of empathy in infant studies supports the idea that therapists either can interact with coactive and alternating patterns of mutual influence or they can not. This ability is learned either during early infancy from a good partner or not at all, unless it is through an intense psychotherapeutic experience. Recent infant studies of the earliest forms of empathy reinforce the "pedagogical commonplace [that] as a rule, students learn more about the analytic attitude from undergoing their own personal analysis and the supervision of their clinical work" (Schafer, 1983, p. 4) than they do from didactic experience. What is certainly needed is a way to test therapists for their ability to join in coactive or altering patterns of interaction. To do so would move the therapeutic professions to a new level of effectiveness.

In summary, the convergence of clinical observations and infant–mother studies supports mutual-influence theory. Mutual influence contributes to building psychic structure, occurs across modes of experience and perception, facilitates communication, and contributes to negative affects when misattunement occurs. Infant studies also support the idea that psychotherapy is a much more effective undertaking if it is more collaborative, if, in fact, it incorporates some form of twinship transference.

integration of trauma needed

self-delineation —

can be offered by therapist

pt. supported by the therapist

expression of developmental ~~longings~~ longings

fear of retraumatization —

24

Toward a General Theory

The idea of three major paradigms in the history of psychological healing—religious healing, classical analysis and self psychology—is a frame of reference for the development of a theory of psychotherapy. Our major interests have been in the emergence of the self psychology paradigm to challenge classical analysis, and, on the basis of this paradigm, in affording clinicians new insights into a broad range of clinical material, especially that relating to the narcissistic disorders.

The emergence of the self psychology paradigm, through the intellectual leadership of Heinz Kohut, took place gradually over a period of 25 years. Step by step, Kohut developed the concepts that became the building blocks of the new paradigm, many of which had been adapted from the remains of past conceptualizations scattered throughout the psychoanalytic literature. Employing empathy as his method and making the transformation of narcissism his goal, Kohut explored the treatment of patients with narcissistic transferences and discovered the utility of such concepts as the selfobject, the supraordinate self (self as organizing principle and as agent), and transmuting internalization. His was a major intellectual achievement in which he was aided by a significant number of colleagues and students. Nonetheless, Kohut knew that the paradigm was incomplete.

Work on the self psychology paradigm after Kohut—self psychology in the 80s and into the 90s—has been aimed at making it more general and inclusive, with an emphasis on theories of intersubjectivity, impasse, affect, trauma, and mutual influence. Self psychology's broadened inclusiveness may be summarized under four categories: (a) pathological syndromes, (b) treatment modalities, (c) interdisciplinary influence, and (d) other psychotherapy theories.

PATHOLOGICAL SYNDROMES

Pursuing the appeal of the 1950s, self psychology invested in the new theorizing involved in widening the scope of psychoanalysis beyond the treatment of the narcissistic disorders to more severe disorders of the self. Prominent is Galatzer-Levy's (1988) work with manic-depressives; Stolorow, Atwood, and Brandchaft's (1988) efforts with psychotics; Brandchaft's (1988) persistence with patients suffering severe depressive personality disorders; and Ulman and Bothers's (1988) treatment of those with posttraumatic stress disorder. Out of participation, that is "doing," new theory continues to emerge. To the extent that any theory remains static, it becomes a new "prisonhouse" (Goldberg, 1990).

TREATMENT MODALITIES

A self-psychologically informed psychotherapy can achieve considerable structural change and be of greater value in the therapeutic armamentarium than was believed under the classical paradigm. Admittedly, self psychology still sees a significant difference between psychoanalysis and psychotherapy, with psychoanalysis committed to repeatedly interpreting the "here-and-now" transference and to an extensive working-through. But self psychology does not conceive of the two as different in kind, primarily because both make selfobject functions central to the process. Nor is psychotherapy seen as "second class" in self psychology. Acceptance of the growing importance of psychotherapy in producing structural change opens the possibility of, and paves the way for, including other therapeutic modalities: family, marriage, group, within a self psychology paradigm.

INTERDISCIPLINARY INFLUENCE

Self psychology is also open to ideas from other disciplines, especially those having to do with subjective human experience. Compared with classical analysis, long mired in drive theory, self psychology enjoys a relationship of mutual influence, with mutual benefits, to literature, history, philosophy, infant development, and neurophysiology.

Kohut set an inclusive tone as he explored literature. For example, his insights throw new light on Thomas Mann's (1954) *Death in Venice* where Mann illuminates homosexual longings as an attempt to shore up a fragmenting self (Kohut, 1957). Kohut (1976) also had a special appreciation for the value of history in understanding clinical phenomena. For example, he saw the development of Nazism in Germany as an expression of pathological grandiose narcissism in the form of a "group self."

Self psychology also sees philosophy as another field for the enrichment of therapeutic work. Once psychotherapy is linked with the "science of experience" (Atwood and Stolorow, 1984, p. 8), then the insights of such philosophers as Husserl (Nissim-Sabat, 1989), who conceived of phenomenology, become important. So do the existentialists Heidegger and Sarte (Atwood, 1989), as well as Kierkegaard (Rubin, 1989) himself. And as Chessick (1977) reminds us, Descartes, Kant, Schopenhauer, Nietzsche, and Jaspers cannot be ignored as crucial molders and shapers of modern thought. Another philosopher important for self psychology is Maurice Merleau-Ponty (Masek, 1989). Such philosophers have been able to express their own profound subjective experiences as new ways of thinking. Their ideas challenge self psychology to continue the task of broadening the scope of psychoanalysis and psychotherapy.

It is also clear from the work of infant developmentalists, such as Stern (1985), that ideas useful in explaining infant behavior can be another rich source of material for developing new insights about psychotherapy. Through self psychology's openness, the concepts of infant research, for example, "core self," have presented new challenges to the prevailing ideas of the therapeutic establishment.

Neurophysiology is another field of study whose ideas have the potential to influence the concepts of self psychology. Levin (1991) has made "novel and detailed correlations between psychological/psychoanalytic variables, on one hand, and neuroanatomical/neurophysiological considerations on the other" (p. xxi). Reflecting on the neurosciences, Gedo (1991) writes that "the unfolding breakthrough toward a biology of mind promises soon to relegate hermeneutics to a secondary position in the analytic scheme of things and to focus primary attention on learning processes. The fruitful results of this coming revolution are incalculable" (p. xix).

PSYCHOTHERAPY THEORIES

Self psychology in the 80s has continued to explore other theories of psychotherapy. The collection edited by Detrick and Detrick (1989), *Self Psychology: Comparisons and Contrasts*, reflects self psychology's continuing interest in such pioneer thinkers as Jung, Adler, Rank, and Ferenczi; such object relations theorists as Klein, Fairbairn, Balint and Winnicott; and such American pioneers as Sullivan and Rogers; as well as the range of modern theorists from Masterson and Kernberg to Lacan and Mahler.

In an important reversal of self psychology's inclusiveness, Mitchell (1988) has portrayed self psychology as a part of a larger paradigm, which he refers to as a relational theory in contradistinction to drive/conflict theory and to developmental arrest theory. Mitchell conceives of this relational theory as an overarching general theory that includes the interactional theory of Harry Stack Sullivan; British object relations theory, especially that of Fairbairn;

and "certain currents of both self psychology and existential psychoanalysis" (p. 289).

Mitchell actually refers to the relational theory as the "relational-conflict model," because he sees conflict as an inherent property of relatedness. "To regard conflict as the exclusive property of drive theory and to present relational concepts as fundamentally nonconflictual in nature is seriously to limit the clinical utility of relational contributions" (p. 160).

The relational model of Mitchell has three dimensions: "The self, the other, and the space in between the two" (p. 33). Object relations theory, interpersonal theory, and self psychology theorize about these dimensions, but with different emphases. For example, while Mitchell sees self psychology as interested in the "space between" and in the "other," this interest basically subserves a more primary interest in the cohesion of the self.

Mitchell sees the relationship among these three major psychotherapy theories as follows:

> Interpersonal theory, object relations theory, and self psychology generate what is essentially the same story line, but in different voices. These traditions regard mind as developing out of a relational matrix, and psychopathology as a product of disturbances in interpersonal relations. The *differences* among these traditions concern the various kinds of questions they pursue, based on these same fundamental assumptions. They tend to generate complementary interpretations, and the question they pose and the answers they generate do not provide alternative visions, but instead, different angles for viewing the same, consensually acknowledged scene [p. 35].

Associated with this relational model Mitchell offers a penetrating criticism of the developmental arrest model of psychopathology. He depicts the developmental arrest model as assuming that psychopathology exists because of the needy infant in the adult, a need that originally arose from faulty parental responding. Mitchell agrees that unempathic parenting is an important source of this pathology but persuasively argues that psychopathology is best conceived of as maladaptive (rather than infantile) forms of relating to ensure some kind of relational bond despite the faulty parental responding. He says, "Psychopathology is not a state of aborted, frozen development, but a cocoon activity woven of fantasied ties to significant others" (p. 163).

In reply to Mitchell, self psychology can claim that its paradigm is much broader than an arrested development model. Admittedly, (as discussed in chapter 16), in an effort to differentiate itself from drive theory, self psychology resorted to a developmental arrest model. However, developmental arrest in the sense of the "baby in the adult" as Mitchell uses it, has never been crucial to the self psychology paradigm. Kohut began with the centrality of the narcissistic transferences, that is, with transferences presupposing a relational model and then developed his concepts of the selfobject (the "other") and of the self to encompass both the organization of experience and the sense of personal agency.

With these constructs of self and selfobject, self psychology has had the conceptual tools to examine the relational model from multiple perspectives. For narcissistic patients, for example, when therapist and patient "relate," the relationship may be perceived by a third party as two selves interacting with each other. From the point of view of the therapist, however, the relationship is between a selfobject and a self, with the therapist serving as a selfobject for the patient. From the patient's view, there may be no perceived relationship at all, just one self, that is, the patient, with the therapist as an extension of that self. A self psychology theorist looking at this same relationship may see a selfobject–self and self–selfobject engaged in a complex interaction. Given these possibilities of relating, self psychology can make the case that its model is more useful than the interactional model because it covers more dimensions of meaning. Similarly, a strong case can be made for self psychology's balanced interest among the major components of Mitchell's relational model, and for self psychology's broad paradigm having room for both the object-relational and interpersonal models.

Additionally, self psychology has developed a concept of conflict that is not drive based and, especially through the intersubjectivists, has been able to incorporate a nondrive-based concept of conflict into its expanding paradigm. Mitchell's work does suggest an interesting convergence between some theoretical developments in self psychology and the work of other theorists who have attempted to develop a nondrive-oriented paradigm for psychotherapy.

The trend in self psychology toward a more general theory reveals a creative ferment in process. Thus, when self psychology is referred to as a new paradigm, it really is new: it is still being formed. Any fear that with the death of Kohut the creative fires would die out, has been quelled by evidence of the productivity of the 80s. If anything, that decade witnessed a remarkable burst of publications revealing an even greater expansion of theory, and showing that self psychology was well prepared to grow beyond the work of its founder.

Before Kohut died, he told his wife that even though he had accomplished what he had set out to do for psychoanalysis, his work remained incomplete.

> [My husband] expressed the hope that his colleagues, particularly those of the younger generation, would do further research on the many questions he has raised during the course of his work. He also expressed the hope that his thoughts would stimulate them to raise questions of their own, in order to continue the advance of the science of psychoanalysis [Kohut, 1984, p.].

We think the theory and practice of psychotherapy after Kohut is not only well, but thriving. Our belief is that if Kohut were alive and present at the self psychology conferences of today, his eyes would have a proud gleam.

References

Abraham, K. (1919), A particular form of resistance against the psycho-analytic method. In: *Selected Papers*. New York: Basic, pp. 303-311.

Aichhorn, A. (1951), *Wayward Youth*. London: Imago.

Alexander, F. (1953), Current views on psychotherapy. *Psychiat.*, 16:113-123.

——— French, T. (1946), *Psychoanalytic Therapy: Principles and Application*. New York: Ronald Press.

Allport, G. (1937), *Personality: A Psychological Interpretation*. New York: Holt.

Als, H. (1986), A synactive model of neonatal behavioral organization: Framework for the assessment of neurobehavioral development in the premature infant and for support of infants and parents in the neonatal intensive care environment. *Physical & Occupat. Ther. in Pediatrics*, 6:3-55.

Anderson, B., Vietze, P. & Dokecki, P. (1977), Reciprocity in vocal interactions of mothers and infant. *Child Devel.*, 48:1676-1681.

Anderson, J. (1985), *Winnicott the Therapist*. Unpublished manuscript.

Applebaum, S. (1977), *The Anatomy of Change*. New York: Plenum.

Applegarth, A. (1971), Comments on aspects of the theory of energy. *J. Amer. Psychoanal. Assn.*, 19:379-416.

Arlow, J. (1977), Affects and the psychoanalytic situation. *J. Psychoanal.*, 58:157-170.

Atwood, G. (1989), Psychoanalytic phenomenology and the thinking of Martin Heidigger and Jean Paul Sartre. In: *Self Psychology: Comparisons and Contrasts*, ed. D. Detrick & S. Detrick. Hillsdale, NJ: The Analytic Press, pp. 193-212.

——— Stolorow, R. (1984), *Structures of Subjectivity: Explorations in Psychoanalytic Phenomenology*. Hillsdale, NJ: The Analytic Press.

——— ———Trop, J. (1989), Impasses in psychoanalytic therapy. *Contemp. Psychoanal.*, 25:554-573.

Bacal, H. (1985), Optimal responsiveness and the therapeutic process. In: *Progress in Self Psychology, Vol. 1*, ed. A. Goldberg. New York: Guilford Press, pp. 202-226.

——— (1988), Reflections on "optimal frustration." In: *Learning From Kohut: Progress in Self Psychology, Vol. 4*, ed. A. Goldberg. Hillsdale, NJ: The Analytic Press, pp. 127-132.

——— (1989), Winnicott and self psychology: Remarkable reflections. In: *Self Psychology: Comparisons and Contrasts*, ed. D. Detrick & S. Detrick. Hillsdale, NJ: The Analytic Press, pp. 259-274.

Balint, M. (1936), The final goal of psychoanalytic treatment. *Internat. J. Psycho-Anal.*, 17:206-216.

——— (1952), *Primary Love and Psycho-analytic Technique*. London: Hogarth Press.

——— (1958), Sandor Ferenczi's Last Years. *Internat. J. Psycho-Anal.*, 39:68.

——— (1968), *The Basic Fault*. New York: Brunner/Mazel.

——— (1969), Trauma and object relations. *Internat. J. Psycho-Anal.*, 50:429-435.

Basch, M. (1975a), Toward a theory that encompasses depression: A revision of existing causal hypotheses in psychoanalysis. In: *Depression and Human Existence*, ed. E. Anthony & T. Benedek. Boston: Little, Brown, pp. 485-534.

——— (1975b), Perception, consciousness, and Freud's "Project." *The Annual of Psychoanalysis*, 3:3-19. New York: International Universities Press.

——— (1980), *Doing Psychotherapy*. New York: Basic.

——— (1983a), Affect and the analyst. *Psychoanal. Inq.*, 3:691-703.

——— (1983b), Empathic understanding: A review of the concept and some theoretical considerations. *J. Amer. Psychoanal. Assn.*, 31:101-126.

——— (1983c), The significance of self psychology for a theory of psychotherapy. *In: Reflections on Self Psychology*, ed. J. Lichtenberg & S. Kaplan. Hillsdale, NJ: The Analytic Press, pp. 223-238.

——— (1985), Development and defense in psychotherapeutic interventions in adolescence. Presented to the American Society of Adolescent Psychiatry, Dallas, TX, May 17 (Tapes #1, 204-1a, b, c available through Informdix, Garden City, CA 92643).

——— (1986), Can this be psychoanalysis? In: *Progress in Self Psychology, Vol. 2*, ed. A. Goldberg. New York: Guilford, pp. 18-30.

——— (1988a), *Understanding Psychotherapy*. New York: Basic.

——— (1988b), Empathy and theory. In: *Frontiers in Self Psychology: Progress in Self Psychology, Vol. 3*, ed. A. Goldberg. Hillsdale, NJ: The Analytic Press, pp. 55-58.

——— (1988c), Psychosis and failure of cognitive development. In: *Frontiers in Self Psychology: Progress in Self Psychology, Vol. 3*, ed. A. Goldberg. Hillsdale, NJ: The Analytic Press, pp. 143-149.

Beach, F. (1956), Characteristics of masculine sex drive. In: *Nebraska Symposium On Motivation, Vol. 4*, ed. M. Jones. Lincoln: Nebraska University Press, pp. 1-32.

Beebe, B. (1985), Mother-infant mutual influence and precursors of self and object representations. In: *Empirical Studies of Psychoanalytic Theories, Vol. 2*, ed. J. Masling. Hillsdale, NJ: The Analytic Press. pp. 27-48.

——— Lachmann, F. (1988), Mother-infant influence and precursors of psychic structure. In: *Frontiers in Self Psychology: Progress in Self Psychology, Vol. 3*,

ed. A. Goldberg. Hillsdale, NJ: The Analytic Press, pp. 3-26.
Bergen, M. (1958), Effect of severe trauma on a four year old child. *The Psychoanalytic Study of the Child*, 13:407-429. New York: International Universities Press.
Bexton, W., Heron, W. & Scott, T. (1954), Effects of decreased variation in the Sensory Environment. *Can. J. Psychol.*, 8:70-76.
Bibring, E. (1941), The development and problems of the theory of instincts. *Internat. J. Psycho-Anal.*, 22:102-131.
——— (1954), Psychoanalysis and the dynamic psychotherapies. *J. Amer. Psychoanal. Assn.*, 2:745-770.
Biegler, J. (1974), A commentary on Freud's treatment of the Rat Man. Presented to the Chicago Psychoanalytic Society.
Bloch, D., Silber, E. & Perry, S. (1956), Some factors in the emotional reaction of children to disaster. *Amer. J. Psychiat.*, 113:416-422.
Blum, H. (1974), The borderline childhood of the wolf man. *J. Amer. Psychoanal. Assn.*, 22:721-742.
——— (1982), Theories of the self and psychoanalytic concepts: Discussion. *J. Amer. Psychoanal. Assn.*, 30:959-978.
Boisen, A. (1960), *Out of the Depths.* New York: Harper.
Bowen, M. (1978), *Family Therapy in Clinical Practice.* New York: Aronson.
Boyer, L. & Giovacchini, P. (1967), *Psychoanalytic Treatment of Schizophrenic, Borderline and Characterological Disorders.* New York: Aronson.
Brandchaft, B. (1983), The negativism of the negative therapeutic reaction and the psychology of the self. In: *The Future of Psychoanalysis*, ed. A. Goldberg. New York: International Universities Press, pp. 327-359.
——— (1986), British object relations theory and self psychology. In: *Progress in Self Psychology, Vol. 2*, ed. A. Goldberg. New York: Guilford, pp. 245-272.
——— (1988), A case of intractable depression. In: *Learning From Kohut: Progress in Self Psychology, Vol. 4*, ed. A. Goldberg. Hillsdale, NJ: The Analytic Press, pp. 133-154.
——— (1989), Klein, Balint and Fairbairn: A self-psychological perspective. In: *Self Psychology: Comparisons and Contrasts*, ed. D. Detrick & S. Detrick. Hillsdale, NJ: The Analytic Press, pp. 231-258.
Brenner, C. (1974), On the nature and development of affects: A unified theory. *Psychoanal. Quart.*, 43:532-566.
——— (1982), *The Mind in Conflict.* New York: International Universities Press.
Breuer, J. & Freud, S. (1893-95), Studies on hysteria. *Standard Edition*, 2:1-305. London: Hogarth Press, 1965.
Brinton, C. (1963), *The Shaping of Modern Thought.* Englewood Cliffs, NJ: Prentice-Hall.
Burke, J., Borus, J., Burns, B., Millstein, K. & Beasley, M. (1982), Changes in children's behavior after a natural disaster. *Amer. J. Psychiat.*, 139:1010-1 014.
Campbell, D. (1969), A phenomenology of the other one: Corrigible hypothetical and critical. In: *Human Action: Conceptual and Empirical Issues*, ed. T. Mischel. New York: Academic Press, pp. 41-69.
——— (1975), On the conflicts between biological and social evolution and between psychology and moral tradition. *Amer. Psychol.*, 30:1103-1126.

Chappell, P. & Sander, L. (1979), Mutual regulation of the neonatal-maternal interactive process. In: *Before Speech: The Beginning of Interpersonal Communication*, ed. M. Bullova. Cambridge: Cambridge University Press, pp. 89-109.

Chassel, J. (1953), Report of panel on psychotherapy. *J. Amer. Psychoanal. Assn.*, 1:550.

Chessick, R. (1974), *Technique and Practice of Intensive Psychotherapy*. New York: Aronson.

——— (1977), *Great Ideas in Psychotherapy*. New York: Aronson.

——— (1980a), *Freud Teaches Psychotherapy*. Indianapolis, IN: Hacket.

——— (1980b), The problematic self in Kant and Kohut. *Psychoanal. Quart.*, 49:456-473.

——— (1985), *Psychology of Self and the Treatment of Narcissism*. New York: Aronson.

——— (1989), *The Technique and Practice of Listening in Intensive Psychotherapy*. Northvale, NJ: Aronson.

Chomsky, N. (1959), Review of *B.F. Skinner. Verbal Behavior Language*, 35:26-58.

Church, J. (1961), *Language and the Discovery of Reality*. New York: Random House.

Clebsch, W. & Jaekle, C. (1964), *Pastoral Care in Historical Perspective*. Englewood Cliffs, NJ: Prentice-Hall.

Cohen, J. (1980), Structural consequences of psychic trauma: A new look at "Beyond the Pleasure Principle." *Internat. J. Psycho-Anal.*, 61:421-432.

Condon, W. & Sander, L. (1974), Neonate movement is synchronized with adult speech. *Science*, 183:99-101.

Corcoran, J. (1982), The concentration camp syndrome and USAF Vietnam prisoners of war. *Psychiat. Annals*, 12:991-994.

Curtis, H. (1983), Review of *The Search for the Self: Selected Writings of Heinz Kohut, 1950-1978*, ed. P. Ornstein. *J. Amer. Psychoanal. Assn.*, 31:272-285.

——— (1986), Clinical consequences of the theory of self psychology. In: *Progress in Self Psychology, Vol. 2*, ed. A. Goldberg. New York: Guilford, pp. 3-17.

Darwin, C. (1872), *The Expression of Emotions in Man and Animals*. Chicago: University of Chicago Press.

Decasper, A. & Carstens, A. (1980), Contingencies of stimulation: Effects on learning and emotion in neonates. *Infant Behav. & Devel.*, 4:19-36.

——— Fifer, W. (1980), Of human bonding: Newborns prefer their mothers' voices. *Science*, 208:1174-1176.

Demos, E. (1988), Affect and the Development of the Self: A new frontier. In: *Frontiers in Self Psychology: Progress in Self Psychology, Vol. 3*, ed. A. Goldberg. Hillsdale, NJ: The Analytic Press, pp. 27-54.

——— Kaplan, S. (1987), Motivation and affect reconsidered: Affect biographies of two infants. *Psychoanal. Contemp. Thought*, 10:147-221.

Detrick, D. (1985), Alterego phenomenon and alterego transference. In: *Progress in Self Psychology, Vol. 1*, ed. A. Goldberg. New York: Guilford, pp. 240-256.

——— (1986), Alterego phenomena and the alterego transferences: Some further considerations. In: *Progress in Self Psychology, Vol. 2*, ed. A. Goldberg. New York: Guilford, pp. 299-304.

——— Detrick, S. (1989), *Self Psychology: Comparisons and Contrasts*. Hillsdale, NJ: The Analytic Press.

Deutsch, F. (1957), Footnote to Freud's "Fragment of an Analysis of a Case of Hysteria." *Psychoanal. Quart.*, 26:159-167.

Donaldson, M. & Gardiner, R. (1985), Diagnosis and treatment of traumatic stress among women after childhood incest. In: *Trauma and Its Wake*, ed. C. Figley. New York: Brunner/Mazel, pp. 356-377.

Dorpat, T. (1990), Review of *The Shattered Self*. *Psychoanal. Rev.*, 77:455-457.

Dowd, J. & Tronick, E. (1983), Methods for the quantitative analysis of infant limb movements. In: *Manual Specialization and the Developing Brain*, ed. G. Young. New York: Academic Press, pp. 307-317.

Eissler, K. (1953), The effect of structure of the ego on psychoanalytic treatment. *J. Amer. Psychoanal. Assn.*, 1:104-143.

Ekman, P. (1971), Universal and cultural differences in facial expression. In: *Nebraska Symposium on Motivation, Vol. 19*, ed. J. Cole. Lincoln: University of Nebraska Press, pp. 207-283.

——— (1977), Biological and cultural contributions to body and facial movement. In: *Anthropology of the Body*, ed. J. Blacking. New York: Academic Press, pp. 39-84.

——— (1983), Autonomic nervous system activity distinguishes among emotions. *Science*, 221:1208-1210.

——— Friesen, W. (1975), *Unmasking the Face*. Englewood Cliffs, NJ: Prentice Hall.

——— Levenson, R. & Friesen, W. (1983), Autonomic nervous system activity distinguishes among emotions. *Science*, 221:1208-1210.

Emde, R. (1980), Toward a psychoanalytic theory of affect: II. Emerging models of emotional development in infancy. In: *The Course of Life, Vol. 1*, ed. S. Greenspan & G. Pollock. Washington, DC: National Institutes of Mental Health, pp. 63-84.

——— Gaensbauer, T. & Harmon, R. (1976), Emotional expression in infancy: A biobehavioral study. *Psychological Issues*, Monogr. 37. New York: International Universities Press.

Fairbairn, R. (1940), The schizoid factors in personality. In: *Psychoanalytic Studies of the Personality*, London: Routledge & Kegan Paul, 1981, pp. 3-27.

——— (1941), A revised psychopathology of the psychoses and psychoneuroses. In: *Psychoanalytic Studies of the Personality*. London: Routledge & Kegan Paul, 1981, pp. 28-58.

——— (1944), Endopsychic structure considered in terms of object-relations. In: *Psychoanalytic Studies of the Personality*. London: Routledge & Kegan Paul, 1981, pp. 82-132.

——— (1951), A synopsis of the development of the author's views regarding the structure of personality. In: *Psychoanalytic Studies of the Personality*. London: Routledge & Kegan Paul, 1981, pp. 162-179.

Federn, P. (1933), Obituary, Sandor Ferenczi. *Internat. J. Psycho-Anal.*, 14:467-485.

Fenichel, O. (1945), *The Psychoanalytic Theory of Neurosis*. New York: Norton.
Ferenczi, S. (1913), Stages in the development of a sense of reality. In: *Sex in Psychoanalysis*. New York: Basic, 1950, pp. 213-239.
——— (1920), The further development of an active therapy in psycho-analysis. In: *Further Contributions to the Theory and Techniques of Psycho-Analysis, Vol. 2*, ed. J. Rickman. New York: Boni & Liveright, 1927, pp. 198-217.
——— (1925), Contraindications to the active psychoanalytic technique. In: *Further Contributions to the Theory and Techniques of Psychoanalysis, Vol. 2*, ed. J. Richman. New York: Boni & Liveright, 1927, pp. 217-229.
——— (1927), The adaptation of the family to the child. In: *Final Contributions to the Problems and Methods of Psychoanalysis, Vol. 3*, ed. M. Balint. New York: Brunner/Mazel, 1980, pp. 61-76.
——— (1928), The elasticity of psycho-analytic technique. In: *Final Contributions to the Problems and Methods of Psychoanalysis, Vol. 3*, ed. M. Balint. New York: Brunner/Mazel, 1980, pp. 87-101.
——— (1933), Confusion of tongues between adults and the child. In: *Final Contributions to the Problems and Methods of Psychoanalysis, Vol. 3*, ed. M. Balint. New York: Brunner/Mazel, 1980, pp. 156-167.
——— Rank, O. (1924), *The Development of Psychoanalysis*. New York: Nervous & Mental Disease.
Figley, C. (1985), *Trauma and its Wake*. New York: Brunner/Mazel.
Fish, S. (1989), *Doing What Comes Naturally*. Durham, NC: Duke University Press.
Flexner, J. (1967), *George Washington in the American Revolution*. Boston: Little Brown.
Fliess, R. (1942), The metapsychology of the analyst. *Psychoanal. Quart.*, 2:211-227.
Florell, J. (1971), Crisis intervention in orthopedic surgery. Unpublished doctoral dissertation, Northwestern University.
Frank, J. (1963), *Persuasion and Healing*. New York: Schocken.
Freeman, L. (1972), *The Story of Anna O*. New York: Walker.
Freud, A. (1965), *Normality and Pathology in Childhood*. New York: International Universities Press.
Freud, S. (1895), Project for a scientific psychology. *Standard Edition*, 1:283-397. London: Hogarth Press, 1966.
——— (1896a), Heredity and the aetiology of the neuroses. *Standard Edition*, 3:143-156. London: Hogarth Press, 1962.
——— (1896b), The aetiology of hysteria. *Standard Edition*, 3:191-221. London: Hogarth Press, 1962.
——— (1900), The interpretation of dreams. *Standard Edition*, 4 & 5. London: Hogarth Press, 1953.
——— (1905a), Three essays on the theory of sexuality. *Standard Edition*, 7:125-243. London: Hogarth Press, 1953.
——— (1905b), Fragment of an analysis of a case of hysteria. *Standard Edition*, 7:3-122. London: Hogarth Press, 1953.
——— (1909), Notes upon a case of obsessive neurosis. *Standard Edition*, 10:153-318. London: Hogarth Press, 1955.
——— (1911), Formulations on the two principles of mental functioning.

Standard Edition, 12:215-226. London: Hogarth Press, 1957.
——— (1914), On narcissism. *Standard Edition*, 14:69-102. London: Hogarth Press, 1957.
——— (1915), Instincts and their vicissitudes. *Standard Edition*, 14:111-140. London: Hogarth Press, 1957.
——— (1916), On transcience. *Standard Edition*, 14:305-307. London: Hogarth Press, 1957.
——— (1917), Mourning and melancholia. *Standard Edition*, 14:243-258. London: Hogarth Press, 1957.
——— (1918), From the history of an infantile neurosis. *Standard Edition*, 17:3-122. London: Hogarth Press, 1955.
——— (1921), Group psychology and the analysis of the ego. *Standard Edition*, 18:69-143. London: Hogarth Press, 1955.
——— (1923), The ego and the id. *Standard Edition*, 19:3-66. London: Hogarth Press, 1961.
——— (1925), Preface to Aichorn's Wayward Youth. *Standard Edition*, 19:273-275. London: Hogarth Press, 1961.
——— (1927), Humour. *Standard Edition*, 21:161-166. London: Hogarth Press, 1961.
——— (1933), New introductory lectures in psychoanalysis. *Standard Edition*, 22:3-182. London: Hogarth Press, 1964.
——— (1937), Analysis terminable and interminable. *Standard Edition*, 23:211-253. London: Hogarth Press, 1964.
——— (1940), An outline of psychoanalysis. *Standard Edition*. 23:141-207. London: Hogarth Press, 1964.
Friedman, L. (1978), Trends in the psychoanalytic theory of treatment. *Psychoanal. Quart.*, 47:524-567.
——— (1980), Kohut: A book review essay. *Psychoanal Quart.*, 49:393-422.
Fromm-Reichmann, F. (1950), *Principles of Intensive Psychotherapy*. Chicago: University of Chicago Press.
Galatzer-Levy, R. (1988), Manic-depressive illness: Analytic experience and a hypothesis. In: *Learning From Kohut: Progress in Self Psychology, Vol. 4*, ed. A. Goldberg. Hillsdale, NJ: The Analytic Press, pp. 87-102.
Gardiner, M. (1971), *The Wolf Man*. New York: Basic.
Gay, P. (1976), A foreword. *Bergasse 19* by E. Engelman. New York: Basic.
——— (1988), *Freud: A Life for Our Time*. New York: Norton.
Gazzaniga, M. & Le Doux J. (1978), *The Integrated Mind*. New York: Plenum.
Gediman, H. (1989), Conflict and deficit models of psychopathology: A unificatory point of view. In: *Self Psychology: Comparisons and Contrasts*, ed. D. Detrick & S. Detrick. Hillsdale, NJ: The Analytic Press, pp. 293-310.
Gedo, J. (1966), The psychotherapy of developmental arrest. *Brit. J. Med. Psychol.*, 39:25-33.
——— (1967), On critical periods for corrective experience in the theory of arrested development. *Brit. J. Med. Psychol.*, 40:79-83.
——— (1975), Forms of idealization in the analytic transference. *J. Amer. Psychoanal. Assn.*, 23:485-505.

———— (1976), The wise baby reconsidered. *Psychological Issues*, Monogr. 34/35:357-378.

———— (1979), *Beyond Interpretation*. New York: International Universities Press.

———— (1981), *Advances in Clinical Psychoanalysis*. New York: International Universities Press.

———— (1986), *Conceptual Issues in Psychoanalysis*. Hillsdale, NJ: The Analytic Press.

———— (1988), *The Mind in Disorder*. Hillsdale, NJ: The Analytic Press.

———— (1991), The biology of mind: A foreword. In: *Mapping the Mind* by F. Levin. Hillsdale, NJ: The Analytic Press, pp. xi-xix.

———— Goldberg, A. (1973), *Models of the Mind: A Psychoanalytic Theory*. Chicago: University of Chicago Press.

Geha, R. (1988), Freud as fictionalist. In: *Freud: Appraisals and Reappraisals, Vol. 2*, ed. P. Stepansky. Hillsdale, NJ: The Analytic Press, pp. 103-160.

Gill, M. 1951), Ego psychology and psychotherapy. *Psychoanal. Quart.*, 20:62-71.

———— (1954), Psychoanalysis and exploratory psychotherapy. *J. Amer. Psychoanal. Assn.*, 2:771-777.

———— (1976), Metapsychology is not psychology. In: *Psychology versus Metapsychology: Psychoanalytic Essays in Memory of George S. Klein*, ed. M. Gill & P. Holtzman. New York: International Universities Press, pp. 158-197.

———— (1982), *Analysis of Transference, Vol. 1*, New York: International Universities Press.

———— (1984), Psychoanalysis and psychotherapy: A revision. *Internat. Rev. Psychoanal.*, 11:161-179.

Gillin, J. (1948), Magical fright. *Psychiat.*, 11:387-400.

Giovacchini, P. (1979), *The Treatment of Primitive Mental States*. New York: Aronson.

———— (1987), *A Narrative Textbook of Psychanalysis*. Northvale, NJ: Aronson.

Glover, E. (1931), The therapeutic effect of inexact interpretation: A contribution to the theory of suggestion. In: *The Techniques of Psychoanalysis*, New York: International Universities Press, pp. 253-266.

———— (1943), The concept of disassociation. *Internat. J. Psycho-Anal.*, 24:7-13.

———— (1945), Examination of the Klein system of child psychology, *The Psychoanalytic Study of the Child*, 1:75-118, New Haven, CT: Yale University Press.

Goldberg, A. (1974), On the prognosis and treatment of narcissism. *J. Amer. Psychoanal. Assn.*, 22:243-254.

———— (1978), *The Psychology of Self: A Casebook*. New York: International Universities Press.

———— (1980a), Introductory remarks. In: *Advances in Self Psychology.*, ed. A. Goldberg. New York: International Universities Press, pp. 1-16.

———— (1980b), Self psychology and the distinctiveness of psychotherapy. *Internat. J. Psychother.*, 8:57-70.

———— (1983), Self psychology and alternative perspectives on internalization. In: *Reflections on Self Psychology*, ed. J. Lichtenberg & S. Kaplan. Hillsdale, NJ: The Analytic Press, pp. 297-312.

_______ (1988), *A Fresh Look at Psychoanalysis.* Hillsdale, NJ: The Analytic Press.

_______ (1990), *The Prisonhouse of Psychoanalysis.* Hillsdale, NJ: The Analytic Press.

Green, A. (1983), Dimensions of psychological trauma in abused children. *Amer. Acad. Child Psychiat.*, 32:231-237.

Green, B., Wilson, J. & Lindy, J. (1985), Conceptualizing post-traumatic stress disorder: A psychological framework. In: *Trauma and Its Wake*, ed. C. Figley. New York: Brunner/Mazel, pp. 53-69.

Grosskurth, P. (1986), *Melanie Klein: Her World and Her Work.* New York: Knopf.

Grotstein, J. (1983), Some perspectives in self psychology. In: *The Future of Psychoanalysis*, ed. A. Goldberg. New York: International Universities Press, pp. 165-201.

Guntrip, H. (1969), *Schizoid Phenomena, Object Relations and the Self.* New York: International Universities Press.

Hanly, C. & Masson, J.M. (1976), A critical examination of the new narcissism. *Internat. J. Psycho-Anal.*, 57:49-66.

Hartmann, H. (1939), *Ego Psychology and the Problem of Adaptation.* New York: International Universities Press. 1958.

_______ (1950), Comments on the psychoanalytic theory of the ego, *The Psychoanalytic Study of the Child*, 5:74-96. New York: International Universities Press.

_______ (1952), The mutual influences in the development of ego and id, *The Psychoanalytic Study of the Child*, 7:9-30. New York: International Universities Press.

_______ (1953), Contributions to the metapsychology of schizophrenia. *The Psychoanalytic Study of the Child.* 8:177-198. New York: International Universities Press.

_______ Kris, E. & Loewenstein, R. (1946), Comments on the formation of psychic structure. *The Psychoanalytic Study of the Child*, 2:11-38. New York: International Universities Press.

Hesse, M. (1980), *Revolutions and Reconstructions in the Philosophy of Science.* Bloomington: Indiana University Press.

Holmes, T. & Rahe, R. (1967), The social adjustment rating scale. *J. Psychosomat. Res.*, 11:213-218.

Holt, R. (1976), Drive or wish? A reconsideration of the psychoanalytic theory of motivation. In: *Psychology verses Metapsychology*, ed. M. Gill & P. Holtzman. New York: International Universities Press, pp. 158-197.

Horwitz, L. (1974), *Clinical Prediction in Psychotherapy.* New York: Aronson.

Izard, C. (1971), *The Face of Emotion.* New York: Appleton-Century Crofts.

_______ (1977a), *Human Emotions.* New York: Plenum Press.

_______ (1977b), The emotions and emotion constructs in personality and cultural research. In: *Handbook in Modern Personality Theory*, ed. R. Cattell & R. Dreger. New York: Wiley, pp. 496-510.

Jacobson, E. (1964), *The Self and the Object World.* New York: International Universities Press.

James, W. (1890), *Principles of Psychology.* New York: Dover, 1950.

Janoff-Bulman, R. (1985), The aftermath of victimization: Rebuilding shattered assumptions. In: *Trauma and Its Wake*, ed. C. Figley. New York: Brunner/Mazel, pp. 15-35.

Jones, E. (1920), Recent advances in psycho-analysis. *Internat. J. Psycho-Anal.*, 1:161-185.

——— (1961), *The Life and Work of Sigmund Freud*. Vols. I, II & III. New York: Basic.

Kaye, K. (1982), *The Mental and Social Life of Babies*. Chicago: University of Chicago Press.

Kent, E. (1981), *The Brains of Men and Machines*. Peterborough, NH: Byte/McGraw Hill.

Kernberg, O. (1975), *Borderline Conditions and Pathological Narcissism*. New York: Aronson.

——— Burstein, E., Coyne, L., Applebaum, A., Horwitz, L. & Voth, H. (1972), Psychotherapy and psychoanalysis: Final report of the Menninger Foundation's Psychotherapy Research Project. *Bull. Menn. Clin.* 36:1-275.

Khan, M. (1974), *The Privacy of the Self*. New York: International Universities Press.

Kilpatrick, D., Veronen, L. & Best, C. (1985), Factors predicting psychological stress among rape victims. In: *Trauma and Its Wake*, ed. C. Figley. New York: Brunner/Mazel, pp. 113-141.

Klein, G. (1973), Two Theories or One. *Bull. Menn. Clin.*, 37:102-132.

——— (1976), *Psychoanalytic Theory: An Explanation of Essentials*. New York: International Universities Press.

Klein, M. (1935), A contribution to the psychogenesis of manic-depressive states. In: *Love, Guilt and Reparation, 1921-1945*. London: Hogarth, 1975, pp. 262-289.

Kohut, H. (1957), Death in Venice by Thomas Mann: A story about the disintegration of artistic sublimation. In: *The Search for the Self*, ed P. Ornstein. New York: International Universities Press, 1978, pp. 107-130.

——— (1959), Introspection, empathy, and psychoanalysis. In: *The Search for the Self*, ed. P. Ornstein. New York: International Universities Press, 1978, pp. 205-232.

——— (1966), Forms and transformations of narcissism. In: *Self Psychology and the Humanities*, ed. C. Strozier. New York: Norton, 1985, pp. 97-123.

——— (1971), *The Analysis of the Self*. New York: International Universities Press.

——— (1975), The future of psychoanalysis. *The Annual of Psychoanalysis*, 3:341-370. New York: International Universities Press.

——— (1976), Creativeness, charisma, group psychology. In: *Self Psychology and the Humanities*, ed. C. Strozier. New York: Norton, 1985, pp. 171-211.

——— (1977), *The Restoration of the Self*. New York: International Universities Press.

——— (1978), *The Search for the Self*, Vols. 1 & 2, ed. P. Ornstein. New York: International Universities Press.

——— (1979), The two analyses of Mr. Z. *Internat. J. Psycho-Anal.*, 60:3-27.

——— (1980), Reflections. In: *Advances in Self Psychology*, ed. A. Goldberg. New

York: International Universities Press, pp. 473-554.

_______ (1983), Selected problems of self-psychological theory. In: *Reflections on Self Psychology*, ed. J. Lichtenberg & S. Kaplan. Hillsdale, NJ: The Analytic Press, pp. 387-416.

_______ (1984), *How Does Analysis Cure?* ed. A. Goldberg & P. Stepansky. Chicago: University of Chicago Press.

_______ Wolf, E. (1978), Disorders of the Self and their treatment. *Internat. J. Psycho-Anal.*, 59:413-425.

Kris, E. (1951), Ego psychology and interpretation in psychoanalytic therapy. *Psychoanal. Quart.*, 20:15-30.

Krystal, H. (1978), Trauma and affects. *The Psychoanalytic Study of the Child*, 33:81-116. New Haven, CT: Yale University Press.

Kubie, L. (1975), The language tools of psychoanalysis. *Internat. Rev. Psycho-Anal.*, 2:11-24.

Kuhn, T. (1962), *The Structure of Scientific Revolutions*. Chicago: University of Chicago Press.

Langer, S. (1951), *Philosophy in a New Key*. Cambridge, MA: Harvard University Press.

Langs, R. (1976), *The Therapeutic Interaction, Vol. 2*. New York: Aronson

Lax, R. (1975), Some comments on the narcissistic aspects of self-righteousness: Defensive and structural considerations. *Internat. J. Psycho-Anal.*, 56:283-292.

Layton, E., Pineau, R. & Costello, J. (1985), *And I was There*. New York: William Morrow.

Lee, R. (1979), Totemic therapy. *J. Rel. & Health*, 18:21-28.

_______ (1981), *Clergy and Clients*. New York: Seabury.

_______ (1988), Reverse selfobject experience. *Amer. J. Psychother.*, 42:416-424.

Lévi-Strauss, C. (1963), *Structural Anthropology*. New York: Basic

Levin, F. (1990), Psychological development and the changing organization of the brain. *The Annual of Psychoanalysis*, 18:45-61. Hillsdale, NJ: The Analytic Press.

_______ (1991), *Mapping the Mind*. Hillsdale, NJ: The Analytic Press.

_______ Vuckovitch, D. (1991), Psychoanalysis and the two cerebral hemispheres. In: *The Mapping of the Mind* by F. Levin. Hillsdale, NJ: The Analytic Press.

Lichtenberg, J. (1988), Infant research and self psychology. In: *Frontiers in Self Psychology: Progress in Self Psychology, Vol. 3*. Hillsdale, NJ: The Analytic Press, pp. 59-64.

_______ (1989), *Psychoanalysis and Motivation*. Hillsdale, NJ: The Analytic Press.

Lindemann, E. (1944), The symptomatology and management of acute grief. *Amer. J. Psychiat.*, 101:141-146.

Lipton, S. (1977), The advantages of Freud's technique as shown in his analysis of the Rat Man. *Internat. J. Psycho-Anal.*, 58:255-273.

Loewald, H. (1960), On the therapeutic action of psychoanalysis. *Internat. J. Psycho-Anal.*, 41:16-23.

_______ (1973), Review of *The Analysis of the Self* by H. Kohut. *Psychoanal. Quart.*, 42:441-451.

London, N. (1985), An appraisal of self psychology. *Internat. J. Psycho-anal.*, 66:95-107.

Lorand, S. (1966), Sandor Ferenczi. In: *Psychoanalytic Pioneers*, ed. F. Alexander, S. Eisenstein & M. Grotjahn. New York: Basic Books, pp. 14-35.

Lorenz, K. (1966), *On Aggression*. New York: Bantam.

Macalpine, I. (1950), The development of the transference. *Psychoanal. Quart.*, 19:501-539.

MacLean, P. (1962), New findings relevant to the evolution of psychosexual functions of the brain. *J. Nerv. Ment. Dis.*, 135:289-301.

Magid, B. (in press), Self psychology meets the Wolf Man. In: *Freud's Case Studies: A Self-Psychological Perspective*, ed. B. Magid. Hillsdale, NJ: The Analytic Press.

Mahler, M. (1979), *The Selected Papers of Margaret S. Mahler. Vol. 2*, New York: Aronson.

——— Pine, F. & Bergman, A. (1975), *The Psychological Birth of the Human Infant*. New York: Basic.

Mahony, P. (1984), *Cries of the Wolf Man*. New York: International Universities Press.

——— (1986), *Freud and the Rat Man*. New Haven, CT: Yale University Press.

Malin, A. & Grotstein, J. (1966), Projective identification in the therapeutic process. *Internat. J. Psycho-Anal.*, 42:26-31.

Manchester, W. (1988), *The Last Lion: Winston Spencer Churchill. Alone, 1932-1940*. Boston: Little-Brown.

Mann, T. (1954), *Death in Venice*. New York: Vintage.

Markson, E. & Thomson, P. (1986), The relationship between psychoanalytic concepts of conflict and deficit. In: *Progress in Self Psychology, Vol. 2*, ed. A. Goldberg. New York: Guilford, pp. 31-40.

Masek, R. (1989), On Maurice Merleau-Ponty and the psychology of the self. In: *Self Psychology: Comparisons and Contrasts*, ed. D. Detrick and S. Detrick. Hillsdale, NJ: The Analytic Press, pp. 175-192.

Mason, R. (1980), The psychology of the self: Religion and psychotherapy. In: *Advances in Self Psychology*, ed. A. Goldberg. New York: International Universities Press, pp. 407-425.

Masson, J.M. (1984), *The Assault on Truth*. New York: Penguin.

Masterson, J. (1981), *The Narcissistic and Borderline Disorders*. New York: Brunner/Mazel.

May, R. (1958), *Existence*. New York: Basic Books.

Miller, G. (1963), What is information measurement? In: *Modern Systems Research for the Behavioral Scientist*, ed. W. Buckley. Chicago: Aldine, 1968, pp. 123-128.

Miller, J. (1988), Kohut's view on integration. In: *Learning From Kohut: Progress in Self Psychology, Vol. 4*, ed. A. Goldberg. Hillsdale, NJ: The Analytic Press, pp. 79-84.

Mitchell, S. (1988), *Relational Concepts in Psychoanalysis: An Integration*. Cambridge, MA: Harvard University Press.

Murray, H. (1938), *Explorations in Personality*. New York: Oxford University Press.

Muslin, H. & Val, E., (1987), *The Psychotherapy of the Self*. New York: Brunner/Mazel.

Newson, J. (1977), An intersubjective approach to the systematic description of mother-infant interaction. In: *Studies in Mother-Infant Interaction*, ed. H.

Schaffer. New York: Academic Press, pp. 47-62.

Nissim-Sabat, M. (1989), Kohut and Husserl: The empathic bond. In: *Self Psychology: Comparisons and Contrasts*, ed. D. Detrick & S. Detrick. Hillsdale, NJ: The Analytic Press, pp. 151-174.

Nunberg, G. & Shapiro, L. (1983), The central organizing fantasy. *Psychoanal. Rev.*, 70:493-503.

Nunberg, H. (1951), Transference and reality. *Internat. J. Psycho-Anal.*, 32:1-9.

Ogden, T. (1979), On projective identification. *Internat. J. Psycho-Anal.*, 60:357-373.

Ornstein, A. (1974), The dread to repeat and the new beginning. *The Annual of Psychoanalysis*, 2:231-248. New York: International Universities Press.

Ornstein, P. (1974), On narcissism: Beyond the introduction, highlights of Heinz Kohut's contributions to the psychoanalytic treatment of narcissistic personality disorders. *The Annual of Psychoanalysis*, 2:127-149. New York: International Universities Press.

——— (1978), The evolution of Heinz Kohut's psychoanalytic psychology of the self. In: *The Search for the Self*, ed. P. Ornstein. New York: International Universities Press, pp. 1-106.

Parson, E. (1985), Ethnicity and traumatic stress: The intersecting point in psychotherapy. In: *Trauma and Its Wake*, ed. C. Figley. New York: Brunner/Mazel, pp. 314-337.

Perry, J. (1980), Neonate-adult head movement. *Developmental Psychol.*, 16:245-250.

Peterfreund, E. (1971), *Information, Systems and Psychoanalysis: An Evolutionary Biological Approach to Psychoanalytic Theory*. New York: International Universities Press.

Piaget, J. (1970), *Structuralism*. New York: Basic.

Polanyi, M. (1965a), On the modern mind. *Encounter*, May, pp. 12-20.

——— (1965b), The structures of consciousness. *Brain*, 88:799-810.

——— (1966), *The Tacit Dimension*. New York: Doubleday.

Popper, K. (1959), *The Logic of Scientific Discovery*. New York: Harper & Row, 1968.

——— (1963), *Conjectures and Refutations*. New York: Harper & Row.

Pribrim, K. (1980), The biology of emotions and other feelings. In: *Emotion: Theory, Research and Experience*, ed. R. Plutchik & H. Kellerman. New York: Academic Press, pp. 245-269.

Pruett, K. (1979), Home treatment for two infants who witnessed their mother's murder. *J. Amer. Acad. Child Psychiat.*, 18:647-657.

Rachman, A. (1989), Ferenczi's contributions to the evolution of a self psychology framework in psychoanalysis. In: *Self Psychology: Comparisons and Contrasts*, ed. D. Detrick & S. Detrick. Hillsdale, NJ: The Analytic Press, pp. 89-109.

Racker, H. (1954), Considerations in the theory of transference. In: *Transference and Countertransference*. London: Hogarth, 1968, pp. 71-78.

——— (1957), The meanings and uses of countertransference. *Internat. J. Psycho-Anal.*, 26:303-357.

Rangell, L. (1981), Psychoanalysis and dynamic psychotherapy. *Psychoanal. Quart.*, 50:665-693.

Rapaport, D. (1959), The structure of psychoanalytic theory: A systematizing attempt. *Psychological Issues*, Monogr. #6. New York: International Universities Press. 1960.

Reik, T. (1937), *Surprise and the Psychoanalyst.* New York: Dutton.

Reiser, D. (1986), Self psychology and the problem of suicide. In: *Progress in Self Psychology, Vol. 2*, ed. A. Goldberg. New York: Guilford, pp. 227-241.

Reiser, M. (1984), *Mind, Brain, Body: Toward a Convergence of Psychoanalysis and Neurobiology*. New York: Basic Books.

Rhodes, R. (1986), *The Making of the Atomic Bomb*. New York: Touchstone.

Ricoeur, P. (1984), *Time and Narrative*. Chicago: University of Chicago Press.

Riviere, J. (1936), A contribution to the analysis of the negative therapeutic reaction. *Internat. J. Psycho-Anal.*, 17:304-320.

Roethlesberger, F. & Dickson, W. (1939), *Management and the Worker*. Cambridge, MA: Harvard University Press.

Rogers, C. (1961), *On Becoming a Person*. New York: Houghton Mifflin.

Rotenberg, C. (1988), Selfobject theory and the artistic process. In: *Learning From Kohut: Progress in Self Psychology, Vol. 4*, ed. A, Goldberg. Hillsdale, NJ: The Analytic Press, pp. 193-214.

Rothstein, A. (1980), Toward a critique of psychology of the self. *Psychoanal. Quart.* 59:423-455.

Rubin, J. (1989), Narcissism and Nihilism: Kohut and Kierkegaard on the modern self. In: *Self Psychology: Comparisons and Contrasts*, ed. D. Detrick & B. Detrick. Hillsdale, NJ: The Analytic Press, pp. 131-150.

Rubinstein, B. (1967), Explanation and mere description: A metascientific examination of certain aspects of the psychoanalytic theory of motivation. In: *Motives and Thought*, ed. R. Holt. New York: International Universities Press, pp. 20-27.

——— (1973), *Psychoanalysis and Contemporary Science: An Annual of Integrative and Interdisciplinary Studies, Vol. 2*, New York: Macmillan.

Rychlak, J. (1968), *A Philosophy of Science for Personality Theory*. Boston: Houghton Mifflin.

Ryle, G. (1949), *The Concept of Mind*. New York: Barnes & Noble.

Salzman, L. (1980), *Treatment of the Obsessive Personality*. New York: Aronson.

Sander, L. (1970), Regulation and organization in the early infant-caretaker system. In: *Brain and Early Behavior*, ed. R. Robinson. New York: Academic Press, pp. 313-331.

——— (1977), The regulation of exchange in the infant-caretaker system and some aspects of the context-content relationship. In: *Interaction, Conversation and the Development of Language*, ed. M. Lewis & L. Rosenblaum. New York: Wiley, pp. 133-156.

——— (1982), Toward a logic of organization in psychobiologic development. Paper presented at the 13th Margaret Mahler Symposium in Philadelphia.

——— (1983), To begin with—Reflections on ontogeny. In: *Relections on Self Psychology*, ed. J. Lichtenberg & S. Kaplan. Hillsdale, NJ: The Analytic Press, pp. 85-104.

——— Sandler, A. (1978), On the development of object relationships and affects. *Internat. J. Psycho-Anal.*, 59:285-296.

Schafer, R. (1959), Generative empathy in the treatment situation. *Psychoanal. Quart.*, 28:342-373.
——— (1968), *Aspects of Internalization*. New York: International Universities Press.
——— (1976), *A New Language for Psychoanalysis*. New Haven, CT: Yale University Press.
——— (1983), *The Analytic Attitude*. New York: Basic.
Schetky, D. (1978), Preschooler's response to the murder of their mothers by their fathers: A study of four cases. *Bull. Amer. Acad. Psychiat. & Law.*, 6:45-47.
Schlesinger, H. (1969), Diagnosis and prescription for psychotherapy. *Bull. Menn. Clin.*, 33:269-278.
Schonberger, R. (1982), *Japanese Manufacturing Techniques*. New York: Free Press.
Schwaber, E. (1980), Self psychology and the concept of psychopathology: A case presentation. In: *Advances in Self Psychology*, ed. A, Goldberg. New York: International Universities Press, pp., 215-242.
——— (1983a), Construction, reconstruction, and the mode of clinical attunement. In: *The Future of Psychoanalysis*, ed. A. Goldberg. New York: International Universities Press, pp. 273-291.
——— (1983b), Psychoanalytic listening and psychic reality. *Internat, Rev. Psycho-Anal.*, 10:379-392.
Schwartz, L. (1978), Review of *The Restoration of the Self. Psychoanal. Quart.*, 47:436-443.
Segal, H. (1974), *Introduction to the Work of Melanie Klein*, 2nd. Ed. New York: Basic.
Selye, H. (1950), *The Physiology and Pathology of Exposure to Stress*. Montreal: Acta.
Senior, N., Gladstone, T. & Nurcombe, B. (1982), Child snatching: A case report. *J. Amer. Acad. Child Psychiat.*, 21:579-583.
Shane, M. & Shane, E. (1980), Psychoanalytic developmental theories of the self; An integration. In *Advances in Self Psychology*, ed. A. Goldberg. New York: International Universities Press, pp. 23-46.
——— (1986), Self change and development in the analysis of an adolescent patient: The use of a combined model with a developmental orientation and approach. In: *Progress in Self Psychology, Vol. 2*, ed. A. Goldberg. New York: Guilford, pp. 142-160.
Sherwood, M. (1969), *The Logic of Explanation in Psychoanalysis*. New York: Academic Press.
Simeons, A. (1962), *Man's Presumptuous Brain*. New York: Dutton.
Spitz, R. (1945), Hospitalism: an enquiry into the genesis of psychiatric conditions in early childhood. *The Psychoanalytic Study of the Child*, 1:53-74, New York: International Universities Press.
Sroufe, L. (1979), Socioemotional development. In: *Handbook of Infant Development*, ed. J. Osofsky. New York: Wiley, pp. 462-516.
Stechler, G. & Kaplan, S. (1980), The development of self. *The Psychoanalytic Study of the Child*, 35:85-105, New Haven, CT: Yale University Press.
Stein, M. (1979), Review of *The Restoration of the Self. J. Amer. Psychoanal. Assn.*,

27:665-680.

Stepansky, P. (1989), Adler, Kohut, and the idea of a psychoanalytic research tradition. In: *Self Psychology: Comparisons and Contrasts*, ed. D. Detrick & S. Detrick. Hillsdale, NJ: The Analytic Press, pp. 49-74.

Stern, D. (1974), Mother and infant at play: The dyadic interaction involving facial, vocal, and gaze behaviors. In: *The Effect of the Infant on its Caregiver*, ed. M. Lewis & L. Rosenblum. New York: Wiley, pp. 187-213.

——— (1977), *The First Relationship: Infant and Mother*. Cambridge, MA: Harvard University Press.

——— (1983), The early development of schemas of self, other, and "self with other." In: *Reflections on Self Psychology*, ed. J. Lichtenberg. Hillsdale, NJ: The Analytic Press, pp. 49-84.

——— (1985), *The Interpersonal World of the Infant*. New York: Basic.

——— Jaffe, J., Beebe, B. & Bennett, S. (1975), Vocalizing in unison and in alternation: Two modes of communication within the mother-infant dyad. *Annals of the New York Academy of Sciences*, 263:89-100.

Stern, M. (1988), *Repetition and Trauma*, ed. L. Stern. Hillsdale, NJ: The Analytic Press.

Stolorow, R. (1975), Addendum to a partial analysis of a perversion involving bugs: An illustration of the narcissistic function of perverse activity. *Internat. J. Psycho-Anal.*, 56:361-364.

——— (1980), Discussion of "Self Psychology and the Concept of Health" by Paul H. Ornstein. In: *Advances in Self Psychology*, ed. A. Goldberg. New York: International Universities Press, pp. 161-165.

——— (1983), Toward a pure psychology of inner conflict. In: *Progress in Self Psychology, Vol. 1*, ed. A. Goldberg. New York: Guilford, pp. 193-201.

——— (1986a), Beyond dogma in psychoanalysis. In: *Progress in Self Psychology, Vol. 2*, ed. A. Goldberg. New York: Guilford, pp. 41-49.

——— (1986b), On experiencing an object: A multidimensional perspective. In: *Progress in Self Psychology, Vol. 2*, ed. A. Goldberg. New York: Guilford, pp. 273-279.

——— (1988), Integrating self psychology and classical psychoanalysis: An experience-near approach. In: *Learning From Kohut: Progress in Self Psychology, Vol. 4*, ed. A. Goldberg. Hillsdale NJ: The Analytic Press, pp. 63-70.

——— Atwood, G. (1979), *Faces in a Cloud: Subjectivity in Personality Theory*. Northvale: NJ: Aronson.

——— ——— Brandchaft, B. (1988), Symbols of subject truth in psychotic states: Implications for psychoanalytic treatment. In: *Frontiers in Self Psychology: Progress in Self Psychology, Vol. 3*, ed. A. Goldberg. Hillsdale, NJ: The Analytic Press, pp. 103-142.

——— Brandchaft, B. & Atwood, G. (1987), *Psychoanalytic Treatment: An Intersubjective Approach*. Hillsdale, NJ: The Analytic Press.

——— Lachmann, F. (1980), *Psychoanalysis of Developmental Arrests*. New York: International Universities Press.

Stone, L. (1951), Psychoanalysis and brief psychotherapy. *Psychoanal. Quart.*, 20:215-236.

_______ (1954), The widening scope of indications for psychoanalysis. *J. Amer. Psychoanal. Assn.*, 2:567-594.

Strachey, J. (1934), The nature of therapeutic action of psychoanalysis. *Internat. J. Psycho-Anal.*, 15:127-159.

Sullivan, H. (1953), *The Interpersonal Theory of Psychiatry*. New York: Norton.

Swales, P. (1986), Freud, his teacher, and the birth of psychoanalysis. In: *Freud: Appraisals and Reappraisals—Contributions to Freud Studies, Vol 1*, ed. P. Stepansky. Hillsdale, NJ: The Analytic Press, pp. 3-82.

_______ (1988), Freud, Katharina, and the first "wild analysis." In: *Freud: Appraisals and Reappraisals—Contributions to Freud Studies, Vol. 3*, ed. P. Stepansky. Hillsdale, NJ: The Analytic Press, pp. 81-166

Swanson, D. (1977), A critique of psychic energy as an explanatory concept. *J. Amer. Psychoanal. Assn.*, 25:603-633.

Tansey, M. & Burke, W. (1989), *Understanding Countertransference: From Projective Identification to Empathy*. Hillsdale, NJ: The Analytic Press.

Terman, D. (1980), Object love and the psychology of the self. In: *Advances in Self Psychology*, ed. A. Goldberg. New York: International Universities Press, pp. 349-362.

_______ (1988), Optimum frustration: Structuralization and the therapeutic process. In: *Learning From Kohut: Progress in Self Psychology, Vol. 4*, ed. A. Goldberg. New York: The Analytic Press, pp. 113-125.

Tichener, J. & Kapp, F. (1976), Family and character change at Buffalo Creek. *Amer. J. Psychiat.*, 133:295-299.

Ticho, E. (1970), Differences between psychoanalysis and psychotherapy. *Bull. Menn. Clin.*, 34:128-138.

Tolpin, M. (1971), On the beginnings of a cohesive self. *The Psychoanalytic Study of the Child*, 26:316-352. New York: Quadrangle Books.

_______ (1980), Discussion of Psychoanalytic developmental theories of the self: An integration by Morton Shane and Estelle Shane. In: *Advances in Self Psychology*, ed. A. Goldberg. New York: International Universities Press, pp. 47-68.

_______ (1983), Corrective emotional experience: A self-psychological reevaluation. In: *The Future of Psychoanalysis*, ed. A. Goldberg. New York: International Universities Press, pp. 363-379.

_______ (1986), The self and its selfobjects: A different baby. In: *Progress In Self Psychology, Vol, 2*, ed. A. Goldberg. New York: Guilford, pp. 115-128.

Tolpin P. (1983a), A change in the self; The development and transformation of an idealizing transference. *Internat. J. Psycho-Anal.*, 64:461-483.

_______ (1983b), Self psychology and dreams. In: *The Future of Psychoanalysis*, ed. A. Goldberg. New York: International Universities Press, pp. 255-272.

Tomkins, S. (1962-63), *Affect, Imagery, Consciousness*, Vols. 1 & 2. New York: Springer.

Torok, M. (1979), L'os de la fin. *Confrontation*, 1:163-186.

Torrey, E. (1972), *The Mind Game*. New York: Emerson Hall.

Trevarthan, C. (1977), Descriptive analyses of infant communicative behavior. In: *Studies in Mother-Infant Interaction*, ed. H Schafer. New York: Academic Press, pp. 227-270.

Tronick, E., Als, H. & Brazelton, T. (1980), Monadic phases: A structural descriptive analysis of infant-mother face-to-face interaction. *Merrill Palmer Quart.*, 26:3-24.

Tylim, I. (1978), Narcissistic transference and countertransference in adolescent treatment. *The Psychoanalytic Study of the Child*, 33:279-292, New Haven, CT: Yale University Press.

Ulman, R. & Brothers, D. (1988), *The Shattered Self.* Hillsdale, NJ: The Analytic Press.

Van der Kolk, B. (1988), Review of *The Shattered Self* by Ulman & Brothers. *J. Clin. Psychiat.*, 49:375-376.

von Bertalanffy, L. (1968), *General System Theory.* New York: Braziller.

Vygotsky, L. (1978), *Mind in Society.* Cambridge, MA: Harvard U. Press.

Waelder, R. (1956), Introduction to the discussion on problems of transference. *Internat. J. Psycho-Anal.*, 37:367-368.

——— (1962), Psychoanalysis, scientific method and philosophy. *J. Amer. Psychoanal. Assn.*, 10:617-637.

Wallerstein, R. (1986), *Forty Two Lives in Treatment.* New York: Guilford.

Weatherhead, L. (1951), *Psychology, Religion and Healing.* London: Hodder & Stoughton.

White, M. & Weiner, M. (1986), *The Theory and Practice of Self Psychology.* New York: Brunner/Mazel.

Winnicott, D. (1951), Transitional objects and transitional phenomena. In: *Collected Papers: Through Paediatrics to Psychoanalysis.* New York: Basic, 1975, pp. 229-242.

——— (1960), The theory of the parent-infant relationship. In: *The Maturational Processes and the Facilitating Environment.* New York: International Universities Press, 1965, pp. 37-55.

——— (1962), The aim of psycho-analytic treatment. In: *The Maturational Processes and the Facilitating Environment.* New York: International Universities Press, 1965, pp. 166-170.

——— (1966), The ordinary devoted mother. Presented to the nursing school association of Great Britain and Northern Ireland, London branch.

——— (1971), Creativity and its origins. In: *Playing and Reality.* London: Tavistock, 1971, pp. 65-85.

Wise, C. (1951), *Pastoral Counseling: Its Theory and Practice.* New York: Harper & Row.

——— (1966), *The Meaning of Pastoral Care.* New York: Harper & Row.

Wolf, E. (1980a), On the developmental line of self object relations. In: *Advances in Self Psychology*, ed. A. Goldberg. New York: International Universities Press, pp. 117-135.

——— (1980b), Tomorrow's self: Heinz Kohut's contribution to adolescent psychiatry. *Adol. Psychiat.*, 8:41-50.

——— (1983a), Aspects of neutrality. *Psychoanal. Inq.*, 3:675-689.

——— (1983b), Empathy and countertransference. In: *The Future of Psychoanalysis*, ed. A. Goldberg. New York: International Universities Press, pp. 309-326.

——— (1988), *Treating The Self.* New York: Guilford.

Zetzel, E. (1956), An approach to the relation between concept and content in psychoanalytic theory (with special reference to the work of Melanie Klein and her followers). *The Psychoanalytic Study of the Child*, 11:99-121. New York: International Universities Press.

Author Index

H

I

J

K

L

M

Subject Index